S0-ACI-615

A HISTORY OF
MESSIANIC SPECULATION IN ISRAEL

Abba Hillel Silver was born in 1893 in Lithuania. He attended public school in New York city and was graduated from the University of Cincinnati in 1915. He received his D.D. degree from Hebrew Union College in 1925, a Litt. D. from Western Reserve in 1928, a D.H.L. from Hebrew Union College in 1941, and an H.H.D. from the University of Tampa, Florida. While serving as rabbi in Wheeling in 1917 he was called to The Temple of Cleveland, the largest liberal Jewish congregation in America. An active Zionist, Rabbi Silver has served both as chairman and co-chairman of the United Palestine Appeal, as co-chairman of the United Jewish Appeal, with the National Child Labor Committee, the Advisory Committee of the American Birth Control League, and the Ohio Race Betterment Association.

His other books include DEMOCRATIC IMPULSE IN JEWISH HISTORY, RELIGION IN A CHANGING WORLD, WORLD CRISIS AND JEWISH SURVIVAL, and VISION AND VICTORY.

A HISTORY
OF
MESSIANIC SPECULATION IN ISRAEL

From the First through the Seventeenth Centuries

By ABBA HILLEL SILVER

With a new preface by the author

BEACON PRESS BEACON HILL BOSTON

First published, 1927, by The Macmillan Company
First Beacon Paperback edition published, 1959

Printed in the United States of America

Library of Congress Catalog Card Number: 59-6395

CONTENTS

Part I. Messianic Calculation

CONTENTS

CONTENTS

TO
VIRGINIA

FOREWORD

Three factors contributed to the spread of the Messianic belief in Israel: the loss of national independence and the attendant deprivations, the will to live dominantly and triumphantly as a rehabilitated people in its national home, and the unfaltering faith in divine justice by whose eternal canons the national restoration was infallibly prescribed. Helplessness in the face of overwhelming odds, a masterful love of life, and an unyielding hold upon the basic morality underlying all national experiences constituted the physical, psychic and ethical elements out of which the Messianic faith was fashioned. The Messianic ideal was a group conception into which political aspirations, religious imperialism and moral vindications merged.

In the beginning the Messianic ideal was temporal and political, colored by that intense mystico-religious imperialism of the nation which was the legacy of prophetism. The ideal evolved into supernaturalism as the task of national redemption and universal conversion appeared progressively more difficult of accomplishment through human effort alone. While the human character of the Messiah and his religio-political mission were never entirely lost sight of, certain miraculous potencies were added to his personality in proportion to the nation's realization of its own impotence. Only the cataclysmic intervention of a divinely endowed being, at the moment of the nation's deepest degradation, could destroy the wicked powers which oppressed it, restore the people, cleansed by suffering, to its ancient glory and rebuild the broken harmonies of the world. The nation could not save itself—except through repentance. Moral purification could prepare the way for the advent of the redeemer. But only as a penitent sinner could Israel play a part in the drama of its national salvation.

Messianism thrives on suffering. It is its soil and sap. And in Israel suffering was continuous throughout the centuries, if only the suffering which derives from the consciousness of the loss of national independence and a national home. The Jew never forgot, even when others did not cause him to remember, his exile.

Also he never forgot the divine promise of Redemption! In his darkest hour he never doubted it. He knew his exile to be penance and atonement—a long and dreadful penance and an unprecedented atonement. But he also knew that in a world of providential justice no penance can be everlasting. "Behold, we who are in this long and bitter exile," writes Moses Albelda (16 c.), "are warranted in hoping for our Redemption for three reasons: first, because of God's compassion, 'for the mercies of the Lord are unending'; second, because of the vindication of God's name which has been profaned among the nations; and, third, because of God's promise, for He is certain to keep His word."[1]

Again, this mundane cycle cannot terminate, as it must terminate after it had traversed its span of 6000 years, without human life first attaining to absolute perfection. This was the certain law of human progress. Israel entertained an active faith in the life ascendant, rising through defeat until it reached its consummation in universal harmony and well-being. By that token its own redemption was inevitable.

Redemption was certain, however long deferred. But when *would* it come? The troubled heart wished to know. "When will be the end of the wonders?" It turned to the Sacred Text for answer. It sought to discover the secret by reading the riddle of the cryptic texts of Daniel, by interpreting the phrases, words and letters of other prophetic texts, by conjecture and computation—an enterprise of pathetic futility, but one which slaked a thirst, one which comforted and cheered.

At times Messianic calculations seemed so real, so plausible and so clearly implied in prophecy as to set the whole

[1] *Sha'are Dim'ah*, Venice, 1586, p. 138 b.

nation agog with vivid expectation and stampede it into disastrous Messianic movements. At times these calculations were so authoritatively delivered as to cause the migrations of whole communities to the Holy Land on anticipatory Messianic pilgrimages. Some of the pseudo-Messiahs in Israel were as much the creatures of these "literary" Messianic speculations of the people as the up-thrusts of the untoward political conditions of their times.

Too little attention has been paid to the rôle which the practice of "calculating the end" played in the successive Messianic movements from the first century onward.

To trace the story of these Messianic calculations in Israel from the destruction to the Shabbetai Ẓebi movement, to analyze their method and technique, to point to their historic consequences, and also to disclose the consistent opposition to them throughout the centuries are the objects of this study.

PREFACE

The nucleus of this book is the doctorate thesis which I presented to the faculty of the Hebrew Union College in 1925. I have, since, considerably enlarged the original work and completely revised it.

I wish to express my profound gratitude to my friend, the eminent scholar and historian, Professor Jacob Mann, of the Hebrew Union College, for the many valuable suggestions and helpful criticisms which he generously offered me during the preparation of this book. He made me doubly his debtor by assisting me in the revision of the proofs.

I am also indebted to Professor Alexander Marx of the Jewish Theological Seminary of America, Mr. Adolph S. Oko, Librarian of the Hebrew Union College, Dr. Joshua Bloch, Chief of the Jewish Division, New York Public Library, and Mr. Gordon W. Thayer, Librarian of the John G. White Collection, Cleveland Public Library, for their unfailing courtesy in placing at my disposal such books as I required in the prosecution of these studies.

A. H. S.

May, 1927

PREFACE TO BEACON PRESS EDITION

This book, which I wrote a little more than 30 years ago, carries the story of Messianic speculation in Israel through the 17th Century. This appeared a logical place to stop: for the Messianic movements of that century marked the climax of such movements in Jewish history since the rise of Christianity and their catastrophic denouement.

The Shabbetian Movement swept through all the ranks of world Jewry, excited the highest hopes — and led to spiritual debacle and national humiliation. It had shaken the Jewish community to its very depths. The sober leaders of the people, once they had rediscovered their voice and their courage, determined not to permit such a thing to happen again. They frowned upon all further speculation inasmuch as such speculation always contributed to the rise of Messianic pretenders. Nevertheless speculation persisted, for the Messianic hope itself persisted among the people. It glowed like a flaming star in the darkness of their lives. The tragic conditions of the times, especially as they affected Polish Jewry, lent desperate urgency to that hope. The study of the Zohar, and of Lurianic Kabbala generally, continued unabated. Such study always provided fertile soil for the Messianic complex. This was especially true among those circles which refused to abandon their belief in the Messianic role of Shabbetai Ẓebi even after his conversion to Islam in 1666 and his death in 1676.

Unlike all other Messianic movements since the time of Jesus, that of Shabbetai Ẓebi persisted even after his death; his followers spread Shabbetian doctrines, or those ascribed to him — some of them not without Trinitarian and Incarnation overtones — far and wide. Foremost among them was Abraham Miguel Cardoso (c. 1630-1706) a Morrano, from Spain or Portugal; Mordecai Mochiaḥ (c. 1650-1729); Daniel Bonafoux (second half of 17 c.); Jacob Querido (d. 1690), brother-in-law of Shabbetai Ẓebi, and his son, Berechiah. In Poland, Ḥayyim Mal'ak and Löbele Prössnitz (d. 1750) were active Shabbetian propagandists. Among these leading followers some claimed to be Messiahs themselves or the incarnations of Shabbetai Ẓebi or the Messiah ben Joseph, the forerunner of the Messiah ben David.

When the miracle year, 1666, failed to usher in the anticipated redemption, and, in fact, witnessed the conversion of the proclaimed Messiah to Islam, his baffled but undismayed followers turned to the year 1668 as the true year of deliverance. They saw in the apostasy of the Messiah only the necessary preliminary stage in fulfillment of his mission which was to descend into the lowest depths and bring up the souls lost among the *kelipot,* the shells of uncleanness — the demonic powers, and by his personal degradation atone for Israel's sins and save the generation from the birth pangs of the Messianic times. Calculations were soon forthcoming pointing to the year 1668 as the true year of redemption. When this year too disappointed the hopes of believers, other calculations were discovered which pointed to the year 1673, 1674 or 1675. It might be noted, in passing, that the year 1674 witnessed a strong Messianic agitation in Morocco where Joseph ben Ẓur announced himself as the Messiah ben Joseph and prophesied that the actual redemption, through Shabbetai Ẓebi, would take place in the year 1675. (See Gershon Shalom, *Shabbetai Ẓebi,* Tel Aviv, 1957, Vol. II, p. 770.) Not even the death of Shabbetai Ẓebi put an end to the speculations. It was held that he would arise again and return to complete his work. In fact it was argued that the whole Jubilee period from 1640 to 1690 was the destined period of redemption. When the Jubilee ended in disappointment, the faithful continued to project still other but more remote dates.

One of the most colorful and dynamic of the Shabbetian apostles, whose activities in Amsterdam created a bitter controversy and a rift in that community, was Neḥemiah Ḥiva Ḥayyun. He had wandered through Palestine, Egypt, Turkey and Italy and was an old man when he finally arrived in Amsterdam in 1713. His reputation as a Shabbetian had preceded him as well as the fact of his excommunication.

In his Kabbalistic commentary on the Pentateuch "Dibre Neḥemiah" (Berlin, 1713) Ḥayyun calculates the time of the redemption. The exile has lasted through the Fifth Millenium (240-1240 C.E.). The first half of the Sixth Millenium (1240-1740 C.E.) also belongs to the exile and is called Night. The Night is divided into three watches during which God mourns over the destruction of His Temple and the dispersion of His people (Ber. 3a). This Night which is divided into three watches thus lasts 1500 years. During the first watch the Judgments prevail and the evil *Kelipot* wax strong. During the second watch the *Kelipot* are divided and their strength begins to wane. It is during the third watch (1240-1740 C.E.) that the people of Israel will go forth from exile: "In the morning behold the men were sent forth" (Genesis 44.3) — that is, redeemed from exile — (Dibre Neḥemiah, p. 60 a, b).

In 1699 Judah Ḥasid of Poland, himself not a Shabbetian, but a mystic and an ascetic, undertook a pilgrimage to Palestine with hundreds of followers who called themselves Ḥasidim — pietists, believing that the year of Redemption was at hand. Many who accompanied him perished on the way. He himself died three days after he arrived in Jerusalem and his group of followers was scattered, many of them returning to Europe, some abandoning their faith altogether. The Shabbetian, Ḥayyim Mal'ak, joined this pilgrimage of Judah Ḥasid, and for a time remained in Palestine. He believed that the Messiah would come in the year 1706. The reason for it was that Moses kept the Jews in the wilderness for forty years before he led them to the Promised Land, so Shabbetai Ẓebi would arise from the dead and redeem the people in 1706 — forty years after his first appearance (1666).

The Shabbetai Ẓebi movement reached its lowest depths in the Messianic adventures of Jacob Frank and his followers. They were tainted with grossness and moral corruption, not unlike the Christian sect of the Carpocratians of the 2nd Century which plagued the early Church so grievously. One of their doctrines was that the way to purge one's soul from sin was through physical debauchery. The Frankists, of course, encountered the fierce opposition of the responsible leaders of Jewry, and they became bitter enemies of the rabbis as well as of the Talmud. They called themselves Zoharists out of their devotion to the "Zohar." They succeeded in forcing some of the rabbis of Poland into public disputations (1757; 1759) reminiscent of the disputations into which Spanish Jews were forced in the 13th and 14th centuries. They even charged their fellow Jews with the dread blood accusation. As a result of their activities the Talmud was ordered publicly burned. The Frankists finally went over to Christianity *en masse* (1759), but not before they had brought much shame and confusion upon the household of Israel.

The disruptive consequences of the Shabbetai Ẓebi movement lasted far into the 18th Century. A disastrous controversy, continuing for more than six years, raged between Jacob Emden (1698-1776), doughty champion of anti-Shabbetianism, like his father before him, the Ḥaham Ẓebi (1658-1718) — and Jonathan Eibeschuetz (1690-1765), Chief Rabbi of the triple community — Altona, Hamburg and Wandsbeck. Eibeschuetz, one of the foremost Rabbinic authorities of his day, was accused by Emden of Shabbetian heresies, and of having inserted the name of Shabbetai Ẓebi in certain amulets which he had distributed. The controversy soon spread "from Lorraine to Podolia, from the Elbe to the Po" (Graetz) and engulfed many of the foremost Rabbis of Europe. The bitter feud, in which both sides resorted to the most extreme measures and to unrestrained and abusive attack succeeded in nothing so much as in undermining, irreparably, the prestige and influence of the Rabbinate with the people. This ruinous controversy in Western Europe and the violent convulsions wrought in the East by the Frankist movement, may be said to have brought to a close the calamitous century-long Shabbetian complex in Jewish history.

Thereafter, while Messianic speculation continued, and occasionally a mystic visionary like Moses Ḥayyim Luzzatto (1707-1747) may have secretly harbored, or may have been accused of harboring, Messianic pretentions, no Messianic movement of any consequence centered in a living personality makes itself manifest among European Jewry.

In Yemen, however, there arose in 1861, a prophet, Judah bar Shalom, who claimed to be the messenger of Elijah, and announced the near advent of the Messiah. He is described by contemporaries as a poor, honest, middle-aged artisan much given to Kabbala and the study of the Zohar, and slightly unbalanced.

Rumors of his miracle-making powers spread far and wide. His Messianic prophesies must have aroused the suspicions of the ruler of the province, for at his command he was waylaid in the mountain passes back of his village and assassinated. His head was sent to Sana and there exposed on the gates leading to the Jewish quarter.

But some three years later a man arose who claimed to be the resurrected Judah bar Shalom — and men believed him.

On Passover, in 1867, he announced that at the end of the month he would attack the city of Sana with a large host of soldiers from the tribes of Gad and Reuben, and also with Arab soldiers. The Imam of Yemen threatened to destroy all the Jews. The Jews were thrown into utter despair. They fasted and prayed. The good offices of the ruler of the city of Sana were employed and for a very liberal consideration he interceded for them. They were spared.

The neo-Judah bar Shalom quoted Scripture to prove the authenticity of his mission. Gen. 49.1 reads: "Gather yourselves together, that I may tell you that which shall befall you in the end of days." The Gematria of באחרות הימים — "the end of days" is 621, or 1861, the year in which the Messianic vision came to Judah.

Arabia, Egypt and Palestine were profoundly stirred by this Messianic pretender. The repercussions were felt in Turkey, Babylon and Bombay. Jews in Alexandria assembled in the synagogues at midnight, prayed, chanted psalms and diligently studied the Zohar. The Yemenite Jews seem to have been completely bewitched. Those who dared to question Judah's claims were hounded and persecuted and compelled to flee the country. (See Jacob Saphir, *Eben Saphir,* Mainz, 1874, Vol. II, pp. 149-152.)

While the Ḥasidic movement of the 18th Century, founded by Israel Baal Shem Tov (c. 1700-1760) was not a by-product of the Messianic fervor of the 17th and early 18th centuries it undoubtedly reflected the mood and temper of that age, so steeped in Kabbalistic lore and so riven by the appalling tragedies of the Chmielnicki massacres.

Ḥasidism was not centered in Messianism, although the hopes of the coming of the Messiah were as strong among the Ḥasidim as among all other believing Jews. Occasionally one hears of a Ḥasidic leader like Rabbi Moses Teitelbaum (1759-1841), in Hungary, who so eagerly and confidently awaited the coming of the Messiah that he kept his holiday garb and his silver cane ready at hand at his bed-side so as not to lose any time when the Shofar of the Messiah would be blown. But not many were so eager or so impatient. Occasionally too, one hears of a Ḥasidic wonder Rabbi, like Israel Ruzhyner (c. 1797-1850), of Sadagora, founder of the famed Friedmann dynasty, who may have harbored Messianic pretensions which were of a rather non-active sort. That too is very rare. The Ḥasidic Ẓadikim did not assume Messianic roles. They greatly loved and revered the Holy Land and many of their leaders settled there. The Baal Shem himself and his great disciple Rabbi Joseph HaKohen (d.c. 1782) set out for Palestine but were forced to turn back. Rabbi Naḥman of Brazlav (1777-1811), great grandson of the Baal Shem, lived for a time in Palestine. In 1777 a group of some three hundred Ḥasidim settled in Palestine under the leadership of Rabbi Menaḥem Mendel of Vitebsk.

We do not find, however, any extensive speculation as to the actual time of the advent of the Messiah in Ḥasidic literature, though much space, of course, is devoted to the concepts of Messiah and Redemption. A more spiritual and less activist approach to the subject is in evidence. The Baal Shem himself wrote of an encounter which he had with the Messiah in a vision. When he questioned him as to the time of his appearance on earth, the Messiah replied:

> "It shall be a sign unto you when your doctrine shall become known and the fountains of your wisdom shall be poured forth; when all other men shall have the power of performing the same mysteries as yourself, then shall disappear all the hosts of impurity and the time of great favor and salvation shall arrive."

In a similar vein did Rabbi Ḥayyim of Czernowitz interpret the Messianic moment in history:

> "After all the evil in the world shall have been overcome and goodness and holiness shall have ascended to power in the highest degree, and all the sparks and souls which are held captive in the *Kelipot* shall have been purified and released, then will our righteous Messiah most certainly come and set us free; for this is the essence of the redemption. When the good will be redeemed from the evil and all the souls and holy sparks will go forth purified from the exile of the *Kelipot,* then their physical bodies too will go forth and will be redeemed in a perfect redemption after which there will never again be any exile."

("Be'er May'im Ḥayyim, Par. Toledot) This is a recurrent theme in Ḥasidic literature.

In the closing half of the 18th and in the 19th centuries the Messianic movement in Judaism ceased to be a compelling historic actuality. The dogma, of course, remained. It was never rejected but progressively it receded into the background.

The consequences of attempting to concretize the Messianic idea had proved disastrous. It had lead to disillusionment, apostasy, moral chaos and danger. It had disrupted the peace of many communities.

But now new winds had begun to blow through the Jewish world. In Western Europe the age of Mendelssohn and of the Haskala was dawning. The Middle Ages were coming to a close. A new age was soon to be born. Secular studies would before long force the mystic lore of the Kabbalist and all Messianic romancing into the dim background. The French Revolution and the armies of Napoleon would soon batter down the ghetto walls and Jewish life would begin to move rapidly into the mainstream of European life and culture.

Even in the East, where Medievalism would hold sway longer, and social and political emancipation would lag behind, a recoil from the Kabbalistic Messianic obsession was inevitable. The responsible leaders of Jewry, both lay and rabbinical, came to realize the dangers which threatened the integrity of their communal life and their very faith. They, accordingly, resorted to a number of drastic disciplinary measures, including formal excommunication. They succeeded finally in checking the license of the Messianic adventurers and the mass hysteria which resulted from their activities. The study of Lurianic Kabbala was prohibited by the Council of the communities of Southern Poland, which met in Brody in 1756, to all men under 40, and the study of the Zohar and the works of Cordevero to men under 30, and then only if the student had first made himself fully proficient in Talmudic studies.

This recalls similar though somewhat less dramatic action which was taken by the leaders of Spanish Jewry in the 14th Century, when they found themselves confronted with situations similar, in many ways, to those of Polish Jewry in the 18th Century.

In the 19th Century there were certain years which were hopefully looked forward to as Messianic years by many for whom the dogma had not lost its force.

The year 1840 was counted on by many as the Messianic year. The deliverance of the Jews of Damascus, who were threatened by a blood accusation, was looked upon as the beginning of the Redemption. The Zohar names 1840 as one of the Messianic years. (See p. 91.) A Gematria for the year is found in the SONG OF SONGS (2.12): "The time of singing is come and the voice of the turtle-dove קול התר is heard in our land." The numerical value of התר is 5600 or 1840.

Judah Alkalai (1788-1878), the precursor of political Zionism, whose writings and activities may be said to represent the transition from the purely religious Messianic hope of Restoration to a practical program of action on the part of the people themselves to rebuild Zion, regarded the year 1840 as the year of the Messiah b. Joseph, soon to be followed by the Messiah b. David. (See Minḥat Yehudah, Vienna, 1843.)

The year 1860 was another such year. Many Jews neglected their business activities in confident anticipation of the advent of the Messiah. The letters of the Hebrew word meaning "Crown" כתר add up to 1860.

Aḥad Ha-Am records that among the Ḥasidim of Sadagora — his own father was a Sadagora Ḥasid — the year 1866 was looked to as the Messianic year. They had for their authority their Rabbi who based his calculation on the numerical value of the initials as well as of the final letters of the Biblical phrase (Lev. 16.30). "For on this day shall atonement be made for you, to cleanse you, from all your sins you shall be clean before the Lord." ("Reshumot" — VI, p. 553.)

The Zionist movement, secular and political in the main though it was, nevertheless attracted many who saw in it the preparatory stage for the Messianic Ingathering and Restoration. On the other hand it was attacked by some orthodox religionists as an unwarranted act of "crowding the End" — and as an attempt to accomplish with human hands that which could only be achieved by divine intervention.

The establishment of the State of Israel in 1948 has been viewed by many as Messianic fulfillment — by others only as a partial fulfillment. The complete Messianic hope is the spiritual redemption of the whole of mankind, when the world will be perfected in justice, brotherhood and peace under the kingdom of the Almighty — "when the Lord shall be One, and His name shall be One."

The Messianic hope sustained the Jewish people through centuries of darkness and tragedy, of homelessness and persecution.

PREFACE TO BEACON PRESS EDITION

In its prophetic expression as the beckoning vision of a redeemed humanity, it continues to guide, inspire and sustain men of goodwill everywhere.

August, 1958 A. H. S.

ERRATA

Page 62. Line 14 should read אמוני.

Page 65. Line 6 should read בארמוני and belongs at the beginning of line 5.

Page 87. Note 24 should read בגד.

Page 89. Line 26. *Ibbur* should read *Gilgul.*

Page 99. Line 23 should read *Palestinian.*

Page 104. Line 10 should read *Senior.*

Page 115. Note 11 should read *inserere.*

Page 127. Line 4 and 7 should read 531 and 1531.

Page 129. Line 24, should read קבלת הראשונים.

Page 138. Note 112, should read האר"י.

Page 151. Line 4 should read *Annus Mirabilis.*

Page 158. Note 13 should read החסידות.

Page 185. Note 81 should read דמקרא,

Page 187. Note 96 should read עמוקות.

Page 189. Note 104 should read אחד מכם גולה לברברי ואחד מכם לסמטרי (Sarmatia) דומה כמו שגליתם כולכם . . . ונשתעבדתם בע' אומות.

Page 200. Note 25 should read *χρόνους ἤ τοὺς καιροὺς.*

Page 209. Line 13 should read באחרית הימים.

Page 220. Note 61 should read ספר נצחון.

A HISTORY OF MESSIANIC SPECULATION IN ISRAEL

Chapter I

THE TALMUDIC PERIOD

A. Before 70 c. e.

The pathetic eagerness to read the riddle of Redemption and to discover the exact hour of the Messiah's advent was shared in common by Jews in Palestine and throughout the Diaspora, and continuously from the time of the loss of their national independence. In spite of rabbinic injunction and the admonitions of the more discerning among them, the quest proceeded with varying intensity clear down the ages. At times it seems to be the idle speculation of leisure minds, intrigued by the mystery; at other times it is the desperate search of men in great tribulation. Saadia, analyzing the *locus classicus* of Messianic prophecy—the Book of Daniel—appears in the rôle of a pious exegete, mystically biased, attempting to unravel a knotty problem. Isaac Abarbanel, an exile, crushed by the tragedy of the Spanish expulsion, seeks refuge and hope for himself and his afflicted brethren in the selfsame field of adventism.

The critical events in the history of the world which affected Jewish life invariably stimulated interest in such speculation. Great political changes, boding weal or woe for Israel, accelerated the tempo of expectancy. Wars, invasions, migrations of peoples, the rise and fall of dynasties were fraught with significance for the scattered Jewish communities, and the rich fancy of the people, stirred by the impact of these great events, sought to find in them intimations of the Great Fulfilment. The

Maccabean wars, the struggle with Rome, the fall of the Temple, the Bar Kochba uprising, the Perso-Roman wars, the fall of Rome, the rise of Islam, the Crusades, the coming of the Tartars, the expulsions, the Ottoman conquests, the religious wars of the sixteenth and the seventeenth centuries, the Cossack rebellion of 1648, and many other momentous occurrences intensified, each in its time, the Messianic hope among the people and precipitated adventist speculations and movements in Israel.

That successive calculations proved false and seemingly certain forecasts never materialized did not at all discourage renewed essays in the field. The troubled heart would not surrender this precious enterprise. In dark hours the Messianic promise was the one prop and stay of suffering Israel, and the desperate wish for Redemption expressed itself in Messianic prognostications, even as desires often fulfil themselves in dreams. The forecasts were, of course, doomed to non-fulfilment, and the people in consequence suffered from disillusionments commensurate with the ardor of their expectations. Leaders in Israel, aware of the demoralizing effects of such frustrated hopes, attempted to dissuade the people from continuing their efforts to solve the mystery, but without avail. The dire urgencies of their life forced them to seek surcease from despair in apocalyptic fancies and Messianic romanticism.

These calculators sought, and apparently found, support in the Bible. The Bible seemed to offer precedent and warrant for such an occupation. The Book of Daniel, the one canonized apocalyptic tract out of the many which were widely circulated and held in high regard by the people, dwelt upon the mystery of the "end of days" and seemingly gave a clue to its solution. There were many other Biblical passages which seemed to point to the Messiah, and which, if properly interpreted, could be made to yield up the secret of his coming. All the ingenuity of rabbinic method in hermeneutics and homiletics was therefore brought into play, and words, phrases and letters, vowels, accents and tropes, and all the mystic science of letter and numeral were marshaled into service.

Prior to the first century the Messianic interest was not excessive, although such great historical events as the conquest of Persia by Alexander, the rule of the Ptolemies and the Seleucides, the persecutions under Antiochus, the revolt of the Maccabees, and the Roman aggression find their mystic-Messianic echo in the apocalyptic writings of the first two pre-Christian centuries. Calculations, however, as to the exact hour of the Messiah's appearance are wanting.[1] Mention of the Messiah is made in some of the books of the Apocrypha, e.g., in Enoch (2 c. B. C. E.), in the Psalms of Solomon (1 c. B. C. E.) and at times in a well-defined technical sense; but it is significant that such books as Tobit (3 c. B. C. E.) which, through Persian influence, contains a rather well-developed eschatology and angelology, Ben Sirach (3 c. B. C. E.) and the Wisdom of Solomon (1 c. B. C. E.) make no mention whatever of the Messiah. Even in the apocalyptic Book of Jubilees (2 c. B. C. E.) he is mentioned only once.

The first century, however, especially the generation before the destruction, witnessed a remarkable outburst of Messianic emotionalism. This is to be attributed, as we shall see, not to an intensification of Roman persecution but to the prevalent belief induced *by the popular chronology of that day* that the age was on the threshold of the Millennium.

In the procuratorship of Cuspius Fadus (44 C. E.) the false prophet Theudas appeared, "and many were deluded by his words. However, Fadus did not permit them to make any advantage of his wild attempt but sent a troop of horsemen out against them, who, falling upon them unexpectedly, slew many of them and took many of them alive. They also took Theudas alive and cut off his head and carried it to Jerusalem."[2] The Romans' severity was undoubtedly due to the fact that Theudas either enter-

[1] Unless Josephus' account of the predictions of the Pharisees in the case of Herod's brother Pheroras, and the eunuch Bagoas, implies such a calculation (*Antiquities* XVII. 2. 4. See also Schürer, *Geschichte*, II.[4], p. 599).

[2] Josephus, *op. cit.*, XX. 5.1.

tained Messianic notions himself or announced himself as the Messiah. The Messianic hope, of course, always implied the overthrow of the Roman power in Palestine.

The movement gained headway under the procuratorship of Felix (52–60 C. E.). Numerous outbreaks are reported. "There were such men as deceived and deluded the people under the pretense of divine inspiration, but were for procuring innovations and changes of the government; and these prevailed with the multitude to act like madmen, and went before them into the wilderness, as pretending that God would there show them *the signals of liberty*; but Felix thought the procedure was to be the *beginnings of a revolt*; so he sent some horsemen and footmen, both armed, who destroyed a great number of them."[3] An Egyptian prophet, undoubtedly an Egyptian Jew, now appears on the scene, whose short Messianic career brought sharp reprisals upon the Jews.[4]

When Jesus came into Galilee, "spreading the gospel of the Kingdom of God and saying the *time is fulfiled* and the kingdom of God is at hand,"[5] he was voicing the opinion universally held that the year 5000 in the Creation calendar, which is to usher in the sixth millennium—the age of the Kingdom of God—was at hand.[6] It was this chronologic fact which inflamed the Messianic hope of the people rather than Roman persecutions. There is no evidence anywhere to show that the political fortunes of the people in the second quarter of the first century of the common era—the period of many Messianic movements—were in any degree lower than those in the first quarter, in which no Messianic movements are recorded.

Jesus appeared in the procuratorship of Pontius Pilate (26–36 C. E.). The first mention of the appearance of a Messiah in Josephus is in connection with the disturbances during the term of office of the procurator Cuspius Fadus (c. 44 C. E.). It seems likely, therefore, that in the minds

[3] Josephus *Wars* II. 13.4; *Ant.* XX, 8.6.

[4] *Ibid.* The Egyptian prophet is also mentioned in Acts 21. 38.

[5] Mk. 1.14–15.

[6] See also Mk. 9.1, 13.30; Matt. 10.23. See *infra*, pp. 16 ff.

of the people the Millennium was to begin around the year 30 C. E.

Be it remembered that it is not the Messiah who brings about the Millennium; it is the inevitable advent of the Millennium which carries along with it the Messiah and his appointed activities. The Messiah was expected around the second quarter of the first century C. E., because the Millennium was at hand. Prior to that time he was not expected, because according to the chronology of the day the Millennium was still considerably removed.

The central theme of the preachment of Jesus and of John the Baptist, whom Jesus hailed as the Elijah who was to announce the advent of the Millennium,[7] as well as of the disciples of Jesus, was repentance. The day of repentance will precede the actual Millennium. Thus *The Assumption of Moses*, which was probably written during the very lifetime of Jesus, states: "And receive thou this writing that thou mayest know how to preserve the books . . . until *the day of repentance* in the visitation wherewith the Lord will visit them in the consummation of the end of the days." (1.17–18). Only those who would repent would be spared the purging and cleansing process antecedent to the Millennium—"the wrath that is to come."[8]

Jesus' essential mission was apocalyptic, not prophetic. He was more of the mystic than the moralist. His impassioned concern was not to reconstruct society but to save it from the winnowing and retributive judgment which was imminent in the van of the approaching Millennium. He sought to save men from the birth-throes of the Messianic times. The ethical counsel which he gave to his followers was for a world *in extremis*. It was to help them survive the terrors to come and to be worthy of the perfect Kingdom, the new order of existence which the Millennium would usher in. The Kingdom will be not the moral achievement of men but the pre-ordained act of divinity. The whole epic of Jesus must be read in the light

[7] Mal. 3.23; Matt. 11.11–15.
[8] Matt. 3.7.

of this millenarian chronology of his day, or it remains unintelligible.

Passionately did Jesus strive to convey this message of the impending crisis to the people. Ardently he strove to warn them of the approaching catastrophe. He was profoundly perturbed and impatient because the people did not seem to realize it: "Ye hypocrites, ye know how to interpret the face of the earth and the heaven; but how is it that ye know not how to interpret this time?"[9] Though he would not, because he could not[10] definitely state the exact hour of the coming of the Kingdom and advised against speculation upon the subject,[11] he nevertheless was completely overwhelmed by the thought of its nearness: "And being asked by the Pharisees when the kingdom of God cometh, he answered them and said, The kingdom of God cometh not with observation (i. e. cannot be ascertained through the popular methods of calculation). Neither shall they say, Lo, here! or there! but lo, the kingdom of God *is* in the midst of you."[12] "Verily I say unto you, there are some of them that stand here, who shall in no wise taste of death till they see the Son of Man coming in his kingdom."[13]

The crash and doom of the world was at hand and therefore there was no longer time for the ordinary pursuits of life, for its commonplace commerce and traffic, for concerns about food, raiment, and shelter: "Be not therefore anxious, saying, What shall we eat? or, What shall we drink, or, Wherewithal shall we be clothed?"[14] The end is approaching! The unquenchable fires of Judgment are upon us! Therefore, "Seek ye first His kingdom and

[9] Luke 12.56.

[10] Matt. 24.36: "But of that day and hour knoweth no one, not even the angels of heaven, neither the son, but the Father only" *Cf. Yoma* 9b: "To my heart alone have I revealed it, not even to the ministering angels."

[11] *Cf.* Acts 1.6–7: "They therefore when they were come together asked him saying, Lord, dost thou at this time restore the kingdom to Israel. And he said unto them, It is not for you to know time or seasons," referring to the "times" and "seasons" of Dan. 7.25 and 12.7.

[12] Luke 17. 20–21.

[13] Matt. 16. 28; also 10.23.

[14] Matt. 6.31.

His righteousness."[15] A man must disencumber himself of all those things which are likely to keep his mind and soul entangled in the affairs of this perishing world. Wealth, Jesus felt, would of all things prove the most difficult obstacle in the way of men's preparation for the Kingdom. Wherefore he counsels a rich man who seeks after the perfection which will admit him into the Kingdom: "Sell that which thou hast, and give to the poor."[16] There is no time to waste. A disciple cannot be spared from the desperately needed ministry of proclamation even long enough to go and bury his own father.[17] Jesus does not permit himself the enjoyment of even a moment's relaxation in the bosom of his family.[18] He is convinced that many could be saved from the impending doom, but that there were too few "laborers for the harvest."[19]

Jesus' attitude toward the Law was determined by his views concerning the approaching end. He did not oppose the Law in part or in whole. He did not seek to abrogate it. He did not wish to substitute for it. It was not necessary. The incoming Millennium would of itself do away with the Law entirely. This was the view commonly held by the contemporaries of Jesus.[20] However, "until all things be accomplished," the Law must be obeyed. Not, however, as most men obey it, formally and mechanically, but with a soul-searching intent and intensity, so that it may prove a real help to that spiritual lustration required for initiation into the Kingdom. Jesus' real attitude to the Law is admirably summed up in Matt. 5.17–20:

> Think not that I am come to destroy the Law or the prophets; I come not to destroy but to fulfil. For verily I say unto you, till heaven and earth pass away, one jot or one tittle shall in no wise pass away

[15] Matt. 6.33.
[16] Matt. 19.21.
[17] Matt. 8.21–22.
[18] Matt. 12.46–50; Mk. 3.31–35; Luke 8.19–21.
[19] Matt. 9.35–38.
[20] *Cf. Nid.* 61b: מצות בטלות לעתיד לבא. ("All commandments are abolished in the world to come.")

> from the law, till all things be accomplished. Whosoever shall break one of these least commandments and shall teach men so, shall be called least in the kingdom of heaven; but whosoever shall do and teach them, he shall be called great in the kingdom of heaven. But I say unto you, that except your righteousness shall exceed the righteousness of the scribes and Pharisees, ye shall in no wise enter into the kingdom of heaven.

Jesus proceeds to indicate what he means by a righteousness which exceeds the righteousness of the scribes and Pharisees.[21] In no instance does he call for a new Law or the abrogation of the old Law, but for the correct "intensive" attitude toward the existing Law.[22]

Why should men fulfil the law with such inner intentness? Not that they will thereby bring the Kingdom about. The Kingdom comes through the grace of God, not through the works of men: "For it is your Father's good pleasure to give you the kingdom."[23] Its advent is pre-ordained in the cosmic scheme. It is inevitable. It cannot be hastened or retarded. But those who will fulfil the Law in truth and in sincerity will be spared the "pangs of the Messianic times" and will be privileged to enter the Kingdom.

Similarly was Jesus' attitude toward the government determined by his apocalyptic premises. He was not a revolutionist. He did not attempt to deliver his people from the yoke of Rome. He counseled no political action. It was no longer necessary. The Millennium was near and Rome would be crushed by a power greater than that of man. Her doom was sealed, even as the doom of all malefactors of society. Therefore until the hour of universal reckoning is come, "render unto Caesar the things that

[21] Matt. 5.21 ff.

[22] Jesus' attitude toward divorce (Matt. 5.31–32) was the attitude of the school of Shammai, and was expressed *within* the framework of the Law. So also were his strictures concerning oaths and his pacifist doctrines (Matt. 5.33–39) shared by many Pharisees of his day.

[23] Luke 12.32.

are Caesar's, and unto God the things that are God's."[24]

The thought of the approaching end dominates almost all the writings of the New Testament. Paul was as much convinced of the imminence of the new order as Jesus.[25] So were those to whom Paul addressed himself. Like Jesus, he advised his followers not to speculate about the apocalyptic "times and seasons" of Daniel. The great cataclysm is at hand, but it will come "as a thief in the night," and no one can know the exact hour.[26]

Paul never assumed that Jesus would bring the Kingdom about. Jesus merely proclaimed the gospel of repentance in view of the world's approaching crisis. His death and resurrection were in the eyes of Paul the supreme proof of his divine commission to make this proclamation. It further established beyond a doubt that he was the Messiah, awaiting the pre-ordained moment of the actual inauguration of the Kingdom to reappear. Jesus may have doubted his own Messiahship and may have looked forward to the coming of the Son of Man—the real Messiah. If he believed himself to be the Messiah, he clearly did not make this the essential part of his proclamation. Paul, however, was certain that Jesus was the Messiah. The vision which had come to him of the resurrected Jesus proved to be the all-compelling fact in his life.[27] So that Paul proclaimed not only the imminence of the end but Jesus as the Christ, who is soon to reappear with the advent of the Millennium. It followed, therefore, that one's preparation for the Kingdom must include not only the intensive ethical self-discipline preached by Jesus but also an acknowledgment of the Messianic rôle of Jesus. Thus a dogma of faith was added to a code of conduct. This is the vital distinction between the gospel of Jesus and the gospel of Paul. Paul was keenly aware of this distinction. He baptized not according to "John's baptism," which was "the

[24] Mk. 12.17.
[25] I Cor. 1.7 ff., 4.5, 7.29 ff., 10.11; Rom. 13.11 ff.; I Thess. 3.13, 4.15-18.
[26] I Thess. 5.1 ff.
[27] I Cor. 15.12 ff.

baptism of repentance,"[28] but "in the name of the Lord Jesus."[29] To Paul it was insufficient to know "only the baptism of John."[30]

When Jesus died his disciples and followers continued in their profound convictions touching the imminence of the Kingdom. This was now coupled with another conviction, that Jesus would return with the coming of the Kingdom, to complete his Messianic work. Their chief prayer was their Master's prayer, "Thy Kingdom come," and their motto as summarized in the Didache was, "Watch for your life's sake; let your lamps not go out, and your loins not be relaxed, but be ready; for ye know not the hour in which our Lord cometh."[31]

As the crisis approached in the life of the nation with the sack of Jerusalem and the destruction of the Temple, the Messianic excitement of the people was at fever heat. While the Temple was burning a prophet appeared announcing that the Messiah was at hand. "A false prophet was the occasion of these people's destruction, who had made a public proclamation in the city that very day that God commanded them to get up upon the Temple and that there they should receive miraculous signs of their deliverance. Now there was then *a great number of false prophets* suborned by the tyrants (i. e. the Zealots—the militant patriots) to impose upon the people, who denounced this to them that they should wait for deliverance from God."[32]

Josephus also recounts a Messianic calculation popularly held at the time of the destruction based upon "an ambiguous oracle that was also found in their sacred writings, how 'about that time, one from their country should become governor of the habitable earth.'"[33] Josephus applies this prophecy to Vespasian.

Tacitus recounts the high Messianic expectation, based

[28] Acts 19.4.
[29] Acts 19.3–5.
[30] Acts 18.25.
[31] The Didache, Chap. XVI. Cf. Matt. 25. 1 ff.
[32] Josephus *Wars* VI. 5.2.
[33] *Ibid.*, VI. 5.4.

upon an authoritative tradition, held at the time of the destruction: "The majority were deeply impressed with a persuasion that it was contained in the ancient writings of the priests that it would come to pass that *at that very time*, that the East would renew its strength and they that should go forth from Judea should be rulers of the world."[34] So also Seutonius: "A firm persuasion had long prevailed through all the East that it was fated for the empire of the world *at that time* to devolve on someone who should go forth from Judea. This prediction referred to a Roman emperor, as the event showed, *but the Jews applying it to themselves broke out into rebellion*."[35]

With the final collapse of the state, the destruction of the Temple, and the tragic dispersion of the people, Messianism assumes preëminence in the national consciousness. In it the race voices its invincible hope of survival and Redemption. It should be borne in mind that Messianism was essentially a political ideal. It was bound up with the restoration of the Davidic dynasty and with the reconstitution of the independence of Israel. Certain eschatological and supernatural features were combined with it, but essentially it was and remained a this-world, temporal, national ideal.

B. 70 C. E.—175 C. E.

The century following the destruction—the age of the Hadrianic persecutions and the Bar Kochba revolution—witnessed not only a remarkable spread of the Messiah idea among the people, but also many definite speculations as to the time of his advent.

1. *Yoḥanan ben Zakkai* (1 c.), just before his death, turned to his disciples and said: "Remove all vessels lest they be rendered unclean, and prepare a throne for Hezekiah, king of Judea, who is come."[36] King Hezekiah, whom the Rabbis held in highest regard as defender and champion of the Torah[37], was regarded by some of them

[34] *History* V. 13.
[35] *Life of Vespasian*, par. 4.
[36] *Ber*. 28b.
[37] *San*. 94b.

as the Messiah. This is clearly the meaning of Rabbi Hillel's dictum: "Israel no longer need expect the Messiah, for he was already consumed (he already appeared) in the days of Hezekiah."[38] Another teacher, Bar Kappara of Sepphoris (2-3 c.), indicates, that this belief was held by some of his colleagues: "The Lord wished to make Hezekiah Messiah, but Justice protested and said, 'Master of the Universe, David, King of Israel, who sang so many songs and praises unto thee, Thou didst not make Messiah. Hezekiah, in whose behalf Thou hast already performed so many miracles, and who did not sing praises unto Thee, wilt thou make him Messiah?' Wherefore it (the letter ם in לם'רבה [Is. 9.6]) was closed."[39]

Ben Zakkai, who died about a decade after the destruction of the Temple, expected the Messiah, then, in the immediate future (c. 80 C. E.).

2. *Rabbi Eliezer ben Hyrcanus* (1-2 c.) believed that the "days of the Messiah" (ימות המשיח) would last forty years. His belief, according to one Baraita, was based on Ps. 95.10: "For forty years was I wearied with that generation." According to another Baraita, on a combination of Deut. 8.3: "And he afflicted thee and suffered thee to hunger and fed thee with manna" (40 years in the wilderness); and Ps. 90. 15: "Make us glad according to the days wherein thou hast afflicted us."[40] According to *Midrash Tehillim* 90.17, it was Rabbi Akiba, whose faith in the restoration never wavered[41] and who heroically championed the cause of Bar Kochba, who entertained this belief.[42]

It is, of course, difficult to establish exactly what the

[38] *San.* 99a.

[39] *San.* 94a. Geiger suggests that the Hezekiah here mentioned is identical with Hezekiah the Galilean, who was killed by Herod and whose son Judah was the founder of the party of the Zealots. Judah's son Menaḥem played an important rôle in the revolt of 66. This family may have claimed Davidic descent and entertained Messianic ambitions (see *Jüdische Zeitschrift*, VIII, pp. 35 ff.)

[40] *San.* 99a. See discussion of this passage in Bacher's אגדות התנאים, I, pp. 102–3 and notes.

[41] *Makkoth* 24a, b.

[42] See also *Pesiḳ. Rab.* I, ed. Friedmann, p. 4a.

Rabbis meant by "the days of the Messiah." There is not only a difference of opinion among them as to the duration of these days, but also as to their character. It is clear that some Rabbis understood by it the years *following* the appearance of the Messiah, and continuing up to the establishment of the New Order—the Millennium. Others took it to mean the period of Messianic travail immediately *preceding* the coming of the Messiah. Still others included in it the whole epoch from the preparatory period prior to the appearance of the Messiah to the destruction of the world *at the end* of the Millennium. This may account in part for the wide disparity as to the supposed length of these "days of the Messiah" varying from forty years to two thousand years.[43]

It is of interest, however, to note that the Rabbis of the first and the early part of the second centuries—those who lived during the destruction of the Temple, and those who lived before, during or immediately after the Bar Kochba revolution—all gave a comparatively *brief* term to the Messianic age: Rabbi Eliezer ben Hycranus, 40 years; Rabbi Eleazar ben Azariah, 70 years; Jose the Galilean, 60 years. Whereas those who lived after the Bar Kochba revolution, and in the succeeding centuries, gave comparatively *long* terms to the Messianic age: Rabbi Dosa, 400 years (600 years); Judah ha-Nasi, 365 years. Even longer terms are attributed to Samuel, Naḥman bar Isaac, and to the anonymous Tanna debe Eliyahu.

The explanation may lie in the fact that the earlier Rabbis took the "days of the Messiah" to mean the days of travail immediately *preceding* the advent of the Messiah, and they expected the Messiah to appear *in the very near future.* The Bar Kochba revolution shattered these Messianic hopes and brought tragic disillusionment into the hearts of the people, so that the Rabbis who lived after this fateful apocalyptic debacle sought to project the Messianic hope to a more distant future, thereby discouraging, if possible, a recrudescence of such intense hopes in the immediacy of the Messiah's advent.

[43] See *San.* 99a; also *Pesiḳ. Rab.* chap. 1.

Rabbis and laymen of the first and the early half of the second centuries generally believed that they were living at the close of the fifth millennium—the last millennium before the thousand years of peace which were to close this mundane cycle. This fact seems generally to have been overlooked by scholars who unconsciously employ the present Creation calendar, which did not make its appearance until considerably later. There are but two references to the Creation calendar in the Talmud, *'Ab. Zar.* 9b (4231 A. M.) and *San.* 97b (4291 A. M.) The latter date is given in connection with R. Joseph bar Ḥiyya (4 c.). The next mention of a Creation date is found in the Baraita of R. Samuel, where the date 4531 A. M. or 771 C. E., is given.[44]

The Messianic hopes were rife in Israel at this time, not only because the people were suffering under Roman oppression, but also because their chronology led them to believe that they were on the threshold of the Millennium. There did not, of course, exist as yet a fixed and authoritative tradition regarding the age of the world. For some centuries thereafter this subject was debated, among Jews as well as among Christians, but it is evident that the men of the first and the early part of the second centuries had an approximate idea of the place of their age in the creation cycle. They were very near the year 5000!

The Rabbis generally believed on the basis of the Biblical Creation week, that "The world will last 6,000 years and will be in chaos 1,000 years."[45] The thousand years prior to the destruction of the world (5000–6000) would be the years of consummation and universal blessedness.

The closing chapter of the apocalypse IV Ezra gives a very explicit date: "And I did so in the seventh year of the sixth week *of 5,000 years of the creation*, and three months and twelve days."[46] The author of this apocalypse

[44] See Bornstein's article "תאריכי ישראל" in the התקופה, IX, pp. 222 ff., and Mahler's *Handbuch der jüd. Chronologie*, p. 156.

[45] *San.* 97a.

[46] 14.48.

anticipated the swift approach of the "consummation of the times." The writer of the original source of IV Ezra, living just 35 years after the destruction,[47] believed in the imminent collapse of the Roman Empire and the speedy restoration of Israel. In answer to the preplexed Salathiel (Ezra), who could not reconcile Israel's suffering with the justice of God, the angel replies: "If thou survive, thou shalt see, and if thou livest long, thou shalt marvel, for the age is hastening fast to its end."[48] The final redactor of IV Ezra, living in the early reign of Hadrian (c. 120 C. E.) expected the Messiah to come during or directly after the reign of this emperor.[49]

II Baruch, a composite work of the latter half of the first century, clearly expresses this same thought regarding the age of the world, and the expectations of an early denouement: "For truly my redemption has drawn nigh, and is not far distant as aforetime."[50] "And at that time, after a *little interval*, Zion will again be builded."[51] "For the youth of the world is passed, and the strength of the creation already exhausted, and the advent of the times *is very short* . . . and the pitcher is near to the cistern, and the ship to the port."[52] In 28.2 the writer seems even to give a cryptic date, which, however, is undecipherable: "For the measure and reckoning of that time are two parts a week of seven weeks."

Josephus, too, gives clear indication that the men of his generation took their age to be at the close of the fifth millennium. His *Antiquities*, which give an historical account from Creation to the year 66 C. E., cover an itemized period of approximately 5,000 years. He wrote the first book of his *Contra Apionem* (93 C. E.) to substantiate his claim of the great antiquity of the Jewish people. He

[47] 3.1. See Charles, *The Apocalypse and Pseudepigrapha*, II, p. 552.

[48] 4.26. See also verses 44–50: "The fire and the rainstorm have already gone by, only the smoke and the drops remain"; and 5.55: "The creation is growing old."

[49] 12.27–32.

[50] 23.7.

[51] 68.4.

[52] 85.10.

writes: "Those *Antiquities* contain the history of 5,000 years, and are taken out of our sacred books."[53] Josephus, in his writings, largely presented the accepted Pharisaic view of his day.

So that the Rabbis, immediately following the destruction, believing themselves to be in the final cycle of the fifth millennium, thought that the "days of the Messiah" would last 40, 60 or 70 years, and expected the Messiah to come during the second century; to be more exact, within the first half of the second century; for it is very likely that the destruction of the Temple was soon regarded by them as the beginning of this Messianic age—the *terminus a quo*. The Messianic age was to begin at a time when the fortunes of the people were at their lowest ebb. It was quite natural, therefore, for them to assume that "on the day when the Temple was destroyed the Messiah was born."[54] If this is correct, the Messianic age, beginning with the destruction of the Temple and lasting 40, 60 or 70 years, would culminate in the years 110, 130 or 140 C. E. The Bar Kochba revolution was, in a sense, the political upthrust of these perfervid Messianic expectations, based on the Millenarian chronology of the early second century, the immediate occasion being Hadrian's prohibition of circumcision, and his avowed intention to restore the Temple as a shrine for Jupiter Capitolinus.

The collapse of this movement at the close of the putative fifth millennium prompted the Rabbis not only to project the Messianic date to a more distant future, but also to *revise their notion of the Creation calendar*. They were living not at the close of the *fifth* but at the close of the *fourth* millennium. The people need not despair of the Messiah. He is still to come. He may come at any time within the fifth millennium, not necessarily at its close; perhaps in 4231 A. M. or 4250, or 4291.[55] The Messianic age has actually begun with the destruction of the Temple,

[53] Bk. I.1
[54] *Jer. Ber.* II, 5a; *Mid. Ekah. R.* 1.57.
[55] See *infra*, p. 26.

but before its final denouement 365 or 400 years or more may elapse.

Christian polemics may also have been responsible for this 1000-year revision in the Creation calendar, which took place before the third century. Christian propagandists from the first century on maintained that Jesus was the fulfilment of prophecy, and that he was born at the close of the fifth, or in the first part of the sixth millennium, when, according to prophecy, the Messiah would be born. St. Augustine preserves the tradition that Jesus was born in the year 5000 A. M.[56] Theophilus (2 c.), the first of the Christian chronologers, traces 5,529 years from Creation to the birth of Jesus.[57] So do also Hippolytus[58] (2-3 c.), Clement of Alexandria (2 c.)[59] and Julius Africanus[60] preserve the tradition that he was born c. 5500. "For the Jews . . . have handed down to us by their extant Hebrew histories the number 5,500 years as the period up to the advent of the Word of Salvation, that was announced to the world in the time of the sway of the Caesars." The Rabbis found it necessary to counter this by asserting that this claim is false, inasmuch as the sixth millennium is still far off. The church fathers and later Christian writers accused the Rabbis of deliberately falsifying the Creation calendar in order to deny the Messiahship of Jesus.[61]

3. *Rabbi Eleazar ben Azariah*, a contemporary of Rabbi Eliezer, believed that the Messiah would come 70 years

[56] See *De Civ.* XXII. 30.5.

[57] *To Antolycus*, Bk. III, chap. 20–28.

[58] See *infra*, p. 34.

[59] See his *Stromata*, Bk. I, chap. 21.

[60] Fragment I of the *Five Books of The Chronology*.

[61] See Graetz, *Monatschrift*, II, p. 433.

The Mohammedan chronologer Albiruni (973–1048) gives evidence that such a charge was made even in his day by Christian scholars against the Jews. He writes: "The Christians reproach the Jews with having diminished the number of years with the view of making the appearance of Jesus fall into the fourth millennium in the middle of the seven millennia, which are, according to their view, the time of the duration of the world, so as not to coincide with that time at which, as the prophets after Moses had prophesied, the birth of Jesus from a pure virgin at the end of time, was to take place." (*The Chronology of Ancient Nations*, ed. C. E. Sachau, London, 1879, p. 18.)

after the destruction (that is, c. 140 C. E.), and based his judgment on Is. 23.15: "And it shall come to pass in that day that Tyre shall be forgotten 70 years, according to the days of one king"—the one king being the Messiah.[62]

4. *Rabbi Jose, the Galilean,*[63] a contemporary of Rabbi Eliezer and Rabbi Eleazar ben Azariah, thinks that the Messiah will come three generations (60 years) after the destruction (i. e., c. 130 C. E.), and bases his opinion on Ps. 72.5: "They shall fear thee while the sun endureth, and as long as the moon, throughout all generations." (דור דורים=3 generations.)

This may also have been the opinion of Rabbi Ishmael (2 c.)[64]. Rabbi Ishmael is quoted by Rabbi Nathan (2 c.) as basing a Messianic computation upon Ps. 80.6: "Thou hast fed them with the bread of tears and given them tears to drink in a threefold measure," =שליש= three generations.[65]

All the above-mentioned teachers lived during or shortly after the fall of Jerusalem, and believed that the Messiah would appear in the very near future. Akiba, too, who credited the Messianic mission of Bar Kochba, believed that the end was near. He is quoted by Rabbi Nathan (2 c.) as basing his hope for an early appearance of the Messiah on Haggai 2.7. "Yet a *little while longer* and I will shake the heavens and the earth."[66] This seems also to have been the hope of the Tanna, Jose ben Ḳisma (2 c.), who was an eye witness of the Bar Kochba insurrection. His disciples asked him: "When will the son of David come?" He answered: "When this gate will fall and rise, and fall and rise again, and fall a third time, then the Messiah will come before they have time to rebuild it."[67]

[62] *San.* 99a.

[63] We follow the version of *Mid. Tehillim* 90.17 rather than that of the Baraita in *San.* 99a, which reads "Rabbi" who offered another date.

[64] We follow Klausner's suggestion that in place of Simlai, an Amora of the third century, we should read "Ishmael", a contemporary of Rabbi Akibà (see הרעיון המשיחי בישראל, p. 25, note 1).

[65] *San.* 97b.

[66] *San.* 97b.

[67] *San.* 98a.

"This gate" probably refers to the gate of Jerusalem; the first and second fall to the first and second destruction; and the third to the fall of Jerusalem before Julius Severus. The Rabbi expected the deliverance to come soon after the great catastrophe, probably through a victory of the Parthians over the Romans.[68]

M. Friedmann correctly remarks: "In the first generation after the destruction, when Rabbi Yoḥanan ben Zakkai, who had said, 'Prepare ye a throne for Hezekiah, king of Judea, who is come,' had died, the hearts of the great men and teachers in Israel were filled with hope that within a short time the visions of the prophets (concerning the restoration) would be fulfilled."[69] They searched Holy Writ for intimations. Especially did they peruse the Book of Daniel. R. Nathan states that certain Rabbis deduced the Messiah's date from an interpretation of Dan. 7.25: "And they shall be given into his hand until a time and times and half a time."[70]

From the first century we also have the testimony of Josephus that the Book of Daniel was held to contain prophecies concerning the ultimate redemption from the "Roman" yoke. In his *Antiquities* he writes: "In the very same manner Daniel also wrote concerning the Roman government, and that our country should be made desolate."[71] Josephus seems also to have known of a definite interpretation of the "beasts" and "times" visions of Daniel, which, however, he quite deliberately withholds from his readers: "Daniel did also declare the meaning of "the stone" to the king, but I do not think proper to relate it, since I have only undertaken to describe things past or things present, but not things of the future; yet if anyone be so very desirous of knowing truth, as not to wave such points of curiosity, and cannot curb his inclination for understanding the uncertainties of futurity, and

[68] See *infra*, p. 28.

[69] *Seder Eliahu rabba und Seder Eliahu zuta*, Vienna, 1902, Intro., p. 21 *et passim* and chap. iii.

[70] *San.* 97b.

[71] Bk. X, 11.7.

whether they will happen or not, let him be diligent in reading the Book of Daniel, which he will find among the sacred writings."[72] So also the author of IV Ezra, who, quite consciously, is supplementing and interpreting the visions of Daniel, writes: "The eagle which they saw come up from the sea is the fourth kingdom which appeared in vision to thy brother Daniel."[73]

The Rabbis of the period immediately after the destruction even discussed the day and month of the Messiah's coming. Rabbi Joshua (1-2c.) said: "In Nisan (the 14th day) were they (the children of Israel) redeemed, in Nisan will they again be redeemed." Rabbi Eliezer (1–2c.) believed that the Redemption would take place in Tishri (on New Year's day). The latter bases his conclusion on a combination of Ps. 81.4–5 and Is. 27.13, and the former on Ex. 12.42.[74]

It is of interest to note how many of the above-mentioned teachers who deliberated upon the Messianic advent were of a definite mystic bias. Yoḥanan ben Zakkai studied and taught Ma'aseh Merkabah.[75] Rabbi Eliezer ben Hyrcanus was fond of employing the mystic technique of Notarikon[76] in interpreting the Bible[77] and was even accused of Christian leanings.[78] Rabbi Akiba was one of the four who entered the Pardes (engaged in esoteric philosophy) but escaped heretical taint. He too was a student of the Merkabah,[79] and later ages regarded him as the author of the mystic text, *Othiot d. R. Akiba.* Rabbi Joshua is highly praised by Yoḥanan ben Zakkai for his great knowledge of Ma'aseh Merkabah.[80] Rabbi Jose the Galilean was looked upon as a miracle worker[81] and as late as the tenth century men invoked him in prayer:

[72] *Ant.*, Bk. X, 10. 4.
[73] 12.10.
[74] *R. H.* 11b.
[75] The mystic lore concerning the Heavenly Chariot (Ezek. 1). *Hag.* 14b.
[76] See *infra*, pp. 244 ff.
[77] *Sab.* 55b; *Mid. R. Num.* 23.2.
[78] *'Ab. Zar.* 16b.
[79] *Hag.* 14b.
[80] *Hag.* 14b.
[81] *Jer. Ber.* 9b.

"R. Jose the Galilean, heal me!"[82] and R. Ishmael b. Elisha was a great Aggadist[83] and was by later ages regarded as the author of the *Hekalot* and *Shi'ur Ḳoma.*

That the Rabbis of the latter half of the first and those of the early half of the second centuries actually believed that the redemption from the yoke of Rome and the restoration of the people to political independence would take place in the proximate future is also apparent from the many Talmudic passages which give a definite Messianic content to the political and social conditions of their times. The Rabbis regarded the demoralization which set in the life of the people as a result of the fall of Jerusalem, the unsuccessful rebellion of Bar Kochba, and the subsequent persecutions, as the *ḥeble Mashiaḥ*, the travail pains of the Messianic Age. These teachers, in the passages which we are about to quote, were not describing theoretically, in an academic vein, the conditions which would prevail at some future time when the Messiah would come. They were concretely depicting the unprecedented conditions which actually were existing in their own time, and they were sincerely anticipating a swift change through the advent of the Messiah. That these conditions actually did prevail is clear from a reading of the tragic catalogue found in the *Mishnah Sotah* IX 12–15: "From the day the Temple was destroyed the 'Shamir' (a worm that cuts stones with its glance) ceased to exist, and the 'Nofet Ẓufim' (honeycomb) as well as the men of faith. . . . From the day the Temple was destroyed there is no day which does not bring with it a curse; the dew never descends for a blessing, the taste is gone from the fruit, even the fat from the crops. . . . From the day the Temple was destroyed the Ḥaberim (scholars living under a rigid regime of Levitical purity) and the men of excellence have been put to shame, the men of action have been impoverished, but the men of violence and slander have become powerful and no one seems to seek or inquire after God. . . From the day the Temple was destroyed the Ḥakamim

[82] See Pinsker, לקוטי קדמוניות, App. p. 32.

[83] *M.K.* 28b.

(the sages) have become like the Soferim (scribes), the Soferim like the Ḥazzanim (teachers of children), the Ḥazzanim like the 'Ame ha-Areẓ, (the unlettered ones), and the 'Ame ha-Areẓ are growing poorer and poorer." It is only *after* the enumeration of this list that the *Mishnah* sharply and significantly turns to a catalogue of the conditions which will prevail just prior to the coming of the Messiah—'be'ikbata di-Meshiḥa'—conditions which are the exact parallel "in extenso" of those just given. The *Tosefta Soṭah,* describing the condition of the times, makes no mention of the Messiah at all.

These conditions ushering in the Messiah, enumerated in the *Mishnah,* are given anonymously. In *San.* 97a they are attributed to three rabbis, all three of the second century.

1. *Rabbi Judah* (2 c.) said: "In the generation when the son of David will come, the scholars' meeting place will be turned into a place of debauchery. Galilee will be destroyed, the Gablan (Gabalene—very fertile land) will be desolate, and its men will wander helplessly about from city to city, and the wisdom of the scribes will be held in ill repute, and sin-fearing men will be disdained, and the face of the generation will be like the face of a dog, and truth will nowhere be found."[84]

2. *Rabbi Neḥorai* (2 c.) said: "In the generation when the son of David will come youths will put old men to shame, and old men will be compelled to stand in the presence of youths, and a daughter will rise up against her mother, and a bride against her mother-in-law . . . and a son will not respect his father."

3. *Rabbi Neḥemiah* (2 c.) said: "In the generation when the son of David will come, insolence will increase and high prices will prevail, the vine will yield abundantly but the price of wine will be high, and the whole kingdom will be

[84] See also II Baruch 70.3–5. The interpretation of the "last black waters": "And they shall hate one another, and provoke one another to fight, and the mean shall rule over the honorable, and those of low degree shall be extolled above the famous. And the many shall be delivered into the hands of the few, and those who were nothing shall rule over the strong, and the poor shall have abundance beyond the rich, and the impious shall exalt themselves above the heroic, and the wise shall be silent, and the foolish shall speak."

converted to apostasy (minut) and no amount of censure will avail."

A similar opinion is expressed by Rabbi Eleazar ben Simon (2 c.): "The son of David will not come until all judges and officers have disappeared from Israel."[85] An anonymous Baraita reads: "The son of David will not come until the acts of informing (delivering a man over to the government) will increase, the number of students will decrease, and the last coin will disappear from the purse, and men will begin to despair of redemption."[86]

Palestinian teachers of the third century, like Rabbi Ḥanina ben Ḥama and Rabbi Yoḥanan ben Nappaḥa, and those who, like Rab and Samuel, came under the Palestinian influence, retained this tradition, but only as a general feature of Messianic times

C. 175 C. E.—500 C. E.

Following the frustration of the Messianic hope in the second century, the next Messianic date seems to have been generally, though not exclusively, placed about four hundred years after the destruction, somewhere in the fifth century. The Rabbis no longer pointed to a date in the near future, but projected it into a relatively distant future. The Bar Kochba disaster had taught them a bitter lesson. The figure 400 was quite naturally fixed upon as it corresponded with the number of years of the first exile—the Egyptian.[87] The principle was laid down that the final redemption would be exactly like the first redemption.[88]

1. *Rabbi Dosa* (2–3 c.) stated that the Messiah would come at the end of 400 years. He derived his figure from a comparison of Ps. 90.15 with Gen. 15.13: "And they shall afflict them 400 years."[89]

2. According to a Baraita in *San.* 99a, Rabbi Judah ha-Nasi (c. 135–220 C. E.), the redactor of the *Mishnah*, believed that the Messiah would come 365 years after the

[85] *San.* 98a.
[86] *San.* 97a.
[87] Gen. 15.13.
[88] *Mid. R. Num.* 11.3.
[89] *San.* 99a.

destruction (i. e. c. 435 C. E.). The number corresponds to the number of days in the solar year, and the ground for his opinion he finds in Is. 63.4: "For the day of vengeance that was in My heart and My year of redemption are come," that is, one year for every day in the solar year. An anonymous Baraita[90] states that the Messiah would come 354 years after the destruction (i. e. c. 425 C. E.), according to the number of days in the lunar year.

3. *Rabbi Ḥanina* (3 c.) likewise believed that the Messiah would appear 400 years after the destruction. "If 400 years after the destruction a man says to you 'Buy my field, which is worth one thousand dinars, for one dinar,' do not buy it."[91] The Messiah will appear that year, and land will be distributed free to everybody. A Baraita is also quoted there to the same effect: "If in the year 4231 A. M. (c. 470 C. E.) a man says to you 'Buy my field, which is worth a thousand dinars, for one dinar,' do not take it."

4. The legend of the mysterious scroll found in the archives of Rome seems to point to a similar Messianic date. Rabbi Ḥanan ben Taḥlipa sent word to Rabbi Joseph (4 c.): "I happened upon a man who had in his possession a scroll written both in Assyrian and Hebrew script (i. e. in square characters and in the Hebrew language). I asked him where he got it, and he told me that he had hired himself out as a servant in the Roman army, and that he had found this scroll in the archives of Rome. In it is written: 4291 years after Creation the present order of the world will come to an end. The Wars of the Serpents will then take place, and the Wars of Gog and Magog, following which the Messianic age will set in."[92] It is probable that the figure originally read 4231 (i. e. c. 470 C. E.).[93]

[90] *Mid. Tehil.* ed Buber. Ps. 90.17, note 93.

[91] *'Ab. Zar.* 9b.

[92] *San.* 97b.

[93] The Wars of the Serpents are an echo of the Tehom-myth, whose classic expression in the Bible is found in Is. 27-1 (see W. O. E. Oesterley, *The Evolution of the Messianic Idea*, Chap. V.) Gog and Magog are the legendary enemies of Israel. They will lead the hosts of the heathen nations in their final attack upon Israel, but they will be utterly discomfited.

5. A similar prediction is contained in the revelation made to Rabbi Judah, brother of Rabbi Sela Ḥasida, (3 c.) by Elijah himself: "The world will endure no less than 85 jubilees (4250 years), and in the last jubilee the son of David will come" (i. e. between 440 and 490 C. E.). Rabbi Judah inquired whether he would come toward the beginning or the end of that period, or at the very end, but Elijah replied that he did not know.

Rab Ashi, who lived in the beginning of the fifth century —the Messianic century—sought to avert any evil consequences which might follow upon the failure of the Messianic hope, by interpreting this statement of Elijah to mean, "Before the 85th jubilee you need not expect him at all. After the 85th jubilee you *may* expect him."[94]

6. A teacher of the school of Elijah expressed the belief that the Messiah could have come as early as 240 C. E., but the sins of the people delayed his coming. "The world will exist 6000 years. The first 2000 years were those of chaos (without the Torah), the second 2000 years were those under the Torah, and the last 2000 years are the Messianic years. But because of our many sins there have already elapsed the years which have gone by (and the Messiah has not yet come)."[95] According to this belief those living after 240 C. E. are definitely within the Messianic cycle and may expect his coming at any time, provided the people are prepared through repentance and self-purification to receive him.

As the fifth century approached the Messianic expectation became vivid and intense. That century witnessed the final scenes in the decline and fall of Rome, mistress of the world for six hundred years. It was a distraught and turbulent century, seething with unrest, marked with the swift movements of barbarian peoples upon Rome; the invasion of Alaric, king of the Visigoths, and the sack of Rome (410 C. E.), the migration of the Vandals through Spain and their conquest of Africa under Gaiseric (430 C. E.), a second sack of Rome by these Vandals (455

[94] *San.* 97b.
[95] *San.* 97a, b; *'Ab. Zar.* 9a.

C. E.), and another invasion of Italy by Attila and his Huns (452 C. E.). The year 476 C. E. witnessed the end of the Western Empire. Such times are favorable for prophecy and high hopes. Israel saw in these successive misfortunes which befell her ancient enemy 'the footprints of the Messiah.' "A certain general (Roman) asked one of the men of Beth Silanus, 'Who will rule the kingdom after us?' The man brought blank paper and took a pen and wrote upon it, 'and after that came forth his brother, and his hand (Jacob's—Israel) had hold of Esau's (Edom-Rome) heel.'" The ascendancy of Israel will follow swiftly upon the decline of Rome.[96] The Christian world, too, believed that the fall of Rome would bring Antichrist on earth and usher in the end of things.[97]

From the fall of Jerusalem to the fall of Rome the people of Israel watched and prayed for the defeat of Rome. The people hung with fervent anticipation upon the outcome of every war waged against Rome. "If you see kingdoms contending with one another, expect the footsteps of the Messiah," said Eleazar ben Abina, a Palestinian Amora, who lived in the fourth century.[98] In the second century the Rabbis placed their hope in the Parthians, who were at that time at war with Trajan and Marcus Aurelius. Before Rabbi Jose ben Ḳisma (2 c.) died, he requested his disciples to bury him in a deep grave: "For there will be no palm tree in Babylonia to which the horses of the Parthians will not be tied, and no coffin in Palestine from which the horses of the Medes will not feed."[99] Rabbi Simeon ben Yoḥai (2 c.) said: "If you see the horse of a Persian (Parthian) tied to a post in the land of Israel, expect the footsteps of the Messiah." This opinion is confirmed by an interpretation of Micah 5.4: "And this shall bring about the Peace—Assyria" = Persia. Jewry of the second century was favorably disposed towards the Parthians

[96] *Mid. R. Ber.* 63.13.

[97] See Bryce, *The Holy Roman Empire*, p. 3. This synchronization of Jewish and Christian Messianic speculation is not unique. It occurs again, as we shall see, in the tenth, twelfth and seventeenth centuries.

[98] *Mid. R. Ber.* 42.7.

[99] *San.* 98a, b.

because of the kindly treatment which they enjoyed at their hands, and because they seriously menaced the supremacy of Rome. Rabban Gamaliel (1–2 c.) and Rabbi Akiba (2 c.) both find very laudable qualities in the Persians.[100]

The attacks launched upon the Roman Empire by the new Sassanian dynasty of Persia in the third century again stirred high hopes. Abba Bar Kahana, a contemporary of Rab (3 c.), declared: "If you see benches filled with Babylonians in the land of Israel, expect the footsteps of the Messiah." He substantiates his opinion with a characteristic reading of Lam. 1.13: פרש רשת לרגלי ("The Persian is a net for my foot")—he will bring about my advent. The play is upon the word פרש=to spread, and פרס=Persia.[101] This hope in the third century was further fed by the condition of anarchy and revolution which prevailed in Rome and in the Roman provinces. At this time twenty emperors ruled in Rome in less than a half century (235–284 C. E.).

In the fifth century these hopes reached their fever point. The Empire was breaking up; the long anticipated collapse was about to take place. Furthermore, the conditions of the Jews in the fifth century were most unfavorable. Palestinian Jewry touched bottom in its political and economic fortunes. Roman oppression was intensified. Under Theodosius II. the patriarchate was abolished (c. 425 C. E.). The few remaining schools were closed. The latter half of this century likewise saw a turn for the worse in the condition of the Jews in Babylonia, now the greatest center of Jewish life. A period of persecution and forced conversions set in. Sherira Gaon mentions the fact that "in the year 781 of the Seleucidean era (469 C. E.) all the schools in Babylon were shut down and the Jews were handed over to the Magians."[102]

The Messianic expectations so widely held were not without their historical consequence. During the middle

[100] *Ber.* 8b.
[101] *Mid. R. Ekah.* 1.13.
[102] אגרת לרב שרירא גאון, ed. Neubauer, in *Med. Jew. Chron.*, I, p. 34.

of the fifth century a pseudo-Messiah actually did appear in Crete, who bore the name of Moses. He won a following among the Jews of Crete. On the day appointed for their departure for Palestine, Moses led them to a promontory overlooking the sea, and commanded them to throw themselves into the sea, in the hope that the waters would part for them as they did in the days of the first redeemer, Moses. It is said that many perished.[103]

It is worthy of note that most of the Talmudic passages touching the coming of the Messiah come from Palestinian and not Babylonian sources. The Babylonian teachers were not given to excessive speculations upon this subject. In fact, the one clear negation of the whole Messianic faith emanates from a Babylonian teacher, Hillel (4 c.).[104] Rab maintained that "all forecasts are at an end." Ulla (3–4 c.) declared, "I would rather not see the Messiah when he comes"; and so did Raba (4 c.). The Jews of Babylonia fared far better than their Palestinian brethren up to the time of the persecutions of Jazdegerd II (454-5) and of Peroz (469-70). Under Parthian and Persian rule they enjoyed, except in the few intervals of persecution, comparative security and prosperity. Their schools of Sura, Nehardea and Pumbedita flourished while the Palestinian schools of Yamnia, Lydda, Usha, Sepphoris and Tiberias were shut down one by one. Hence the desperate urge was lacking among Babylonian Jewry for great Messianic anticipations and speculations.

D. Christian Adventism

Pari passu with the spread of Messianic hopes amongst the Jews was the spread of second adventist hopes among the Judeo-Christians and Pagan-Christians. The Christians of the first century were, of course, compelled by the very death of Jesus and his failure to bring about the Kingdom, to postulate his resurrection and his return—an early return. Quite naturally they turned to the Bible for corroboration even as they had turned to it for confirmation of their faith in the Messiahship of Jesus, and for cor-

[103] See *J. E.*, IX, p. 64.
[104] See *infra*, p. 197.

respondence between the prophecies in Scriptures and their fulfilment in Jesus. The Bible soon became in their hands an apocalypse, prophetic of the whole epic of the Messiah Jesus. In this regard they anticipated the Jewish Messianic speculators, whose major effort to make of the Bible a Messianic book did not take place until the second century and especially until after the collapse of the Bar Kochba insurrection.

The writings of the New Testament bespeak the same profound conviction as regards the immediacy of the advent and the establishment of the New Jerusalem, as do the Jewish apocalypses and the sayings of the Rabbis of the first and second centuries.

Paul and the Synoptic Gospels give clear evidence that they expected the early return of Jesus.[105] John, the author of Revelations, who wrote his apocalypse in 95, holds out the promise of the impending advent of the Messiah to the churches whom he addresses: "Behold, he cometh with clouds; and every eye shall see him, and they also which pierced him";[106] "Behold, I come quickly";[107] "for the hour of his judgment is come."[108]

The same hopes are entertained by the Apostolic Fathers. Clement of Rome (end of first century) writes in his Epistle:[109] "Of a truth, soon and suddenly shall His will be accomplished, as the Scripture also bears witness, saying, 'Speedily will He come and will not tarry';[110] and 'The Lord shall suddenly come to His temple.'"[111]

Barnabas (end of first century) quotes Daniel to show that the end is near:[112] "For the day is at hand on which all things shall perish with the evil (one). The Lord is near and His reward."[113]

[105] See *supra*, p. 11 ff.
[106] *Loc. cit.*, 1.7.
[107] *Ibid.*, 3.11 and 22.7,12,20.
[108] *Ibid.*, 14.7.
[109] Chap. 23.
[110] Hab. 2.3.
[111] Mal. 3.1.
[112] Epistle, chap. 4.
[113] *Ibid.*, chap. 21.

These vivid anticipations continue throughout the second and third centuries. At the end of the second century the Montanist movement spread in Christendom and stirred it profoundly. It was heralded by a group of ecstatic prophets, Montanus, Prisca and Maximilla, who announced in the name of the Paraclete promised by Jesus the imminent advent of Christ in the village of Pepuza, in Phrygia. "In the feverish expectation of the last day, country, family and all earthly ties were disregarded. Marriages were dissolved and community of goods and the most severe asceticism prevailed. This state of mental exaltation was fostered by the words of the possessed prophets; the voice of the Paraclete was heard and his exhortations animated them afresh."[114] In the days of Hippolytus (2–3 c.) a similar exodus of rapt expectants took place in Syria. In Pontus a bishop predicted the end of the world during that current year. "His people sold their cattle and left their land untilled to prepare for the great day. In the third century a prophetess of Cappadocia is mentioned, who started an immense multitude en route to Jerusalem."[115]

The early Christian Church borrowed not alone its entire apocalyptic paraphernalia, already completely developed in apocalyptic and pseudepigraphic literature, from Judaism, but also the very method and matter of Messianic chronology. It too turned to the *locus classicus* —the Book of Daniel—for the key to the solution of the mystery, and it too employed pseudo-historical chronology and hermeneutic methods in pursuit of the solution. In fact, the early Christians made more extensive use of the Book of Daniel than did the Jews, both in establishing the Messiaship of Jesus and in discovering the time of his second advent. The Book of Daniel was their strongest argument. Athanasius (4 c.) declared: "Perhaps with regard to the other (prophecies) they (the Jews) may be able to find excuses and to put off what is written to a future time. But what can they say to this, (the prophe-

[114] Abbé Duchesne, *The Early History of the Christian Church*, I, p. 197.
[115] *Ibid.*, note 1.

cies of Daniel), or can they face it at all?[116] From the second century on the Church turned also to the Revelations of John.

The New Testament writers took the prophecies of Daniel to apply to their own times.[117] "The Fourth Kingdom and the Fourth Beast" are Rome. The Son of Man who came with the clouds of heaven[118] is Jesus. The Book of Revelations actually paraphrases Dan. 12.7: "And I heard the man clothed in linen, who was above the waters of the river, when he lifted up his right hand and his left hand unto heaven and swore by Him that liveth forever, that it shall be for a time, times and half a time." Revelations reads: "And the angel which I saw stand upon the sea and upon the earth, lifted up his hand to heaven and sware by Him that liveth forever and ever, who created heaven and the things that therein are, and the earth, and the things that therein are, and the sea, and the things which are therein, *that there should be time no longer.*"[119]

The meaning of the author is clear. The prophecy of Daniel refers to his (the author's) time. The time, times and half a time are already exhausted. There shall no longer be "time." The impending advent of Christ will fulfil the prophecy.

Justin (2 c.) debates the meaning of "time, times and half a time" with Trypho, the Jew.[120] Clement of Alexandria (2–3 c.) gives a complete exposition of the twelfth chapter of Daniel.[121] The seventy weeks[122] are the seventy years which elapsed between the birth of Christ and the destruction. The 2300 evenings and mornings[123] are the "six years and four months during the half of which Nero

[116] "De Incarnatione," Chap. xxxix, in *Nicene and Post-Nicene Fathers*, Second Series, iv. 6.

[117] E.g. Matt. 24.15; Mk. 13.14.

[118] Dan. 7.13.

[119] *Loc. cit.*, 10.5–6.

[120] See *Dialogue*, Chap. 22.

[121] In his *Stromata*, Bk. I, chap. 21.

[122] Dan. 9.24.

[123] Dan. 8.14.

held sway; and for a half, Vespasian, with Otho, Galba and Vitellius reigned."

Tertullian (2–3 c.) goes to great length, in his *Answer to the Jews*, to show that Daniel's prophecies and computations refer to Jesus.[124] Concerning the 70 hebdomads of Daniel, he writes that from the first year of the reign of Darius to the 41st year of the reign of Augustus, when Christ was born, elapsed 437½ years, which are equal to 62½ hebdomads, leaving 7½ hebdomads, which are the 52½ years from the birth of Christ to the subjection of the Jews in the first year of the reign of Vespasian.

Origen (2–3 c.), pupil and disciple of Clement who twice visited Palestine and who was acquainted with R. Hoshaiah and Judah II, believed in the imminence of Christ's return and applied Messianic exegesis to Daniel: "The weeks and years which the prophet Daniel had predicted, extending to the leadership of Christ, had been fulfilled." Moreover, he is at hand who in the Book of Job[125] is said to be about to destroy the huge beast."[126]

Hippolytus (2–3 c.), who called Daniel "a prophet and witness of Christ," gives a complete exposition of that book. The four beasts are Babylon, Persia, Greece and Rome. The "little horn"[127] is the Antichrist. The "stone that smites" is Christ. The "time, times and half a time" are the three and a half years of the reign of the Antichrist, which are equal to the 1290 days of Dan. 12.11.[128] He computes the time of the return of Christ. He bases his calculation on Ex. 25.10—the dimensions of the ark in the Tabernacle (Christ). "The length of the ark is 2½ cubits, its breadth 1½ cubits, its height 1½ cubits, a total of 5½ cubits. These are equal to the 5½ millennia from Creation to the birth of Christ. "From the birth of Christ, then, we must reckon the five hundred years that remain to make up the six thousand (years)

[124] *Op. cit.*, chap. 8.
[125] 41.1.
[126] *De Principiis*, Bk. IV, chap. 1.
[127] Dan. 8.9.
[128] Fragments from Commentaries on Daniel II.

and then the end shall be."[129] Hippolytus, then, like many of his contemporaries and followers, looked forward to the return of Christ in c. 500 C. E. The Jews, as we have seen, also placed their Messianic hope in the fifth century.

Cyril (4 c.), bishop of Jerusalem, while urging upon his catechumens not to be curious as to the time of the end, nevertheless indicates that the Messianic times are at hand, and that the "birth-throes" have already begun. He finds these signs in the war between the Persians and the Romans, in the schisms within the Church, and in the rise of numerous false Christs. He gives his pupils the authentic signs by which the Antichrist and the true Christ can be recognized. He gives an exposition of the Messianic passages of Daniel and calls attention to the fact that the tradition of the Church's interpreters has been that the fourth kingdom of Daniel is Rome.[130] Eusebius (3–4 c.) discusses Daniel at length in his *Demonstratio Evangelica*[131] and again in *Eclogae Propheticai*,[132] He refers to it in his *Church History*.[133]

[129] *Ibid.*

[130] "Cathechetical Lecture," XV, in *Nicene and Post-Nicene Fathers*, Second Series, VII.

[131] Chap. 8.

[132] Chap. 3.

[133] Chap. 6.

CHAPTER II

THE MOHAMMEDAN PERIOD

The failure of the Messiah to appear in the fifth century dampened the ardor of Messianic speculations for a considerable period of time. In fact, such speculations are not in evidence until after the meteoric rise of Islam and its phenomenal sweep through Asia and Africa. The hope of the Messiah did not, of course, at any time disappear in Israel. The literature, largely Midrashic, of the sixth and seventh centuries, abounds in Messianic thought and interest. A few definite Messianic apocalypses come to us from that time, e. g. the Signs of the Messiah (אותות המשיח), which is probably pre-Islamic and which enumerates the ten catastrophic events which will precede the advent of the Messiah;[1] the Agada of the Messiah (אגדת משיח)[2]; and the conclusion of Midrash Wayosha', beginning with: "the Lord will reign forever and ever."[3]

These Midrashim may have been the outgrowth of the national crisis in Babylon during the reign of Kavadh which led to the revolt of the Exilarch Mar Zutra II (520 C. E.) or of the great excitement which prevailed in Palestine during the years 614–28 C. E., when the Persians conquered Syria and Palestine. The return of the Byzantines under Heraclius in 629 resulted in a great persecution of the Jews which lasted until the coming of the Arabs. There are, of course, numerous other Messianic references scattered throughout the Midrashic literature, but there are no definite attempts at computing the end.

[1] See Jellinek, *Bet Ha-Midrash*, II, pp. 58–63; and Eisenstein, *Ozar Midrashim*, II, pp. 390–392.

[2] *B.H.*, III, pp. 141–143; *O.M.*, II, p. 389; found also in *Pesiḳta Zutarti* ed. Buber, IV, pp. 258 ff.

[3] *B.H.*, II, pp. 55–57; *O.M.*, I, pp. 155–156.

But the remarkable victories of the Arabs and the crumbling of the Persian and the Byzantine Empires before their irresistible onslaught set aflame anew the Messianic hopes. The hope was generally entertained that the Arabs would accomplish what the Persians had failed to accomplish—the overthrow of Edom, entrenched in Rome and Byzantium. It was also fervently hoped that they would break the power of Persia, thereby delivering the Jews from the religious intolerance of the Sassanian dynasty. Following these mighty upheavals it was hoped that the Son of David would appear.

A. The Apocalypses

That the Jews regarded the Arabs as their deliverers and read in the mighty events of their day signs of Messianic import is evidenced by the numerous apocalypses of that period which contain Messianic calculations. Among these Midrashic apocalypses may be mentioned the following:

1. Pirḳe de Rabbi Eliezer
2. The Book of Elijah
3. Chapters on The Messiah
4. The Revelations of Simeon ben Yoḥai
5. Midrash of the Ten Kings
6. The Prayer of Simeon ben Yoḥai
7. The Alphabet of Rabbi Akiba (fragment)
8. The Story of Daniel
9. The Book of Zerubbabel

From the practice of the writers of these tracts to count time according to Caliphates, it may be inferred that all these tracts, with the possible exception of the Book of Zerubbabel, were written in Mohammedan lands.

1. *Pirḳe de Rabbi Eliezer.*

The Pirḳe de Rabbi Eliezer, a Pseudepigrapha of Palestinian origin, edited in the eighth century, but containing unmistakable traces of earlier sources, gives three Messianic dates.

In chapter 28[4] the author interprets Abraham's vision of the "covenant between the pieces" found in Gen. 15.[5] God revealed to Abraham the events which would befall his descendants in the generations to come. Four empires would rule over them: Persia, Greece, Rome and Arab. This is suggested in Gen. 15.9. "And he said unto him: Take me a heifer of three years old (Rome), and a she-goat of three years old (Greece), and a ram of three years old (Persia), and an ox (Ishmael), and a young pigeon (Israel)."[6] This is according to Akiba.

According to another view five empires would rule over them: Babylon, Persia, Greece, Rome and Arab. This is suggested in verse 12: "And it came to pass that when the sun was going down a deep sleep fell upon Abram, and lo, a dread (Rome), even a great (Persia) darkness (Greece) fell (Babylon) upon him (Ishmael)." The son of David will flourish "upon him" (Ishmael). In other words, the Messiah will appear after the ascendancy of Islam.

A more specific date is then given. "Rabbi Joshua said: Abraham took his sword and divided them, each one into two parts, as it is said: 'and he took him all these and he divided them in the midst.' "[7] Were it not for the fact that he divided them, the world would not have been able to exist, but because he divided them he weakened their strength, and he brought each part against its corresponding part, as it is said, "and he laid each half over against the other." The author undoubtedly refers to the division of the Roman Empire, which took place after the death of Theodosius in 395 C. E. The Western Empire thus weakened came to an end in 476 C. E. "And the young pigeon," continues the writer, "he left alive, as it is said, 'but the bird he divided not'; hence thou mayst learn that there was not any other bird there except a young pigeon." The young pigeon is, of course,

[4] Ed. Prague, 1784, pp. 13d–14b; Eng. trans. Friedlander, p. 198.

[5] This chapter was regarded as an apocalypse quite early. IV Ezra takes it to refer to the "end of the times" (3.15).

[6] *Cf. Mid. R. Ber.* 44.18.

[7] Gen. 15.10.

Israel.[8] "The bird of prey came down upon them to scatter them and to destroy them. The bird of prey is naught else but David, the son of Jesse, who is compared to a speckled bird of prey, as it is said, "Is mine heritage unto me as a speckled bird of prey."[9] When the sun was about to rise in the east, Abraham sat down and waved his scarf over them, so that the bird of prey could not prevail over them until the raven came (עד שבא הערב)." The writer here clearly refers to the hope for the coming of the Messiah entertained in the fifth century, at the time of the fall of the Western Empire, and explains why the Messiah could not come then. The Messiah was not to appear until after the conquests of the Arabs. The Hebrew word for raven is עֹרֵב, which is a kindred sound to עֲרָב= Arab. If the reading of the first edition is preferred, "until evening (עֶרֶב) set in," the conclusion is unchanged.[10]

"Rabbi Eleazar ben Azariah said: 'From this incident thou mayst learn that the rule of the four kingdoms (Persia, Greece, Rome and Arab) will last only one day, according to the day of the Holy One, blessed be he' " (=1000 years).[11] Friedlander suggests that the period of the four kingdoms mentioned here begins with the Greek persecution under Antiochus Epiphanes, 168 B. C. E. The end of the four kingdoms was therefore to be expected a thousand years later, i. e. c. 832 C. E.[12] It is difficult, however, to understand why the first kingdom should begin with Antiochus Epiphanes. Greek dominion over Palestine did not begin with Antiochus. And what of Persia, which is included in both of the lists of kingdoms enumerated in this chapter? We suggest that the *terminus a quo* is the rebuilding of the Temple, which, according to old Jewish chronology, took place in the year 352 B. C. E.[13]

[8] *Cf.* "Israel is likened unto a pigeon" (*San.* 95a).

[9] Jer. 12.9.

[10] *Cf.* the passage (*Mid. R. Ber.* 50.5): "In the evening (בערב), the evening of Sodom (Rome) came, and her sun set and her sentence was decreed."

[11] Ps. 90.4.

[12] *Loc. cit.*, p. 200, note 6.

[13] See *'Ab. Zar.* 91. Persia ruled 34 years after the rebuilding of the Temple, Greece 180 years, the Hasmoneans 103 years, Herod and Rome 103 years; total, 420 years. The second Temple was therefore built 352 B. C. E.

The four kingdoms, Persia, Greece, Rome and Arab, would last a thousand years; the end of the last kingdom would therefore be c. 648 C. E.

"Rabbi Elazar ben 'Arak said unto him: 'Verily, it is so according to thy word, as it is said, "He hath made me desolate and faint all the day"[14] except for two-thirds of an hour (of God). Know that it is so. Come and see, for when the sun turns to set in the west, during two-thirds of an hour its power is weakened, and it has no light; likewise, whilst the evening is not yet come, the light of Israel shall arise, as it is said, "And it shall come to pass that at evening time there shall be light." ' "[15] Two-thirds of an hour would be about 28 years $\left(\frac{1000}{24}\times\frac{2}{3}=27\frac{7}{9}\text{ years}\right)$. According to Elazar ben 'Arak then, the deliverance of Israel would begin 28 years earlier, i.e. c. 620 C. E. The year of the Hegira was 622 C. E.

The second prognostication is found in chapter 30.[16] "Rabbi Ishmael said: 'In the future the children of Ishmael will do fifteen things in the land (of Israel), in the latter days, and they are . . . and they will build a building in the Holy Place; and two brothers will arise over them, princes at the end; and in their days the branch of the Son of David will arise, as it is said, "And in the days of those kings shall the God of heaven set up a kingdom which will never be destroyed." ' "[17]

It was already pointed out by Zunz[18] that the building spoken of here is the so-called Mosque of Omar, whose foundations were laid by the Caliph Omar in 636 C. E. The two brothers, according to Graetz, are the two sons of Harun al-Rashid—El-Amin and El-Mamun—who ruled over Islam in the first half of the ninth century. This is doubtful. It is not likely that the author would pass over in silence two hundred years of Islamic rule in Palestine,

[14] Lam. 1.13.
[15] Zech. 14.7.
[16] *Op. cit.*, p. 15d; Friedlander, pp. 221–222.
[17] Dan. 2.44.
[18] *Gottesdienstliche Vorträge*, p. 276, note a.

which included the rise of a new dynasty, and settle upon the comparatively unimportant fact of the reign of the two sons of al-Rashid. We believe that the author is writing in the seventh and not in the ninth century. The two brothers are in all likelihood Moawiya, who in 639 was appointed by Omar governor of Syria and Palestine, and who in 661 had himself declared Caliph in Jerusalem, and Ziyad, bastard son of Abu Sofian, father of Moawiya. The latter acknowledged Ziyad as his brother. Ziyad at first opposed Moawiya, but the two were later reconciled and Ziyad became ruler of Basra and the eastern provinces in 665. He died in 672–3. Moawiya died in 680. The author, therefore, expected the Messiah to appear some time in the latter half of the seventh century.

The third prognostication is found in the same chapter 30: "Rabbi Ishmael also said: 'Three wars of trouble will the sons of Ishmael in the future wage on the earth in the latter days . . . one in the forest of Arabia . . . another at sea . . . and one in a great city, which is in Rome . . . from there the Son of David shall flourish and see the destruction of the Gentiles.' "

It has been suggested that these three wars refer to the three stages of the Mohammedan conquest, that of Arabia, Spain and Rome.[19] But this, too, is doubtful. The author living in the seventh century refers to the events of his time. The conquest and consolidation of Arabia was completed under Abu Bekr (d. 634 C. E.). The war at sea refers to the naval engagements between Mohammedan and Byzantine forces from the year 650 C. E. on. In 650 Cyprus was captured by a Mohammedan fleet under Abu Ḳais. In 652 a naval battle was fought near Alexandria between Mohammedan and Byzantine forces, and in 655 the "mast fight"—the naval battle so named because of the numerous ships engaged—was fought between Emperor Constance II and the ships of Caliph Othman, off the coast of Lycia. The war waged in the great city which is in Rome may refer to the conquest of

[19] The last in 830 C. E. (*J.E.*, X, p. 59).

Alexandria by Omar's general, Amr-ibn-el-Ās, in the year 641 C. E., or to the famous attack of the Arabs on Constantinople, the capital of Byzantium, the heir of Rome, in 672. The Byzantines called themselves Romans and their country was called by the Arabs, al-Rūm. This prognostication likewise places the Messianic year somewhere in the middle of the seventh century.

It is of interest to note that a strong Messianic movement began about this time also among the Arabs, nurtured by the civil war which set in between the followers of Ali and those of the Omayyads.[20] The Mahdi (Messiah) idea, derived from Jewish and Christian sources, plays a great rôle in the history of Islam. All Mohammedans looked forward to the coming of a Redeemer who would establish peace and justice on earth. The Shi'ites looked forward to the reappearance of the last of the Imams, who as a child was removed from the earth and remains hidden until his second coming. "Just as many Jewish theologians and mystics have endeavored to compute the exact time of the appearance of the Messiah (based largely on the Book of Daniel), so Sufīites and Shī'ites have calculated, by means of cabalistic use, verses of the Koran and numerical combinations of letters of the alphabet, the exact time of the reappearance of the hidden Imam."[21]

2. *The Book of Elijah.*

The Book of Elijah,[22] in its final redaction, may also be dated from this period. It is a typical apocalypse, and its earlier stratum probably dates from the period of the Perso-Roman struggles in the third century. The angel Michael, after showing Elijah the regions of heaven, reveals to him on Mt. Carmel the time of the end. The Messiah will come in the reign of the last king of Persia. The original apocalypse undoubtedly refers to a Persian ruler of the third century. The final redactor brings the apocalypse "up to date." The Rabbis are made to debate

[20] See Friedlaender, *Die Messiasidee im Islam*, pp. 8 ff; also Goldziher, *Mohammed and Islam*, trans. Seelye, p. 249.

[21] Goldziher, *op. cit.*, p. 243.

[22] *B.H.*, III, pp. 65–68; *O.M.*, I, pp. 26–27.

the name of this last king. One calls him Armilius, another Cyrus. Simeon ben Yoḥai says that his name is הכשרא = Kesra = Chosroes II (590–628 C. E.), who conquered Jerusalem in 614, and his opinion is accepted. The Arabs conquered Persia in 641 C. E. The author expected the Messiah to come shortly after this time, in the second half of the seventh century.

3. *Chapters on The Messiah.*

Chapters on The Messiah[23] contains no definite prognostication, but indicates that the conquests of the Arabs are events presaging the end. The Chapters contains reference to the conquest of Jerusalem and Alexandria, the naval engagements between Islam and Byzantium, and the conquest of Persia by the Arabs. This author likewise intimates that the Messiah would come in the latter half of the seventh century.

4. *The Revelations of Simeon ben Yoḥai.*

The Revelations of Simeon ben Yoḥai,[24] an apocalypse written in Palestine after the year 750 C. E.,[25] which served as a model for other pamphlets of the same character, clearly expresses the thought that the Mohammedans are God's instrument whereby the downfall of Rome will be effected, and definitely places the hour of the Redemption in the period immediately following the fall of the Omayyad dynasty, which took place in the year 750 C. E.

Rabbi Simeon ben Yoḥai, the classic hero of Jewish mysticism, to whom the *Revelations*, as well as the *Prayer of Simeon ben Yoḥai* and the *Zohar* are attributed, is disclosed in his cave[26] ruminating over the passage in Num. 24.21: "And he saw the Kenite (Arab)." He complains to God: "Is it not enough what the kingdom of Edom has done unto us? Must Thou now send upon us also

[23] *B.H.*, III, pp. 68–78; *O.M.*, II, pp. 392–394.

[24] *B. H.*, III, p. 78; *O. M.*, II, pp. 555–557.

[25] See Graetz, Heb. ed., IV, note 16. But *cf.* Steinschneider, "Apocalypsen mit Polemischer Tendenz," in *Zeitschrift der Deutschen Morgenl. Gesellschaft*, Vol. XXVIII, 1874.

[26] *Sab.* 33b.

the kingdom of Ishmael?" Whereupon the angel Metatron (the Revealer) allays his fears: "Fear not, man, the Lord, blessed be He, brings this kingdom of Ishmael upon you only to deliver you from this wicked one" (Edom=Rome=Byzantium). Rabbi Simeon demands proof. The angel adduces Scriptures to substantiate his prophecy: "Go, set a watchman, let him declare what he seeth, and when he seeth a rider, horsemen by pairs, a rider upon an ass and a rider upon a camel, he shall hearken diligently with much heed."[27] The rider upon the ass (=the Messiah),[28] and the rider upon the camel (=the Arabs) are coupled together. The one will follow the other. Again, Is. 60.6 reads: "The caravans of camels (=the Arabs) shall cover thee" (protect and redeem thee).

The angel then proceeds to trace the whole history of Islam from the rise of Mohammed through the line of Omayyad caliphs to the last of the dynasty, Merwan II. Following the death of Merwan II, the angel announces that a cruel king will rule for three months, and the wicked kingdom (Byzantium) will rule over Israel for nine months (a traditional apocalyptic number) . . . then the Messiah ben Joseph will appear and restore the Jews to Jerusalem and rebuild the Temple. . . . But the cruel king Armilius (Antichrist) will then arise, who will be bald and scabby, having small eyes and deaf in one ear[29] . . . who will wage war upon Messiah ben Joseph . . . and Israel will be driven into the wilderness for forty-five days, where the Messiah ben Joseph will die. The Messiah ben David will then appear. The Jews will at first refuse to accept him, saying that the true Messiah had already appeared and been slain, but God will show them that he is in truth the Messiah. He will thereupon slay Armilius. God will then assemble all Israel into Jerusalem, which will be cleansed of all sinners and of all uncircumcised. The heavenly Jerusalem will descend from on high . . . and Israel will dwell in peace for two thousand years, partaking

[27] Is. 21.6–7.
[28] Zech. 9.9.
[29] *Cf.* Midrash Wayosha', end.

of the Behemoth, the Leviathan and the Ziz (fabulous bird). . . . The great Judgment will then take place in the valley of Jehoshaphat.

It is clear that the author of the *Revelations* expected the Messiah to come shortly after the year 750 C. E., the year which marked the fall of the Omayyad dynasty and of Merwan II.

The closing part of the *Revelations*, beginning with "Rabbi Simeon said: 'The Lord will hiss for the fly in Egypt,' " etc. is of a later period and is an abridgment of the second part of the *Prayer of Rabbi Simeon ben Yoḥai* (*q. v.*).

5. *Midrash of The Ten Kings.*

Midrash of The Ten Kings[30] is a composite apocalypse taking the form of a chronicle. Its sources are the *Pirḳe de Rabbi Eliezer* and the *Revelations of Simeon ben Yoḥai.* It enumerates the ten kings who will rule over the world before the advent of the Messiah: (1) God, the first and the last, (2) Nimrod, (3) Joseph, (4) Solomon, (5) Ahab, (6) Nebuchadnezzar, (7) Cyrus, (8) Alexander. This list of eight kings is borrowed *in toto* from *Pirḳe de Rabbi Eliezer*, chapter 11. With some revisions this list is also found in the Targum Sheni on Esther 1.1.

The *Midrash* then continues to tell of the destruction of the Temple, the founding of Yamnia, the Bar Kochba uprising and the Hadrianic persecutions. There is a sudden break here after the words, "and his days will be prolonged in peace." Then follow the prophecies revealed to Rabbi Simeon ben Yoḥai, identical in large measure with the account found in the *Revelations*, though quite distorted. Here, too, the Messiah will appear during the reign of the two brothers, i. e. in the latter half of the seventh century.[31] If the Jews are not found worthy of deliverance at that time, then the Messiah's coming will be postponed until a later time (the time of the fall of the Omayyad dynasty). The author is evidently trying to

[30] Horwitz, *Bet. 'Eked Agadot*, I, pp. 37–65; *O. M.*, II, 461–66.

[31] See *supra*.

combine the two accounts of the *Pirḳe de Rabbi Eliezer* and the *Revelations.*

Toward the end of the *Midrash* the chronological table is resumed. The ninth king will be the Messiah ben David, and the tenth will be God Himself.

6. The Prayer of Rabbi Simeon ben Yoḥai.

The Prayer of Rabbi Simeon ben Yoḥai[32] is modeled closely on the *Revelations.* The first part, ending with the words, "and they will be slain and hung on the trees," is a redaction of the first part of the *Revelations*, ending with the words, "and his sons will be hung on the tree." But while the *Revelations* implies that, soon after the death of Merwan II, 750 C. E., the Messiah will come, the final redactor of the *Prayer* continues his history to the time of the Crusades. One can readily understand how such a Messianic apocalypse and the other apocalypses born out of the turmoil and unrest of the seventh and eighth centuries would be eagerly scanned by the Jews of the equally parlous times of the Crusades, and how such curiosity would result in the revision of these apocalypses so as to bring them into consonance with the events of their own day.

To the chronology of the *Revelations* the author of the first stratum of the *Prayer* adds a reference to the terrible persecutions in Palestine under Emperor Heraclius just prior to the conquest of the country by the Arabs (634 C. E.). He then continues the chronology, as does the author of *Revelations*, to the fall of the Omayyad dynasty. The hope entertained by the Jews that the Messiah would come during the rule of the Arabs is even more forcibly expressed in the *Prayer:* "A troop of camels (Is. 21.7)—i. e. the rule of Ishmael, in whose reign the kingdom of the Messiah will come."

The document now continues: "And it shall come to pass on that day that the Lord shall hiss for the fly that is in the uttermost part of Egypt, and these shall make war

[32] *B. H.*, IV, p. 117; *O. M.*, II, pp. 551–555.

with the Ashkenazim." The term Ashkenazim is a later interpolation. In the *Revelations* the term Egypt is used. The passage seems to refer to the struggle of the Abbasids against the Omayyads. This would account for the fact that the approaching armies are said to hail from the East. The seat of the government of the Abbasids was Bagdad, while that of the Omayyads was Damascus. The reference to the black dress is also clear. Black was the color of the Abbasids. The struggle between the white and the black armies is also referred to in the *Story of Daniel*. If this is correct, then this part of the *Prayer*, like the first part, dates from the eighth century.

Professor Kraus suggests, however, that the Ashkenazim are none other than the Chazars with whom Moawiya waged war. Ḥasdai ibn Shaprut calls the Chazars Ashkenazim, and so does Joseph, king of the Chazars.[33] The Karaite lexicographers, David ben Abraham (10 c.) and Ali Sulaiman (10 c.), also understood Ashkenaz to mean the land of the Chazars.[34] It has also been suggested that this section dates from the period of the Crusades; that Ashkenazim refers to the Crusaders from Germanic lands who were overwhelmed by "the bees from the land of Asshur," viz. the Seljuks. The leader of the Seljuks was the famous Atabek Zangi of Mosul. Asshur is identical with Mosul in medieval Jewish literature.

The author of the final section of the *Prayer* knows of the Crusaders' attack on Egypt, the first of which took place during the Third Crusade (1192). The author also knows of the great siege of Acre (1189–1191) during the Third Crusade. Again, the mention of the Italians may refer to the Fifth Crusade, which set sail for Egypt from Venice in 1218. It is therefore likely that the author of this section, who was also the final redactor of the *Prayer*, lived in the early part of the thirteenth century, and anticipated the coming of the Messiah at that time.[35]

[33] See השלח, XLII, No. 2, pp. 140–141.

[34] See Pinsker, לקוטי קדמוניות, p. 208.

[35] Concerning a Messianic movement in the second decade of the 13 c. see *infra*, pp. 75–76, and concerning Messianic calculations centering in this period, see pp. 65 and 75.

7. The Alphabet of Rabbi Akiba.

The Alphabet of Rabbi Akiba in the Almanzi library,[36] which is in fragmentary form, is a treatise on the mystical significance of the Hebrew letters and contains a clear Messianic calculation. "Eight hundred years after the destruction of the second Temple the Kedarenes will decrease in number . . . at the end of 295 years, according to the calendar of the Gentiles (dating from the Hegira—622 C. E.), this kingdom will vanish from the earth . . . at the end of 304 years according to their calendar the Son of David will come, God willing." This writer evidently expected the Messiah to come in the year 926 C. E.

8. The Story of Daniel.

The Story of Daniel[37] received its final redaction after the First Crusade. The original version probably dates from 9–10 c. It follows the older Midrashim in attempting to give chronologically the list of kings who would rule over Israel up to the end. The narrative and the revelations are here put in the mouth of Daniel. The story abruptly passes from the history of the Persian rulers to Mohammed. The succession of caliphs is given as in the *Revelations*, though not in as accurate a form. A few of the caliphs can be identified. Reference is clearly made to the struggle of the Abbasids against the Omayyads, to the establishment of the seat of the Abbasid dynasty in Bagdad, to Harun-al-Rashid (789–809), and to his sons. The author states that the Messianic age would last 1300 years. This would place his advent in 4700 A. M. or 940 C. E. A later editor introduces a reference to the Crusaders. He believes that the Crusaders will forever destroy Islam.

The final redactor makes allusion to the persecutions of the Almohades in the Magreb toward the middle of the twelfth century, and to their leader Ibn Tumart, who declared himself the Mahdi, the Messiah of the Moslems.[38]

[36] Codex 195; see Steinschneider, *Heb. Bibl.*, V, p. 104; *J. E.*, I, p. 681a.
[37] *B. H.*, V, pp. 117–130; *O. M.*, I, pp. 97–103.
[38] See *O. M.*, I, pp. 101a bottom, 101b top.

9. *The Book of Zerubbabel.*

The Book of Zerubbabel,[39] an apocalypse, the groundwork of which was probably written in Palestine between the years 629 and 636, and was already known to Kalir,[40] contains in its final redaction an important Messianic prognostication. The author of the original Zerubbabel expected the Messiah to come in the immediate future. Later editors substituted later dates.

Zerubbabel, whose name was associated with the first restoration, is transported to Nineveh (Rome), and in the market place finds a "bruised and despised man," who reveals to him his identity.[41] He is the Messiah—Menaḥem ben 'Amiel—doomed to abide there until his hour shall strike. Zerubbabel asks when will the lamp of Israel be kindled. The angel Metatron intervenes and answers that 990 years after the destruction of the Temple (1058 C. E.) the Messiah will come.[42]

Five years prior to the coming of Ḥefẓibah, the mother of the Messiah ben David, the Messiah ben Joseph (Neḥemiah ben Ḥushiel) will appear, but he will be slain by Armilius. Afterwards he will be resurrected by the Messiah ben David.[43]

This book, with its outspoken unequivocal Messianic date, exerted a great influence upon the Messianic thought of the day. The book is mentioned by name in the writings of Rashi, Ibn Ezra and Eleazar of Worms.[44]

[39] *B. H.*, II, pp. 54-57; *O. M.*, I, pp. 159–161.

[40] See Israel Lévi, *Revue des Etudes Juives*, LXVIII, pp. 129 ff; LXIX, p. 108 ff, and LXXI, pp. 57 ff.

[41] *Cf. San.* 98a.

[42]

וכשגמרו עשרה מלכים בה (רומא) והעשירי יחרוב בית המקדש.... ומאותו יום חשוב לך תשע מאות ותשעים שנה תהיה תשועת יהוה ויזכור עם קדשו לגאלם לנטלם לנשאם ולקבצם.

[43] Professor Marx calls attention to a Sefer Zerubbabel which is wedged in between chapter 32.4–40.2 of the *Pirḳe Hekalot* (ed. Wertheimer, Jerusalem, 1890), where the figure 890 instead of 990 is given. This would place the Messianic year in 958 C. E., within a decade of Saadia's date (see *infra*), and would perhaps account for the inquiry which the Jews of the Rhenish country sent to the Palestinian communities concerning the rumor of the Messiah's advent. See *Jew. Quart. Rev.*, New Series, I, pp. 75–76.

[44] See *O. M.*, I, p. 159a.

B. Saadia

Besides this anonymous literature we have at least one known personality of the Mohammedan pre-Crusade period who interested himself in Messianic speculations—Saadia Gaon (882–942 c. e.).

Saadia Gaon, who was probably the first among the Gaonim to attempt to sift the vast Rabbinic opinion on the subject of the Messiah, and whose formulation remained, with slight modification, the accredited and accepted view, devotes the eighth chapter of his *Emunot we-De'ot* to the Final Redemption and dwells at length upon the Messianic predictions in the Book of Daniel. He also treats this subject in his commentary on Daniel, and in his *Sefer ha-Galui*.[45]

In his *Emunot* he endeavors to explain and to harmonize the various figures given in Daniel. He first discusses Dan. 12.6–7: "How long shall it be to the end of wonders? And I heard the man clothed in linen who was above the waters of the river, when he lifted up his right hand and his left hand unto heaven and swore by him that liveth forever, that it shall be for a time, times and a half" (כי למועד מועדים וחצי). This period, Saadia argues, is further explained to Daniel (verse 12) to be 1335 days. The days are here to be reckoned as years. The "times" refer to the two periods during which the kingdom of Israel existed. The first period is that of the 480 years up to the building of the first Temple; the second period is that of the 410 years of the duration of this Temple, giving a total of 890 years; half of this is 445 years; hence "times and a half" is 1335 years.

The second figure is given in chapter 12, verse 11: "And from the time that the continual burnt-offering shall be taken away, and the detestable thing that causes appalment set up, there shall be 1290 days." Saadia argues that this refers to some event which occurred during the second Temple, 45 years after the first prophecy to Daniel. This, then, also gives us the figure 1335.

[45] See S. Poznanski, *Die Berechnung des Erlösungsjahres bei Saadja*, Berlin, 1901, p. 2, notes 3 and 4.

The third prophecy is that in Dan. 8.14: "And he said unto me: Unto 2300 evenings and mornings, then shall the sanctuary be victorious." The number 2300 is to be divided by two, for both nights and days are included in the figure. This gives us the number 1150. This date refers to an event which took place 185 years after the first prophecy to Daniel. Here again we have the figure 1335.

Saadia does not definitely state when this period of 1335 years is to begin. Lacking the *terminus a quo*, we cannot fix the exact year in which Saadia expected the Messiah to come. Professor Malter believes that Saadia had no intention of revealing the Messianic year.[46] He did not have in mind any definite event or dates with which the dates of Daniel are to be connected. "Saadia here proceeds as a mere exegete. His sole purpose is to show that the three prophecies of Daniel do not contradict one another."[47] Professor Malter does believe, however, that Saadia did "harbor some opinion as to when the appearance of the Messiah was to be expected, and though refraining from expressing it, he at least wanted to leave the general impression that the 'end' was not far off."

We are inclined, however, to accept Dr. Poznanski's opinion that the *terminus a quo* here is the third year of the reign of Cyrus, when permission was granted the Jews to return, and which, according to the old Jewish chronology, took place in 367 B. C. E. Saadia's Messianic year would, therefore, be 968 C. E. Dr. Poznanski, basing his opinion upon a Bodleian manuscript of Saadia's unpublished commentary on Daniel, establishes that Saadia's computations point to the year 968 C. E. The event referred to in Dan. 12.11 as having occurred 45 years after the first prophecy (the reorganization of the Temple service by Nehemiah) is described in Nehemiah, chapter 13, and actually took place in the thirty-second year of Artaxerxes-Darius (322 B. C. E.). Accordingly the 1290 years would expire with the year 968 C. E.

Albiruni, the Persian astronomer and chronologer, who

[46] *Journal of Jewish Lore and Philosophy*, I, pp. 45–59.
[47] *Ibid.*, p. 56.

lived a century after Saadia, and who was acquainted with Jewish Messianic movements and speculations, states that the Jews counted the 1335 years from the time of Alexander: "So the Jews expect the coming of the Messiah, who was promised to them at the end of 1335 years after Alexander, expecting it like something which they know for certain. . . . This expectation was based on the assumption that the beginning of this era (Aera Alexandri) [325 B. C. E. not the מנין יונית or מנין שטרות, which began in 312 B. C. E.] coincided with the time when the sacrifices were abolished, when no more divine revelation was received, and no more prophets were sent."[48] This would place the ultimate Messianic year, when the rebuilding of Jerusalem would be completed in 1010 C. E. Forty-five years earlier (the 1290 years of Dan. 12.11) or in 965 C. E. the rebuilding of Jerusalem would *begin*.

It is of interest to note that Salmon ben Yeroḥam, a Karaite contemporary and opponent of Saadia, arrives in his commentary on Daniel at the same date of Saadia—968 C. E.[49] Japheth Ha-Levi (second half of 10 c.) the Karaite scholar and commentator, makes mention of a calculation common among the Rabbis which counted the 1335 day-years from the third year of the reign of Cyrus, and caustically remarks that that date is already past and their opinion flaunted.[50]

As the hoped-for Messianic decade (958–968) approached great excitement prevailed throughout all Israel. The Jews of the Rhine district in 960 sent an inquiry to the school of Jerusalem, asking for a verification of the report of the coming of the Messiah:[51] "I, Isaac bar Dorbelo, saw in Worms a letter which the people of the Rhine sent to Palestine in the year (4) 720 (=960 C. E.) in reference to the report which we have heard about the coming of the Messiah." The reply: "As regards your question about the coming of the Messiah, you do not even deserve a

[48] *The Chronology of Ancient Nations*, ed. C. E. Sachau, London, 1879 p. 18.
[49] Poznanski, *op. cit.*, pp. 5–7.
[50] See Pinsker, לקוטי קדמוניות, p. 81.
[51] *R. E. J.*, XLIV, pp. 238 ff.

reply. For do you not believe in the words of our Sages and their signs (which they specified for the identification of the true Messiah), and these have not as yet come to pass."

That strong Messianic hopes were entertained by the Jews of Germany about this time may also be inferred from the very interesting passage toward the close of the *Itinerary* of Benjamin of Tudela, which is evidently an insertion from an earlier account: "If we were not afraid that the appointed time has not yet been reached, we should have gathered together, but we dare not do so until the time for song has arrived, when the messengers will come and say continually: 'The Lord be exalted.' Meanwhile they send missives to one another, saying: 'Be ye strong in the law of Moses, and do ye, mourners for Zion, and ye, mourners for Jerusalem, entreat the Lord, and may the supplications of those that wear the garments of mourning be received through their merits.'"[52]

Ḥasdai ibn Shaprut (c. 915–970 C. E.), the Spanish statesman and patron of letters, addressed a letter of inquiry to Joseph, king of the Chazars, about the year 960, asking, among other things, concerning any possible information which the king may have touching the time of the Redemption: "Again I would ask of my master, the king, to let me know whether there is among you any tradition concerning the time of the end, for which we have been waiting these many years, during which time we have been going from one captivity to another, and from one exile to another. For one must be very strong, indeed, to refrain from inquiring about it. How can I be silent about the destruction of the Temple of our glory, and about the remnant escaped from the sword, which has passed through fire and water? We who were many are now few, and are fallen from our high estate and dwell in exile. We have no retort to those who say to us daily, 'Every people has a kingdom, but you have none.'" The king of the Chazars replied: "You ask furthermore con-

[52] In Schechter, *Studies*, Third Series, p. 7.

cerning the end of wonders. Our eyes are turned to the Lord, our God, and to the wise men of Israel in the academies of Jerusalem and Babylon, for we are very far from Zion. But we have heard that because of the sins of the people, the calculations have gone astray and we know nothing. . . . We have nothing but the prophecy of Daniel. May the God of Israel hasten the Redemption and gather our exiled and scattered people in our lifetime and in yours, and in the lifetime of the house of Israel, who love His name."[53]

C. The Karaites

It is evident that Messianic speculation was not limited to Rabbinism. The Karaites were equally concerned with it and employed similar methods. Japheth Ha-Levi states that the belief was commonly held among Karaites that the figure 2300 day-years[54] is to be dated from the Exodus, which took place, according to Karaite chronology, in the year 1332 B. C. E. In other words, the Messiah would come in the year 968 C. E. Sahl ben Maẓliaḥ Ha-Kohen (10 c.) seems to have entertained a similar belief, for in his *Sefer Tokaḥot* he writes: "And behold the days of visitation of the nations are at hand, and the time of the salvation of Israel is also at hand. May God hasten that day and deliver us from the two women (the schools of Sura and Pumbeditha = Rabbinism) and cause the Messiah ben David to rule over us."[55] Sahl, who like all Karaites was a strong Messianist, and who points with pride to the Karaite communities of pious and righteous men (known as the "Abele Zion"—"the Mourners for Zion"), established in Jerusalem for the purpose of praying continuously for the coming of the Messiah[56] believed himself to be living in the Messianic milieu. The rejection

[53] *Letter of Ḥasdai ibn Shaprut,* printed with Kuzari, ed. Wilna, 1914, pp. 6–8.

[54] Dan. 8.14.

[55] See Pinsker, לקוטי קדמוניות, p. 43.

[56] *Ibid.*, p. 30. See also Mann, "An Early Karaite Tract," *J. Q. R.*, XII, New Series, pp. 272 ff. Soon after the rise of this movement, groups of Karaites, forsaking home and friends, migrated to Palestine and their fervid yearning for the restoration of the Temple exceeded even that of the Rabbinites.

of Rabbinism, he argued, would hasten his coming. This, too, is the opinion of Elijah ben Abraham.[57] Japheth also mentions the calculation of the great Karaite Benjamin Ben Moses Nahawendi (8–9 c.), who dates the 2300 day-years from the destruction of Shilo (942 B. C. E.), and the 1290 day-years[58] from the destruction of the second Temple (68 C. E.), and thereby arrives at 1358 C. E. as the Messianic year.[59]

D. Pseudo-Messiahs

The four centuries (600–1000 C. E.) produced at least three pseudo-Messiahs: (1) Abu Isa al-Ispahani, (2) Serene, and (3) the disciple of Abu Isa, Yudghan. They also witnessed a revival of interest in the Lost Ten Tribes, which is a concomitant of Messianic speculation.

1. Abu Isa of Ispahan lived in Persia during the stormy period of the Omayyad-Abbasid struggle for supremacy in the middle of the eighth century. An illiterate, and a plain tailor by profession, he was, nevertheless, able to gain a large following among the Jews of Persia when he announced himself as the fifth and last messenger of the Messiah sent to deliver Israel from the yoke of the Gentiles. He felt himself strong enough to rebel against the Caliph. It is likely that Abu Isa's religious views had much to do with his popularity. In his revolt against certain Rabbinic doctrines and practices he was, in a sense, a fore-runner of Anan and the Karaites. Serene and Yudghan likewise entertained views hostile to the Rabbinic tradition. The age was one of revolt against Talmudic authority, and sects were springing up in Jewry culminating in the great Karaite movement of the eighth and ninth centuries.

Abu Isa entertained a wide tolerance for Christianity and Islam. Ḳirḳisani reports of him that he "acknowledged the prophecy of Jesus, the son of Mary, and the prophecy of the Master of the Mohammedans, contending that each of these two was sent to his own people. He advo-

[57] *Ibid.*, pp. 102–3.
[58] Dan. 12.11.
[59] Pinsker, *op. cit.*, p. 82.

cated the study of the Gospels and of the Koran, as well as the knowledge of their interpretation, and he maintained that the Mohammedans and Christians were both guided in their faith by what they possessed, just as the Jews were guided in their faith by what they possessed."[60]

Abu Isa was defeated by the forces of the Caliph at Rai. He himself was killed (755) and his followers were scattered. A sect known as the Isawites survived.[61]

2. Serene (from Shirin) announced himself as the Messiah about the year 720 C. E. He promised to restore Palestine to the Jews after expelling the Mohammedans. He gained a large following. Isador Pacensis, writing in 750, narrates that many Spanish and French Jews, believing implicitly in the Messiahship of Serene, abandoned their homes and their possessions and set out to meet him. The ruler confiscated their property.

Serene was finally captured and haled before the caliph Yazid II. He sought refuge in lying words, saying that he had deliberately planned to mislead and to mock the Jews. The Caliph bound him over to the Jews for punishment.

Judging from the *Responsum* of Naṭronai Gaon, Serene and his followers violated Rabbinic law, and set at naught many of the traditions originating with the Rabbis, even as the followers of Abu Isa had done.[62]

3. Yudghan of Hamadan, surnamed al-Rai, the Shepherd, was a disciple of Abu Isa. He himself did not claim to be the Messiah, only a prophet and the forerunner of the Messiah, but his followers hailed him as the Messiah. Little else is known of his life and of his activities. The Yudghanites likewise took issue with Rabbinism on many important laws and practices.[63]

The second half of the ninth century gave rise to Eldad Ha-Dani, who, though not a false Messiah, brought reports

[60] See Friedlaender, "Jewish Arabic Studies," in *J. Q. R.*, New Series, III, p. 240, who correctly traces these views to Islamic influence.

[61] Harkavy, לקורות הכתות בישראל, in Graetz, Heb. ed., III, pp. 501–502.

[62] *Ibid.*, III, pp. 170–173.

[63] *Ibid.*, III, pp. 453–455, 503.

of the Lost Tribes, whose restoration was an essential feature of the Messianic saga. Eldad's report was the source of the Prester John legend of the twelfth century. Eldad claimed to come from Eastern Africa, where the tribes of Dan, Asher, Gad and Naphtali lived. Eldad, who traveled extensively, spread the news through Babylon, Egypt and Spain of his discovery of the Lost Tribes, whom he found in Persia, Armenia, Arabia and Chazaria, and of the Bene Moshe, who dwelt beyond the River Sambation. His report was universally credited even by leaders of thought, such as Ẓemaḥ Gaon and Ḥasdai ibn Shaprut. Abraham ibn Ezra (12 c.) and Meir of Rothenburg (13 c.) seem to be the only men who in the Middle Ages doubted Eldad's story.

CHAPTER III

THE PERIOD OF THE CRUSADES (11–12 c.)

A. The Background

The terrible tragedies which came upon the Jewish communities of Northwestern Europe in the wake of the successive Crusades—the most devastating in the millennium which followed the destruction of the Temple—find their reflex in the intensified Messianic expectations of the time.

The hordes of the First Crusade (1096 c. e.) swept over the Jewish settlements between the Rhine and the Moselle and laid them waste. Especially did the communities of Metz, Speyer, Worms, Mayence, Cologne and Treves suffer at the hands of the plundering, massacring mobs. Some four thousand Jews were slain or suicided. The black terror of those days speaks to us out of the *Seliḥot*, *Ḳinnot*, and memoirs which have come down to us.

Strange to say, the very year 1096—the year of the First Crusade—was fixed upon generally as the year of Redemption.

1. Solomon ben Simeon (12 c.), the chronicler of the First Crusade, makes mention of this high hope which was entertained by his contemporaries: "And it came to pass in the year 4856 a. m., the 1,028th year of our exile, in the eleventh year of the 256th cycle (=1096 c. e.), when we had hoped for salvation and comfort, according to the prophecy of Jeremiah, 'Sing (רנ״ו=256 in Gematria) with gladness for Jacob and shout at the head of the nation.'[1] But it was turned into sorrow and groaning, weeping and

[1] Jer. 31.7.

lamentation."[2] This seems to be the first clear use of Gematria in Messianic prognostication applied to the Roman exile. Heretofore only actual dates and figures, the length of the earlier exiles or verses suggesting time-periods, were employed. From now on any word or words, however faintly reminiscent of Redemption they might be, are summoned at the behest of Gematria to yield up its secret. The science becomes exceedingly popular, running parallel, no doubt, to its growing popularity in other fields, notably Kabbala and exegesis.

2. Eliezer ben Nathan (12 c.) in his account of the persecutions of 1096[3] likewise states that the eleventh year of the 256th cycle—1096 C. E.—was looked upon as the Messianic year. The same thought is expressed in his Seliḥa, אלהים באזנינו שמענו:[4]

Time and Time again our soul waited
But the end was long delayed and the wound was not healed;
In the season of רָנ"ו we hoped that Redemption would come.
But we hoped for peace, and there was none; for a time of healing
and behold dismay!

3. That the Messianic hopes centering in the year 1096 were widespread is attested also by a reference in the *Lekaḥ Tob*—the Midrashic commentary of Tobiah ben Eliezer, a native of Castoria in Bulgaria, written in 1097. On Ex. 3.20 he writes: "And in the year 4857 A. M., that is to say, the year 1029 since the destruction of the second Temple, which is also the twelfth year in the 256th cycle (מחזור רנ"ו), I, Tobiah, son of R. Eliezer, looked searchingly into our divine books and considered the length of our

[2] Neubauer-Stern, *Heb. Berich. über die Judenverfolgungen während der Kreuzzüge*, p. 1.

[3] *Ibid.*, pp. 36–46.

[4] Reprinted in Bernfeld's *Sefer Ha-Dema'ot*, vol. I, p. 207, and Brody and Wiener's *Anthologia Hebraica*, pp. 223–225.

זמן אחר זמן נפשנו חכתה
וארך הקץ וארוכה לא עלתה
חשבון רָנ"ו ליעקב חכינו יֶשַׁע בְּעִתָּהּ
קוה לשלום ואין טוב, לעת מרפא והנה בְעָתָה

exile, how 'our power is gone and there is none remaining, shut up or left at large;[5] and how *all the ends have passed* and Redemption is now dependent upon repentance alone, as it is written, 'If thou wilt return, O Israel, saith the Lord, yea return unto me,'[6] and again, 'If thou return, then I will bring thee back, thou shalt stand before Me.'[7] We are now looking to the Rock of our Salvation, trusting that even as in the days of Egypt he will now show us wonders."[8]

4. Benjamin ben Zeraḥ, called Baal Shem, who lived in the latter half of the eleventh century (he speaks of the Temple as already 1000 years destroyed), and who probably witnessed the Crusade, writes in his Seliḥa, אדברה וירוח לי[9] of the taunt which the enemies of Israel hurled at the Jews: "Ye have calculated the times of Redemption and they are now past, and the hope of salvation is over and gone."[10]

When in place of Redemption the year 1096 ushered in calamity, the faithful ones, never despairing, began to hope that the very disasters would be the "birth-throes of the Messiah." This hope finds frequent expression in the pathetic prayers which have come down to us from that period.

1. Samuel ben Judah (12 c.) in his dirge-Piyyut for the Sabbath before Shabuot beginning אלהי אקראך במחשב, which mentions the year 1096 as well as the Council of

[5] Deut. 32.36.

[6] Jer. 4.1.

[7] Jer. 15.19.

[8] We use the version of the Florence manuscript. See the Introduction of Buber to his edition of *Lekaḥ Ṭob*, ed. Wilna, 1924, p. 16.

[9] Brody's *A. H.*, pp. 212–215.

עִתֵּי גאלה מניתם ונגמרו
ותקות התשועה פסקה והלכה לה

[10] Benjamin ben Zeraḥ gives no Messianic year of his own. In his Piyyut for the Sabbath before Shabuot beginning אהלל בצלצלי שמע, he quotes from the Letters of Rabbi Akiba, that the world will come to an end in the year 6093 A. M. = 2333 C. E.: "Once in the generation of the Flood (did the world come to an end), and again in the year 6093 A. M." Dr. Günzig erroneously assumes that this refers to the Messianic year, and that ben Zeraḥ is giving an original calculation (see his *Die Wundermänner im jüdishen Volke*, p. 19).

Clermont,[11] prays that the suffering of the age may mark the beginning of the Messianic times:[12]

> Bring nigh the end of the wonders,
> Deliver Thy people from hardship
> Thou, our Redeemer, Lord of Hosts.
> Be Thou not quiet, Lord!

2. Another contemporary, David ben Meshullam, concludes his lament on the martyrs of the Crusades, beginning with אלהים אל דמי לדמי, with a passionate cry for deliverance:[13]

> O living God! Accredit Thou to us the
> merit of their blameless lives (the martyrs)[14]
> and put an end to our suffering.

3. Similarly, David ben Samuel Halevi (12 c.) in his Piyyut אדני אלהי, רבת צררוני מנעורי, cries out:[15]

> Our soul languishes for Thy salvation. When
> wilt Thou comfort us?
> Do it for the sake of Thy holy name. Not for our
> sake, O Lord, not for our sake.

The same cry reaches us from the poetic chroniclers of the Second Crusade (1145–1147) and the Third (1189–1190), and from the intervening disasters, up to the close of the twelfth century.

1. Isaac ben Shalom concludes his Piyyut, אין כמוך באלמים, which sings the mournful story of the massacre in the

11 וּוַעֲדוּ לקרן אפלה. See Graetz, Heb. ed., IV, p. 436, note 1.

12 קָרֵב קץ הפלאות
הצל עמך מתלאות
גואלנו יהוה צבאות
יהוה אל דמי לך

Bernfeld's *S. H.*, pp. 193–197.

13 חַי! זְכוּתָךְ קַוָּם תשמור לנו וצרותינו תגמר

Brody's *A. H.*, pp. 221–223.

14 קַוָּם = line, domain, life. (Ps. 19.5).

15 כלתה נפשנו לישועתך לאמר מתי תנחמנו
למען שם קדשך עשה, לא לנו אדני, לא לנו

Brody's *A. H.*, pp. 215–217. See also Zunz, *Synag. Poesie*, p. 197.

German communities of the twentieth of Nisan, 1147, with the verse:[16]

> Have pity upon Thy scattered ones, O Holy One,
> And with Thy gracious spirit uphold us.
> Arise, our help, deliver us!

2. Ephraim ben Jacob of Bonn (1133–c. 1196), who, as a lad of thirteen, witnessed the horrors of the Second Crusade, and who chronicled it, as well as the story of the Third Crusade, in the Seliḥa, למי אוי למי אֲבוֹי ומדינים, lamenting the destruction of the Jewish community of Blois, 1171, breaks forth in a despairing cry:[17]

> And I, how long shall I hope for Redemption
> At the hands of the son of David and the prophet Elijah?

3. So also Hillel ben Jacob, in his Seliḥa, אטזגי שלמי ישראל, on the slain of Blois, pleads:[18]

> Accept, I pray Thee, my prayer, O God in high!
> Hasten deliverance, and rescue Thy poor people.
> Establish Thy city and Thy dwelling place as of old in beauty
> So that God may swell in Zion.

4. Menahem ben Jacob, too, telling of the tragedy of Boppard (1179), where Jews, wrongfully accused of having slain a Christian woman whose body was found on

16 חמול זרוּיֶיךָ קדושינו
ורוח נדיבה תסמכנו
קומה עזרתה לנו ופדנו.

Bernfeld's *S. H.*, p. 221.

17 ואני עד מתי אצפה להשיבי
ביד בן דוד ואליהו הנביא

Ibid., p 230. See עמק הבכא, ed. Wiener, Leipzig, 1858, App. I.

18 קבל נא צְקוֹנִי אל עליון
חיש מפלט והצל עמך האביון
תשב עירך ונוך כמקדם בצביון
ויהוה שוכן בציון

Ibid., p. 236.

the banks of the Rhine, were thrown into the river and drowned, writes:[19]

And if we be unworthy of redemption,
Remember Thy servants (Hananiah, Mishael and Azariah)
who would not defile themselves.

The Crusades broke the spirit of the Jews in Germany. Their social and political life was sadly worsened and their intellectual life declined. A depressing sense of hopelessness and homelessness gripped them; asceticism and superstition grew apace. All this is fertile ground for Messianic dreams. Again, a mystic emotionalism preceded and attended the Crusades in the Christian world, which could not but infect the Jewish world. The Millenarian hopes, which flared up in Christendom the year 1000, continued without abatement for a long time thereafter, and played a not inconsiderable part in precipitating the Crusades. It was believed that Palestine must come into the possession of the Christians before the second coming of Christ, and inasmuch as his second coming was at hand, the conquest of Palestine should be swiftly accomplished. Throughout the centuries of the Crusades, Christendom was strangely agitated by high Millenarian hopes.[20] The whole world was on tiptoe with expectancy, awaiting vast transformations. Israel was no less expectant.

19 ואם אין אנו כדאים להגאל
זכור משרתיך לא רצו להתגאל

Ibid., p. 241.

20 Guibert, Abbot of Nogent, in his account of the first Crusade, written between 1108–12, giving his version of Pope Urban's plea for a Crusade writes:

"For it is clear that Antichrist is to do battle not with the Jews, not with the Gentiles; but according to the etymology of his name, he will attack Christians. And if Antichrist finds there no Christians (just as at present when scarcely any dwell there), no one will be there to oppose him, or whom he may rightly overcome. According to Daniel and Jerome, the interpreter of Daniel, he is to fix his tents on the Mount of Olive .. .. .. and he will first kill three Kings of Egypt, Africa and Ethopia, without doubt for their Christian faith. This, indeed, could not at all be done unless Christianity was established where now is paganism. .. .. .. Behold, the Gospel cries out, 'Jerusalem shall be trodden down, by the Gentiles, until the times of the Gentiles be fulfilled,' .. .. .. These times, most beloved brothers, will now, forsooth, be fulfilled, provided the might of the pagans be repulsed through you with the co-operation of

B. The Calculators

The Crusades found their echo, as we have seen, in the final recensions of the *Prayer of Simeon ben Yoḥai*, the *Revelations of Simeon ben Yoḥai*, and in the *Story of Daniel*.

We have also definite calculations from four of the outstanding leaders of Jewish thought of the eleventh and twelfth centuries: (1) Rashi, (2) Judah Halevi, (3) Abraham Bar Ḥiyya, (4) Moses Maimonides. We have references to three other calculators. Of the four mentioned above, Rashi alone had direct contact with the events of the Crusades. Halevi, Bar Ḥiyya and Maimonides were influenced as much by the persecutions in the Islamic lands as by the fearful reports reaching them from the lands swept by the Crusades.

The three calculators of whose speculations we have only indirect testimony are: (1) Solomon ibn Gabirol, (2) Hananeel ben Ḥushiel, and (3) Joseph ben Isaac Bekor Shor. Both Gabirol and Hananeel lived in the eleventh century but in a period before the first Crusade.

1. *Solomon ibn Gabirol* (11 c.) is mentioned by Ibn Ezra in his commentary on Dan. 11.30 as having calculated the end on the basis of astrological computations: "also the words of Solomon ibn Gabirol, who sought to make the Redemption contingent upon the great conjunction of Saturn and Jupiter." Gabirol's tract, however, if it was a tract (or perhaps part of a Biblical commentary) in which these calculations appear, is lost to us. This is the first instance recorded of an attempt to calculate the end by means of astrology. Beginning with the eleventh century the practice grows in popularity among the

God. *With the end of the world already near*, even though the Gentiles fail to be converted to the Lord (since according to the apostle there must be a withdrawal from the faith), it is first necessary, according to the prophecy, that the Christian sway be renewed in those regions, either through you, or others whom it shall please God to send before the coming of Antichrist, so that the head of all evil, who is to occupy there the throne of the kingdom, shall find some support of the faith to fight against him." (See August C. Krey, *The First Crusade*, Princeton, 1921, pp. 38–39.)

Jews, whose interest in astrology, due to Arabic influence, now waxes great.

His poems, however, abound in Messianic reflections and invocations. As for example, his poems שוכב עלי מטות זהב[21]; שחר עלה אלי דודי ולך עמי and פתח דודי קומה פתח שער בארמני where he speaks of the persecution of both Rome (חזיר יער = boar) and Arab (פרא = wild ass), and concludes with the phrase: "The end which is sealed added to the sorrow of my heart. There is none to explain it to me, and I am ignorant." And especially his Piyyut, שכולה אכולה למה תבכי[22] which is in the form of a dialogue between God and Israel, in which Israel complains: "Thy end is long drawn, and my gloom has lasted long. How long will the exile last? When will the appointed season arrive? When will Thou resolve what is hidden and sealed?" And the answer is given: "Hope on, hapless one, yet *a little while* longer!" The same thought concerning the proximity of the day of Redemption is voiced in his Piyyut, שופה, נופה בשבלת שטופה "Hearken now, hapless and pilloried one, hope and wait for me, for *very soon* will I send my angel to prepare my way."[23] Gabirol is undoubtedly caught up by the same hope which inspired the author of the Book of Zerubbabel, who announced that the Messiah would come in the year 1058. In one of his poems Gabirol also alludes to the numerous Messianic calculations of the past which have proved vain. In his Piyyut, יהוה תשפת שלום לנו he says: "And how many were the periods which were reckoned since Thy people have been in exile, and the enemies which surround us now say that we have no king."[24]

The calculations of the two other men have come down to us through quotations in the works of others.

2. That of *Hananeel ben Ḥushiel* (11 c.) is quoted by Baḥya ben Asher in his Biblical commentary. He states

[21] *Selected Religious Poems of Solomon ibn Gabirol*, Davidson-Zangwill, pp. 6, 7, 10.

[22] *Ibid.*, p. 22.

[23] *Ibid.*, p. 25.

[24] *Ibid.*, p. 30.

that the Messiah would come in the year 1218 C. E. if the Jews were found worthy.[25]

3. The other is that of *Joseph ben Isaac Bekor Shor* (12 c., French Tosafist and exegete), quoted by Isaac Halevi in his *Pa'aneaḥ Raza.* He believed that the Messiah would come in the year 1403 C. E.[26]

4. *Rashi* (1040–1105) finds that Dan. 8.14 and 12.11–12 clearly point to the year 1352 C. E. as the Messianic year. Verse 14 of chapter 8 reads: "And he said unto me, Unto evening and morning 2300 years, then shall the sanctuary be victorious" (עד ערב בקר אלפים ושלש מאות). ערב and בקר must be taken in their numerical (Gematria) value = 574. Add 2,300 and you have the figure 2,874. The *terminus a quo* is the beginning of the Egyptian captivity. The Jews were 210 years in Egypt; 480 years elapsed from the time of their deliverance to the building of the first Temple; the Temple stood 410 years; the Babylonian captivity lasted 70 years, and the second Temple stood 420 years. This gives you a total of 1590 years from Egypt to the second destruction. Dan. 12.11–12 says that 1290 years must elapse from the time that the continual burnt offering shall be taken away until the time of the Redemption. The offering ceased, according to Rashi, six years before the destruction, i. e. in the 1584th year since the Egyptian captivity; add 1584 and 1290 and you get the figure 2874, the figure of Dan. 8.14. The Temple was destroyed in 68 C. E. The Messiah, according to Rashi, is to appear 1290 years after the cessation of the burnt offering, which took place six years before the destruction (i. e. 62 C. E.). Rashi therefore expected the Messiah to come in the year 1352 C. E.

In his commentary on *San.* 97b, he offers another figure in the name of Samuel ben David Halevi, basing his computation on Ps. 80.6: "And thou hast given them tears to drink in a threefold measure." He states that the present exile would last three times as long as the Egyptian

[25] See *infra*, Baḥya ben Asher.
[26] See *infra*, Isaac ben Judah Halevi.

(400 years) and the Babylonian (70 years) put together, i. e. 1410 years. In other words, the Messiah would come in the year 1478 C. E.

5. *Judah Halevi* (1080–1141). Jewish persecutions at the close of the eleventh and throughout the twelfth century were not confined to France and Germany. The Jews living in some of the Mohammedan lands fared little better. Halevi sums up the story thus: "From the midst of both Edom and Epher (Epher was one of the sons of Keturah, Gen. 25.4, hence Arabs) I cry bitterly unto Thee."[27] Towards the end of his lifetime the followers of the Mahdi Ibn Tumart (d. 1128), founder of the Almohades, conquered Northern Africa, persecuted the Jews and instituted forced conversion.

In his poems Halevi urges upon his brethern not to grow impatient nor to try to find surcease in vain speculations. This seems to be the first of a series of warnings emanating from that period. In his poem beginning יאמץ לבבך ומועדך יְחַלִּי he sings: "Let thy heart be strong, awaiting thine appointed season (of Redemption). Why do you calculate the end of the captivity and grow disturbed? . . . Thou hast done well to wait for thy Redeemer. Do not, therefore, be impatient; thou wilt behold the glory of My work."[28] In another poem, יונה נְשָׂאתָהּ על כנפי נשרים, he doubts the possibility of discovering the end. "And if I ask to know when will be the end of wonders, they (the people) answer: You have asked a difficult question about prophecies."[29]

Halevi knew of a belief commonly held by the generations which preceded his, that the Messiah would appear 1000 years after the destruction, i. e. 1068 C. E. This hope is intimated in *Pirḳe de Rabbi Eliezer*, chapter 18.[30] "She

[27] *Poems*, ed. Harkavy, I, p. 73.

[28] *Ibid.*, pp. 57–58.

[29] ואם אשאל לראות קץ הפלאות
יענו נבואות הקשות לשאול
Ibid., p. 65.

[30] See *supra*, p. 39. From the Arabic original of the Iggeret Teman, end, it is evident that there was an extensive Messianic movement in France about the year 1068.

thought that a thousand years would be the length of her exile, but she was disappointed in all her expectations.[31]

In one of his poems, however, Halevi yields to the temptation of prognosticating the end. He had a dream, he says, in which he vividly saw the downfall of Ishmael. This would occur in the year 1130 C. E.: "In the year 1130 (ושנת תת"ץ) all thy pride (Ishmael) will be shattered. Thou wilt be abashed and ashamed of the things which thou didst devise."[32]

He expresses the belief that Ishmael is the fourth kingdom mentioned in Daniel whose downfall would usher in the Redemption: "Art thou the miry clay in the feet of iron which came at the end and wast exalted?"[33] The march of the Crusaders must have inspired Halevi with the hope that the collapse of the Islamic power was at hand. This hope was grounded in a tradition which prevailed for some time among the Jews in Mohammedan lands. Saadia had declared, basing himself on Rabbinic authority, that the Christians would be in possession of Palestine at the time of the Redemption.[34] Hai Gaon (939–1038 C. E.) in his *Responsum* on the subject of Redemption had declared that the sure sign of the Messiah's coming will be when Edom (The Christians) again rule over Palestine[35]. This was one of the strong motives of the Messianic movements which abounded in the period of the Crusades.

Halevi, in fixing upon the year 1130, follows a belief current in his day among Jews living in Mohammedan

[31] In his poem, יונת רחוקים נדדה יערה (*ibid.*, p. 60). Halevi is writing in the year 1132.

ותחשוב אלף לקץ מועדה
אך חפרה מכל אשר שָׂעֲרָה

[32] *Poems*, II, p. 151.

ושנת תת״ץ תֻּתַּץ לך כל גאוה
תבוש ותחפר מאשר זָמָמְתָּ

[33] *Ibid.*

[34] ותחלתם שאדום יכבשו בית המקדש בעת הגאולה (*Emunot*, VIII, 5).

[35] לפיכך כשאנו רואים ששלטה אדום בארץ ישראל אנו מאמינים שהתחילה ישועתנו טעם זקנים 1854, pp. 59a–61a.

lands, that the Messiah would come 500 years after the rise of Mohammed. In the century preceding Halevi, the belief was held that the Messiah would come 400 years after the Hegira (i. e. 1022 C. E.). Jacob ben Reuben, Karaite commentator of the eleventh century, author of *Sefer ha-'Osher*, mentions this belief: "And it is likely that the Redemption will occur at the end of 400 years of the rule of the little Horn (Islam).[36] When this hope vanished the period was advanced to 500 years. This is borne out by the statement which 'Abd al Mumin, head of the Almohades, made to the leader of the Jews of Morocco when he conquered that country: "I know that your fathers said that your Messiah would come 500 years after the rise of Mohammed, and now the time is past and your Messiah has not yet appeared."[37]

It was not long after Halevi's putative year of Redemption, in 1147, the year of the Second Crusade, that 'Abd al Mumin crossed into Spain and inaugurated a decade of frightful persecution. Synagogues and academies were destroyed, women and children were sold into slavery, the property of the people was confiscated, and many Jews were forced to accept the faith of Islam. The bitter irony of it. . .

6. *Abraham bar Ḥiyya* (d. 1136), contemporary of Halevi, Spanish-Jewish astronomer, mathematician and philosopher, plays an important rôle in Messianic speculation. His book, *Megillat ha-Megalleh*, which has but recently been edited and published[38] shows the author to have been among the first to have engaged in Messianic speculation on a vast and comprehensive scale. He is more thorough than Saadia, the only other author preceding him whose elaborate Messianic calculations have come down to us. Bar Ḥiyya, who seemingly digested all the literature on the subject which had appeared up to his day,[39]

[36] See Pinsker, לקוטי קדמוניות, p. 82.

[37] See Graetz, Heb. ed., IV, p. 198. Somewhat earlier, Yusuf ibn Teshufin, founder of the Almoravid dynasty in Southern Spain (1086), demanded apostasy of the Jews of Lucena on the same grounds (*ibid.*, p. 126).

[38] מגילת המגלה, ed. Adolph Poznanski, Intro. by Julius Guttmann, Berlin, 1924.

[39] *Ibid.*, pp. 2, 83, 84.

influenced to a great degree many of the subsequent Messianic speculations, especially those of Naḥmanides and Abarbanel.

Abraham bar Ḥiyya launches upon his subject with a bold defense of Messianic calculation. It is legitimate. It is sanctioned by the Torah. It finds precedent in the Talmud and in the later Rabbis. It is helpful in that it strengthens faith and enhances the morale of the people.[40] He also vigorously defends his methods of calculation.[41] His calculations derive from four sources: (1), the Creation account in Genesis, (2) the rest of the Torah, (3) the Book of Daniel, and (4) Astrology.[42] He lays greatest value upon the first two, less on the third, and very little on the last, which he utilizes only as a means of convincing those who are given to this science and would not otherwise be convinced.

The world was created solely for the sake of Israel.[43] Every cycle in the Creation story, therefore, is symbolic and prophetic of the history of Israel.[44] The Creation week signifies that the world will last 6000 years, the seventh being the Millennial Sabbath.[45] Each Creation day points to a 1000 years of the world's cycle; for a day in the sight of God is 1000 years, or to be exact, 857$\frac{1}{7}$ years, for it is written, "For a thousand years are in Thy sight as yesterday when it is past *plus* a watch in the night."[46] A watch in the night is equal to a third of a night or four hours.[47] A day of God is therefore equal to $\frac{6}{7}$ of 1000 years, or 857$\frac{1}{7}$, and the seven days of Creation equal 6000 years.[48]

Each day is again divided into seven parts and each part (c. 122 years) is equal to one generation.[49]

[40] *Ibid.*, pp. 1-2.
[41] *Ibid.*, pp. 74 ff.
[42] *Ibid.*, p. 3.
[43] *Sab.*, 88a.
[44] מ. ה., pp. 21–29. ואם העולם כלו נברא בשבילם ראוי הוא שיהיה כל מעשה בראשית רמז עליהם ויהיו הדורות המנוים מאדם הראשון מסורים כנגד הקורות להם (p. 74).
[45] *Ibid.*, p. 19.
[46] Ps. 90.4.
[47] *Ber.* 3a.
[48] מ. ה. p. 20.
[49] *Ibid.*

Through an elaborate maze of figures Bar Ḥiyya arrives at his conclusions, viz. the flood took place at the close of the second day, i. e. 1714 A. M. The Torah was given toward the close of the third day, or more specifically at the beginning of the seventh generation of the third day, i. e. 2448 A. M.[50]

On the basis of this figure, says Bar Ḥiyya, one may calculate that the succeeding three days, at the close of which the Messiah will come, will also last 2448 years, and will terminate in 4896 A. M. The Messiah may therefore be expected in the year 1136 C. E. This is the earliest possible date, perhaps the date when the first signs of his coming will appear.[51] Or one may reckon not from the time of the giving of the Torah but from the conquest of Canaan (2495 A. M.). This would place the year of the Messiah in 4990 A. M. or 1230 C. E. This, according to Bar Ḥiyya, is the more probable date.

Again, says Bar Ḥiyya, one may reason in this wise: In Deut. 28.63 it is stated "and it shall come to pass, that as the Lord rejoiced over you to do you good. . . . so the Lord will rejoice over you to cause you to perish . . ." This implies that the period of suffering will be as long as the period of rejoicing. The period of rejoicing began with the giving of the Torah (2448 A. M.) and closed with the destruction (3828 A. M.). In other words, it lasted 1380 years. The period of suffering will therefore also last 1380 years, i. e. to the year 5208 A. M. or 1448 C. E. This is the outmost figure. The Messiah's coming cannot be delayed beyond it.[52]

There is still a possible fourth calculation. The Torah was given in 2448 A. M., at the close of the third day. This leaves 3552 years for the remaining *four* days of the Creation week, or approximately 890 years per day. The first Temple was destroyed at the close of the fourth day, in 3338 A. M., 890 years after the giving of the Torah. The fifth and sixth days will last 890 x 2 = 1780 years. At the

[50] *Ibid.*, p. 34.
[51] *Ibid.*, p. 36.
[52] *Ibid.*

close of the sixth day the Messiah will come. Add 1780 to 3338 and you get 5118 A. M. or 1358 C. E. as the Messianic year. Bar Ḥiyya writes: "And we believe that in that year Redemption will come without delay."[53] This is approximately also Rashi's date. We shall see that the year 1358 became a favorite one among succeeding speculators. On the basis of the Baraita in *'Ab. Zar.* 9a and *San.* 97a, "six thousand years will the world endure . . ." and Dan. 12.12, Bar Ḥiyya deduces still a fifth date, 1403 C. E., which also proved a popular Messianic date.[54]

Bar Ḥiyya interprets the Messianic verses in Daniel to yield him the same dates. The figure 2300[55] is to be dated either from the time of the building of the first Temple (2928 A. M.), which would yield the Messianic year 5228 A. M.—1468 C. E., or from the preparations for the building which were begun by David twenty years earlier, yielding the Messianic year 1448 C. E.[56] The figure 1290[57] is to be dated from the destruction of the second Temple (68 C. E.). The Messianic year will therefore be 1358 C. E. The figure 1335[58] which is 45 years later, points to the wars of Gog and Magog, which will last 45 years from the time of the appearance of the Messiah.[59]

Bar Ḥiyya apologizes for resorting in his calculations to astrology. The foregoing arguments based on Scriptures and Rabbinic sources are really sufficient, and he would not have stooped to a science which is the creation of the Gentiles but for his desire to convince those who can only be convinced through this method. He was encouraged by the fact that even the Rabbis did not altogether disdain astrology.

All the important events affecting mankind are determined by the conjunctions of the two highest planets,

[53] *Ibid.*, p. 37.
[54] *Ibid.*, p. 46.
[55] Dan. 8.14.
[56] *Op. cit.*, pp. 89-90.
[57] Dan. 12.11.
[58] Dan. 12.12.
[59] *Op. cit.*, p. 107.

Saturn and Jupiter.[60] Bar Ḥiyya traces the whole history of Israel from the Exodus to his own day and shows how the relative positions of these two conjunctions in the Zodiac prefigured the important events which occurred in the life of the people. Three centuries earlier the Arab Alkindi had similarly employed a theory of conjunctions very much like this of Bar Ḥiyya to trace the political fortunes of the Arab Kingdom. And so did Abu Ma'as-char (Albumasar), his pupil.[61]

He defines the five kinds of conjunctions: (1) דבוק קטון, the minor conjunction of the two planets which occurs every 19⅞ years in the ninth sign from the previous conjunction; (2) דבוק אמצעי, the intermediary conjunction of the two planets in the same sign every 60 years; (3) דבוק גדול, the major conjunction of the planets when it occurs in the next trigon after 238 years; (4) דבוק רב the great conjunction when the planets return to the same trigon after 953⅓ years; and (5) דבוק עצום, the grand conjunction when the planets return again to the same sign of the same trigon after 2859 years.[62]

The great conjunction (דבוק רב) of Saturn and Jupiter in the Sign of Pisces in the watery trigon is especially significant for Israel and first occurred in 2365 A. M. It presaged the Redemption from Egypt and the giving of the Torah. This same conjunction will not occur again until after 2859 years, or in 5224 A. M. = 1464 C. E.[63] In the last of the twelve major conjunctions (דבוק גדול) i. e. between 1226–1464 C. E., the Redemption will take place. To be more exact, in the thirteenth year of the seventh minor conjunction (דבוק קטון) within this trigon, or in the year 1358 C. E., the Messiah will appear. However, the first signs of the Messianic times will come earlier, in

[60] *Ibid.*, p. 116.

[61] See Steinschneider, *Die heb. Übersetzungen des Mittelalters*, Berlin, 1893, pp. 562–565; and Thorndike, *History of Magic and Experimental Science*, New York, 1923, I, p. 648.

[62] *Op. cit.*, pp. 116–117. See also Efros, "Pre-Tibbonian Philosophical Terminology," *J. Q. R.*, New Series, XVII, pp. 145 and 152.

[63] *Op. cit.*, pp. 119 and 152.

1129.[64] Another fateful conjunction, the eleventh in the earthly trigon in Capricorn, will take place in the year 1186 C. E., and it will usher in many wars and much suffering in Palestine and in the lands of Edom and Ishmael.[65] The beginning of the downfall of Ishmael would take place twenty years later in 1206 C. E.

As the year 1186 approached Europe and Asia were profoundly stirred, fearing a universal cataclysm.[66]

7. *Maimonides* (1135–1204), too, in spite of his repeated attempts at rationalizing the Messianic idea and at discouraging apocalyptic speculation, fell victim to the fascination of calculating the end. He lived in troubled times. Forced conversions were prevalent and persecutions were widespread. He himself described them: "Forced conversion has been decreed for us in both ends of the earth, both east and west, and Israel is hemmed in by them on all sides."[67] He was convinced that these persecutions were the birth-throes of Messianic times.[68] Evidently many shared this view. In his *Ma'amar Kiddush ha-Shem* he speaks of the many Jews who wrongfully refused to leave the lands where they were forced to accept Islam, thinking that the Messiah would soon appear.

The Yemenite Jews were, in the year 1172, sorely beset by religious persecutions at the hands of the fanatic Shī'ite rulers. They were threatened with forced conversion, apostasy and the menace of a pseudo-Messiah. In their perplexity their leader, Rabbi Jacob ibn Alfayumi, turned to Maimonides—The Light of the Exile—for counsel and guidance. In his reply Maimonides begins with a sharp warning against calculating the end. The end cannot be fathomed. There is even doubt concerning the exact duration of the Egyptian captivity, of which we have clear Biblical data. Maimonides apologizes for Saadia's

[64] *Ibid.*, p. 144.

[65] *Ibid.*, p. 146.

[66] See Fritz Baer, "Eine jüdische Messias-prophetie auf das jahr 1186 und der dritte Kreuzzug" in *Monatschrift für Gesch. und Wissenschaft des Judentums*, March-April, May-June, 1926.

[67] אגרת תימן, ed. Holub., p. 16.

[68] ואין ספק להיות אלו חבלי משיח (*ibid.*).

attempt to fix the end by saying that, in the troubled times in which Saadia lived, he endeavored by these means to strengthen the faith of the people. Maimonides vigorously denounces any attempt at prognosticating the end by means of astrology. He refers slightingly to "one of the smart ones of Spain,"[69] evidently Ibn Alfakar,[70] who attempted this feat and was belied by events, for the very year he fixed upon as the year of Redemption was the year of 'Abd al Mumin's invasion of Spain and the ensuing persecutions (1147). He urges upon the people, however, the belief that the Messiah would surely come, and that when least expected. Furthermore, according to Biblical prophecy, he will come when both Christianity and Mohammedanism will have universally extended their sway, as, "in this, our present time." And then Maimonides continues: "The exact time is not known for a certainty, but there exists among us a great and wonderful tradition which I received from my father, and he in turn from his father, and his grandfather, who likewise received it, and so through a continuous chain to the beginning of the exile from Jerusalem . . . that in Balaam's statement, Num. 23.23, 'Now, is it said of Jacob and of Israel, What hath God wrought?' is found the key to the mystery. From the time of this prophecy one should count the number of years which preceded it from creation. Prophecy will at that time return to Israel, and then the prophets will say, 'Behold what God hath wrought.' This prophecy of Balaam was delivered forty years after the Exodus, i. e. in the year 2488 A. M. The return of prophecy, which is the sign heralding the coming of the Messiah, will therefore transpire in the year 4976 A. M., i. e. 1216 C. E.[71]

It was perhaps this prophecy of Maimonides, and the

[69] אחד מן המחודדים

[70] Ibn Ezra's בן היוצר, com. Dan. 11.31. See אגרת תימן, p. 43, note 202.

[71] *Op. cit.*, pp. 6a–b. This same calculation, based on Num. 23.23, was also known to Abraham Bar Ḥiyya and to his contemporary and townsman, Judah Al-Bargeloni.

That the Yemenite Jews were expecting the Messiah at the close of the twelfth century is indicated in *The Bustan Al-Ukul* written in 1165 by the

earlier prophecy of Hananeel ben Ḥushiel, which inspired three hundred leading Jews of France and England to leave in 1211 for Jerusalem in expectation of the Messiah.[72]

The fascination which these Messianic speculations held for Jewry in the twelfth century may also be gleaned from the account of his travels given by Rabbi Petaḥia of Ratisbon in the latter end of the twelfth century. Petaḥia's travelogue covers the years 1170–1180. "At Nineveh" (Mosul), he writes, "there was an astrologer whose name was Rabbi Solomon. There is among all the sages of Nineveh and Assyria none as expert in the planets as he. Rabbi Petaḥia asked him when would the Messiah come. He replied, 'I have seen this often distinctly in the planets.' But Rabbi Judah the Pious (who transcribed Petaḥia's account) would not write it down lest he should be suspected of believing in the words of Rabbi Solomon."[73]

C. Pseudo-Messiahs

As a result of the untoward circumstances of the people and the consequent aroused Messianic interests, the last quarter of the eleventh and the whole of the twelfth century abound in pseudo-Messiahs and in abortive Messianic movements. Heretofore (up to 1000 C. E.) the Messiahs hailed from Asia Minor, Babylon and Persia. With the shifting of the center of Jewish life to the Medi-

[72] See שבט יהודה, ed. Wiener, p. 113.

[73] *Travels of Rabbi Petachia*, trans. A. Benisch, London, 1861, p. 13.

Yemenite theologian Nathanael ibn Alfayumi, possibly the father of the man to whom Maimonides addressed his Iggeret Teman.

"We hope that that time has drawn near, please God, because we have read it in the explanation of 'moed,' 'moadim' and 'the half,' and they are 'idań,' 'idanim,' and 'the half of idan' given by one of the best commentators. A proof of it is the meaning 'a conjunction, two conjunctions and a half of a conjunction.' That applies to Saturn, as the science of the stars demonstrates most clearly. It presides over our nation, and with its transition to the abovementioned conjunctions God will change the condition of the whole world as He promised, 'For behold I create new heavens and a new earth. Ye shall not remember the first ones.' And to it the prophet alluded when he said, 'At that time shall Michael arise, the great prince who presides over the children of thy people.'" (*The Bustan Al-Ukul*, ed. and trans. David Levine, New York, 1908, p. 101.)

terranean lands, the pseudo-Messiahs now come from Western Europe as well.

1. There was an extensive Messianic movement in Byzantium in 1096 with the coming of the first hordes of the Crusaders. From a Genizah letter published by Neubauer in 1896[74] it appears that great excitement prevailed both among Jews and non-Jews in the Byzantium Empire with the appearance of the Crusaders. Strange signs and portents were reported, prophetic of the Messiah's advent. The Jews of France dispatched a special messenger to Constantinople to obtain reliable information as to whether the time of deliverance had actually come. Seventeen communities of Chazaria left their homes and marched into the desert in the hope of meeting the lost ten tribes. In Salonica it was announced that Elijah had already appeared. Someone had actually received the staff of Elijah, and another had miraculously recovered the sight of both his eyes. Whole communities fasted and prayed and did penance, and many Jews migrated to Salonica on their way to Palestine. Even non-Jews were persuaded that the Messianic times were at hand. Jews were suddenly exempted from taxes and found themselves enjoying great peace and security.

2. Another Messianic movement of the period of the Crusades was brought to light through a Genizah document published by Adler.[75] A certain proselyte, Obadiah by name, relates that he met a Karaite Jew in Palestine, who announced that he would deliver Israel within two and a half months. Dr. Mann has demonstrated that this Obadiah was from Normandy, possibly one of the Crusaders, who was converted to Judaism in 1102 and who made the acquaintance of the Karaite pseudo-Messiah in northern Palestine in 1121.

3. Dr. Mann has also published other Genizah fragments[76] which point to Messianic movements in Chazaria

[74] *J. Q. R.*, IX, pp. 19–27, discussed by Kaufmann, *op. cit.*, X, p. 139, and reprinted and discussed by Mann in the התקופה, XXIII, pp. 253–59.

[75] *R. E. J.*, LXIX, pp. 129–134.

[76] *R. E. J.*, LXXI, pp. 89–93.

and Mesopotamia, in the wake of the First Crusade. The name of the forerunner of the Messiah in Chazaria was Solomon ben Doudji, and his son, Menaḥem, was the Messiah himself. In Mesopotamia in the city of Ba'kouba, a day's journey from Bagdad, a man by the name of ben Chadd[77] arose and claimed to be the Messiah, but he was soon arrested by the Caliph of Bagdad.

4. We have seen that Maimonides' Responsum, *Iggeret Teman*, was evoked by the appearance of a false Messiah in Yemen in 1172. Maimonides thus sums up this occurrence:

> In Yemen there arose a man who said that he was the messenger of the Messiah, preparing the way for his coming. He also announced that the Messiah would appear in Yemen. Many Jews and Arabs followed him. He traversed the country and misled the people, urging them to follow him and to go to meet the Messiah. Our brothers of Yemen wrote to me a long letter informing me about the manner of the man and the innovations which he introduced in the prayers, and what he told them, and reporting also the miracles which he performed, and they solicited my opinion about the matter. I understood from what they wrote that that poor man was ignorant although God-fearing, and that all that men reported concerning his performances was absolutely false. I feared me for the safety of the Jews living there, and so I composed for them three dissertations (or a treatise covering about three quires, וכמו שלשה קונדרסים) on the subject of the King Messiah, and how to know him, and the signs which will usher him in. And I urged upon them to warn that man lest he be lost and lest he also bring destruction upon the (Jewish) communities. The upshot of the matter was that at the end of the year the man was caught and all of his followers deserted him. An Arab king questioned him, and he replied that he had spoken the truth and that he had obeyed the word of God. The king asked him for a sign. He replied, "Cut off my head and I will return to life again." The king

[77] איש אחד הידוע בבן שדד.

said that there could be no greater sign than that, and if his word came true, he and all the world would believe that he spoke the truth. . . . The king commanded and they cut off his head, and the poor man was killed. May his death atone for him and for all Israel. The Jews in many communities were heavily fined. To this day there are ignorant men who believe that he will arise from his grave and appear.[78]

5. Maimonides also mentions in the *Iggeret Teman* a false Messiah who appeared in Fez in 1127: "And similarly, there arose a man in the West in the city of Fez 44 years ago (i. e. 1127), and said that he was the herald announcing that the Messiah would appear that year. His word did not come true, and because of him persecutions befell Israel. A man who witnessed it all told me about it."[79]

This Messianic movement may have been in connection with the Mahdi movement of Ibn Tumart, (d. 1130), founder of the Almohades, or with the general belief that 500 years after the rise of Mohammed the Messiah would appear.[80]

6. Another Messiah appeared in Spain in 1117, says Maimonides: "And ten years before this event there arose in Cordova, Spain, a man who boasted that he was the Messiah, and because of him Israel came very near destruction."[81]

7. And still another Messiah appeared in 1087 (within the Maḥzor רנ"ו). To quote Maimonides: "And 30 years before this time (i. e. 1087) there arose a man in France and announced that he was the Messiah, and performed signs, according to their opinion, and the French killed him, and many other Jews were slain with him."[82]

8. The most spectacular pseudo-Messiah of that period

[78] Letter to the Community of Marseilles, printed in קובץ תשובות הרמב"ם, Leipsic, 1859, II, p. 26a–b. See also Alexander Marx's reprint in *Hebrew Union College Annual*, III, pp. 356–7.

[79] *Op. cit.*, p. 50.

[80] See *supra*, p. 69.

[81] *Op. cit.*, p. 50.

[82] *Ibid.*, p. 51. See however, p. 67, note 30.

is David Alroy, who appeared about 1147, during the Second Crusade. Adventurer, magician and warrior, he announced himself as the Messiah to the Jews of Babylon, and soon won a large following. Benjamin of Tudela,[83] a contemporary, in his itinerary thus sums up Alroy's story: "He took it into his head to revolt against the king of Persia, and to gather around him the Jews who lived in the mountains of Chaftan, in order to war against the Gentiles and to capture Jerusalem. He showed miraculous signs to the Jews, and declared that God sent him to capture Jerusalem and to lead them forth from among the nations, and the people believed in him and proclaimed him the Messiah."

Alroy summoned his followers to wage war upon the Sultan Muktafi's forces and storm the citadel of his native town Amadia in Kurdistan. Little else is known of him that is not legendary. Adler conjectures that he was probably defeated in this attack and slain.[84] Benjamin of Tudela reports that Alroy, after failing to heed the appeal of the Jewish leaders of Bagdad and Mosul, who feared for the safety of their communities, and who had urged upon him to desist from his Messianic pretensions, was finally assassinated by his father-in-law, who was bribed by the governor of Amadia.

We thus have records of at least eight Messianic movements during the first three Crusades: (1) 1096—Byzantium; (2) 1096(?)—Chazaria and Mesopotamia; (3) 1117—Spain; (4) 1121—Palestine; (5) 1127—Morocco; (6) 1147—Babylon; (7) 1172—Yemen, and, (8) the Messianic movement in France in 1087, which antedated by a brief period the First Crusade. The First Crusade began in France, and high expectations were in the air some time before the actual campaign began.[85]

[83] ספר מסעות ר' בנימין, ed. Frankfurt a. M., 1904, p. 72.

[84] *J. E.*, I, .pp. 454-5

[85] See Mann, "The Messianic Movements in the Period of the First Crusades," התקופה, XXIII, pp. 243–261.

CHAPTER IV

THE YEARS 1200–1350

A. The Background

The years 1200–1350 saw no abatement in Messianic speculation. The times did not warrant it. Though the persecutions were not as prolonged as in the twelfth century, they were nevertheless frequent and intense. Christendom made headway against the Moors in Spain, and with its advance came religious intolerance. The thirteenth century was the age of the last five Crusades (1204, 1218, 1228, 1248, 1270), and Europe, Northern Africa and Asia Minor were in the throes of an almost continuous turmoil. That century, too, witnessed the extensions of the Yellow Badge indignity, ordered by the fourth Latern Council of 1215, and the first public burning of the Talmud (1242). The hand of the Church begins to bear down heavily upon the Jews.

In France the Jews suffered under Louis IX. An edict of expulsion was promulgated in 1254, which was, however, later repealed. In 1306 the Jews were again expelled and robbed of their possessions, and in 1320 the Crusade of the Shepherds wrote another bloody chapter in the history of the Jews in France. A year later followed the persecutions of the Lepers. The Jews in England were continuously harassed and mulcted, and in 1290 were altogether expelled. The Rindfleisch (1298) and the Armleder riots (1336) underscore the tribulations of the Jews in Germany and Alsace. In the middle of the fourteenth century the Black Plague swept over Europe and brought with it a long series of disasters. About this time, too, the Flagellants stirred the populace against the Jews. In this century and a half, Jewish life in Western Europe was completely disorganized. Thousands migrated eastward to Bohemia and Austria, to Poland and Lithuania.

Intellectually, the thirteenth century marks the beginning of the decline which was to continue for centuries. Maimonides is furiously attacked, and rationalism is generally discredited. This tendency culminates in the edict of excommunication pronounced by fifteen Rabbis, headed by Solomon ben Adret, against all men under the age of twenty-five who study philosophy (1305). Under the influence of Isaac the Blind, Kabbala begins its ascendency in the realm of Jewish thought. It invades rapidly the whole realm of Jewish literature. Biblical commentary takes a sharp turn away from the rational in the direction of the mystic, the allegoric and the fantastic. At the close of the thirteenth century the *Zohar* makes its appearance. "Talmudic literature, ritualism and Kabbala were almost exclusively cultivated. Poetry, exegesis, philosophy and scientific literature were constantly declining."[1]

B. The Calculators

The period is rich in Messianic speculation. Even the philosopher Gersonides is enticed. Hailing from these times are the speculations of at least eight men, and we have scattered references to still others. These eight men are: (1) Naḥmanides, (2) Isaac Halevi, (3) Abulafia, (4) The author of the *Zohar*, (5) The author of *Sefer ha-Temunah*, (6) Gersonides, (7) Baḥya ben Asher, (8) Joshua ibn Shoeib.

This period likewise presents the names of at least three pseudo-Messiahs, of whom the above-mentioned Abulafia was one. Under the influence of the Kabbalistic exegesis, popularized by Naḥmanides and his followers, in which numerical and literal mysticism—Gematria and Notarikon—is freely employed, the technique of Messianic computation begins to show a marked leaning in that direction. The method of arriving at a date becomes far more involved and supersedes the simpler and the more direct method of the earlier calculators.

[1] Deutsch, *History of the Jews*, p. 63.

1. *Moses Naḥmanides* (1194–1268), in his *Book of Redemption* (*Sefer ha-Ge'ula* or *Sefer ha-Ḳeẓ.*), applies himself zealously to the task of discovering the exact year of Redemption. Azariah dei Rossi marvels at the plausibility of Naḥmanides' arguments and frankly acknowledges that, had he lived in Naḥmanides' days, he too would have been convinced.[2]

Naḥmanides explains the cause of his great interest in this subject. The Messianic belief, he argues, is a truth patent and universally accepted among the wise and the learned. It is the expression of our wish to be nearer to God, to lead the higher life of purity and holiness in the Holy Land, where the Shekinah can dwell in our midst more closely than it can in exile. It is also an expression of our natural desire to triumph over our enemies and to sanctify the name of God before all men.[3]

He sets about to prove four things: (1) that the books of Moses and the later prophetic writings contain definite references to the final Redemption, as well as calculable and ascertainable dates;[4] (2) that Gematria is a legitimate and traditionally sanctioned method of discovering such dates;[5] (3) that the Messianic passages of Daniel refer to the final Redemption;[6] (4) that the Rabbinic injunction against calculating the end is no longer binding because we are so near the end now, and the injunction was made at a time when the end was far off, in order to save the people from heart-breaking disappointments.[7]

Naḥmanides proceeds to harmonize the various dates found in the Book of Daniel, and to deduce from them the exact Messianic year.[8] According to him, Dan. 12.11, "And from the time that the continual burnt offering shall be taken away and the detestable thing that causeth appalment set up, there shall be 1290 days," means that 1290

[2] מאור עינים, ed. Wilna, 1865, Chap. XLIII, p. 100.
[3] ספר הגאולה, ed. Lipschitz, London, 1909, pp. 20–21.
[4] *Ibid.*, pp. 3–16.
[5] *Ibid.*, pp. 3–4.
[6] *Ibid.*, pp. 21–22.
[7] *Ibid.*, p. 29.
[8] *Ibid.*, pp. 27–34.

years after the destruction of the Temple the first Messiah, the Messiah ben Joseph, will appear (i. e. in the year 1358 C.E.).[9] In his public disputation with Pablo Christiani (1263 C. E.), Naḥmanides stated explicitly: "It is now 1195 years since the destruction, or 95 years less than the Messianic figure of Daniel. We believe that the Messiah will come that year."[10] Naḥmanides maintains that the burnt offering was taken away on the day of the destruction, differing in this regard from Saadia. Forty-five years later (i. e. 1403 C. E.) the Messiah ben David will come; hence the second figure of 1335 days found in Dan. 12.13.

The "time and times and half a time"[11] yield the figure 1540; for the "time" refers to the length of the Egyptian bondage, which was 440 years; hence 440 plus 880 plus 220 = 1540. This number represents the number of years which Israel will be under the rule of the fourth kingdom, i. e. Rome, whose rule began with her victory over Greece in 138 B. C. E.

Dan. 8.14, "Unto 2,300 evenings and mornings, then shall the sanctuary be victorious," refers to the number of years which shall elapse from the reign of David (the first Messiah) to the termination of the exile.

Reign of David	40 years
Duration of the first Temple	410 years
The Babylonian captivity	70 years
The duration of the second Temple	420 years
Duration of the last exile	1335 years
	2275 years

or approximately 2300 years. The text means one to understand the figure to be approximate, for its reads עַד עֶרֶב i. e. "*about* the time of the evening." One may even arrive nearer to the figure 2300 by counting from the

[9] See also his commentary on Gen. 2.3, which passage is quoted verbatim approvingly by Baḥya (see *infra*) and by Jacob ben Asher. See his *Commentary on the Torah*, ed. Hannover, 1838, p.2c.

[10] ווכוח הרמב"ן, ed. Steinschneider, Stettin, 1860, p. 15.

[11] Dan. 7.25 and 12.7.

birth of David, which took place thirty years before he ascended the throne, up to the year of the first appearance of the Messiah, which will take place 1330 years after the destruction.[12]

Naḥmanides, who suffered under the rule of Christian Spain, and whose compulsory participation in a religious disputation resulted in his exile, looked toward a new ascendancy of Mohammedan power after 1240 as a preliminary to Redemption. The Jews in Christian lands often looked forward to a Mohammedan victory to prepare the way for the Messiah just as the Jews in Mohammedan lands looked forward to a Christian victory.[13]

Naḥmanides concludes his calculations by adducing a few Gematriot to substantiate them; as e. g. Gen. 15.13, ועִנ"ו את"ם ארב"ע מאו"ת שנה, ("And they will oppress them 400 years"). The Gematria here is 1293, which is the time of the duration of the exile, plus the half of the week (about 3 years), "when he shall cause the sacrifice and the offering to cease."[14] Also Deut. 4.30, בצר ל"ך ומצאו"ך כ"ל הדברי"ם האל"ה באחרית הימים ("In thy distress when all these things are come upon thee in the end of days.") The Gematria here is 1291, which is approximately the number of years between the destruction and the Redemption.[15]

2. *Isaac ben Judah Halevi* (second half of 13 c.), Tosafist of Sens, France, in his commentary on the Pentateuch,[16] which is in the nature of a compilation of the thoughts and interpretations of his teachers and predecessors, quotes the anonymous author of the Biblical commentary, *Gan* (France, 13 c.), as saying that Deut. 28.63 contains a Messianic reference: "And it shall come to pass that as

[12] In his *Disputation*, however, Naḥmanides categorically states that there are no Messianic references in Daniel whatsoever, except at the very end of the book. שאין בפרשה הזאת ולא בכל דברי דניאל קץ לביאת המשיח אלא בסוף הספר (*ibid.*, p. 15). Naḥmanides was forced to take this position because of his opponent's attack.

[13] כי בתחלת האלף הששי תתחדש מלכות אומה שלטת תקיפא ואומתנו יתירא ומתסרבת אל האמת יותר מן הראשונות (Gen. 2.3).

[14] Dan. 9.27.

[15] ספר הגאולה, p. 34.

[16] פענח רזא, *The Revealer of Secrets;* the numerical value of פענח is 208, and of רזא is 208. The author's first name, יצחק, is also 208.

the Lord rejoiced over you (כאשר שָׂשׂ) to do you good . . . so the Lord will rejoice over you (כן יָשִׂישׂ) to cause you to perish." "In these words is found an intimation concerning the end of the exile." This verse is to be taken in connection with Dan. 12.11: "And from the time that the continual burnt offering shall be taken away . . . there shall be 1290 days." The exile will last as long as the period of rejoicing lasted. The period of rejoicing lasted from the sojourn in Egypt (where they multiplied) to the destruction of the first Temple, i. e. 1290 years. Hence the exile will last 1290 years. The other figure given in Dan. 12.12, 1335, which is 45 years later, refers to the complete conquest of the world by the Messiah, which will take place 45 years after his first appearance. "But we do not know when the period of 1290 years begins, or we would know exactly when it will end. . . . It may begin with the taking away of the continual burnt offering in the days of Hyrcan and Aristobulus . . . or it may begin with the reign of Herod, who was not fit to be king over Israel, or perhaps at an even later date, i. e. with the expulsion.[17] At the time of the end when the Messiah will come . . . it shall become clear when the period actually began."[18]

The same computation is quoted almost verbatim in the *Sefer Hadar Zekenim*, another Tosafist Biblical commentary of the fourteenth century,[19] which concludes with the statement: "If the period of the exile (1290 years plus 45 years) is to be counted from the expulsion, then the Messiah will come in the year 5163" (i. e. 1403 C. E.).

An additional calculation is here given. The world, according to the Rabbis, is to last 6,000 years, and then it will be destroyed. The 6,000 years *include* the millennium or the universal Sabbath. The 6,000 years correspond to the six days of Creation plus the seventh day of rest. In other words, the 6,000 years equal the seven days. In the eyes of God a thousand years are equal to

[17] This last would place the Messianic year in 1358 C. E.
[18] *Op. cit.*, ed. Amsterdam, 1698, p. 63a.
[19] ספר הדר זקנים, ed. Leghorn 1840, pp. 72c–73, top.

one day, plus a watch in the night.[20] A day is then equal to 857⅐ years, and six days to 5,142⁶⁄₇ years. The seventh day, or Sabbath—the Messianic day—will then begin in the year 5143 A. M., or 1383 C. E.[21]

Isaac Halevi also attributes to the *Gan* the Messianic interpretation of Deut. 31.18; ואנכי הסת"ר אסתי"ר ("And I will surely hide"), is in Gematria 1335 (not counting the *Aleph of* אסתיר), which is the number given in Dan. 12.12. "When these (years) end, the son of David will come. . . . God will hide His face for the length of time implied in the words הסת"ר אסתי"ר . . . Daniel therefore said, "Blessed is the man who waits until these years are past. There is an indication of the end here.[22]

Isaac Halevi quotes Joseph ben Isaac Bekor Shor[23] in substantiation of his belief that the exile would last 1335 years. Bekor Shor finds his clue in the letters of the alphabet when taken in the reversed order. The first eight letters of the reversed alphabet ,תשר"ק צפע"ס, amount to 1300. By that time the Messiah will have "reigned" ten years (נמל"ך). The next four letters, יטח"ז, amount to 34. This gives you a total of 1334. On the 1335th year (1403 C. E.) joy will come (והד"ג ב"א), i. e. the fish (Leviathan) will come for the feast of the righteous.[24]

3. *Abraham Abulafia* (1240– after 1291), who in 1284, in Sicily, announced himself as the Messiah, prophesied that the Redemption would come during his own lifetime. In his *Sefer ha-Ot*, written in 1285–88, he proclaims: "And the time of salvation and the day of Redemption is come, and no man today pays any regard to this fact."[25] Abulafia wrote his prophecies during the stirring times when the Christian power was breaking before the onslaught of

[20] Ps. 90.4. See Rashi, *ad loc.*.

[21] See *supra.*, p. 70.

[22] *Op. cit.*, p. 64a. This was also known to the author of the מדרש לקח טוב, (c. 1100). See ed. Buber, Wilna, 1924, IV, p. 107.

[23] See *supra.*, p. 66.

[24] *Op. cit.*, 64a. Of the last two words the text says: וכמו הלאסטון= ἡλιαστος =luscious wine. ובאדג שפירוש לשון תענוג perhaps בארג:=effervescent wine, perhaps a pun on כגד (Gen. 30, 11: "fortue has come").

[25] וקץ התשועה ויום הגאולה בא ואין איש אשר ישים לבו היום לדעת זאת in Graetz *Jubelschrift*, עטרת צבי, p. 79. See also p. 68, קץ השקץ הגיע, and p. 69.

Mohammedan forces in Northern Africa, in Syria and in Palestine, and when the Mongolian hosts in the East were threatening the power of the Mohammedans and Christians. Thus in his *Sefer ha-Ot* he speaks of "the three kings who will arise in the three corners of the earth, each pursuing a different faith, and who will wage war upon each other." The king of the South (Mohammedan) will slay the king of the North (Christian) and will in turn be defeated by the king of the East (Mongolian). The Messiah may then be expected.[26]

This mystic, whom Jellinek regards as exceptional among all the pseudo-Messiahs on account of his extensive scholarship, unselfishness and sincerity, was so obsessed by his mission that he actually tried to convert Pope Nicholas III.

The Christian world was not unreceptive to adventist ideas at this time. The thirteenth century was one of great spiritual ferment and mystic exaltation. It was the century of St. Francis of Assisi. Italy and Southern France were especially affected by this mystic mood.

Toward the close of the twelfth century Joachim of Floris had announced that the last of the three ages—The Age of the Holy Spirit—would begin in the year 1260, basing himself on the 1260 days of Rev. 12.6. Preceding it would be the period of great tribulation when the Church would be overthrown by Antichrist.

The views of the Joachimites and the Spirituals had tremendous vogue in the thirteenth century and Apocalyptic hopes were, therefore, very intense and vivid in the second half of this century. The Flagellants appeared in 1260. "The mystic panic spread like wild fire; all men lost their heads, confessed, restored what they had stolen, embraced their enemies and composed canticles. The end of all things seemed to be at hand."[27]

Abulfia was not unaware of these conditions which prevailed in the Christian world and he was not averse to

[26] *Op. cit.*, pp. 83–85.

[27] See Gebhart, *Mystics and Heretics in Italy*, p. 196.

turning to Christendom for support in his Messianic enterprize.

Failing to impress the Jews with his Messianic hopes, Abulafia carried them to the Christian world, which was duly impressed but which preferred to rely upon the efficacy of arms in the conquest of Palestine rather than upon Abulafia. "God commanded him (Abulafia) to speak to the Gentiles of the uncircumcised heart and flesh in His name. He did accordingly and spoke to them and they believed in the message of God. But they did not return unto God, for they put their trust in their sword and bow."[28]

Abulafia claims to have studied Biblical and Talmudic lore, grammar, logic and the natural sciences, philosophy and medicine, and to have had acquaintance with the works of Saadia, Baḥya, Abraham ibn Ezra and Maimonides. These studies brought him knowledge but not the gift of prophecy. It was the mastery of the mystery of the alphabet and numbers that led him to the heights of revelation: "But when I reached to the Names and untied the seal bands, the Lord of all revealed Himself to me and made known to me His secret, and informed me concerning the end of the exile and the beginning of the Redemption through the blood-avenger."[29] Abulafia regards himself as a prophetic Kabbalist, a degree higher than the ordinary Kabbalist. Rising above the conventional themes of Kabbala—En-Sof, Sefirot and 'Ibbur (transmigration of souls), etc.—Abulafia points to the mystery of letters, vowels, numerals and the Tetragrammaton as the highest subjects for speculation. By means of these the whole universe may be controlled. Israel suffers in exile because it has forgotten God's true name,[30] and only by means of the knowledge of the true name of God will the Redemption be brought about.[31] Adret denounced such extravagant

[28] *Op. cit.*, p. 76. Abulafia may be referring to the last Crusade which took place in 1270.

[29] וזאת ליהודה, Letter of Abulafia, contra Solomon ben Adret, in Jellinek's *Auswahl kabal. Mystik*, II, Heb., p. 18. See also his שבע נתיבות התורה in Jellinek's *Philosophie und Kabbala*, I, pp. 21–22.

[30] ספר האות, p. 80.

[31] ואין תשועה כי אם בשם ידוד וגאלתו איננה לאשר לא ידרשוהו על פי שמו (*ibid.*, p. 79).

methods of Biblical interpretation and called Abulafia הנבל, "the scoundrel," but "the scoundrel" stirred his age profoundly. . .

It is likely that the rumors of Abulafia's proclaimed Messiahship, reaching by devious routes the Jews of Germany, contributed in a large measure to the great emigration of Jews, headed by Rabbi Meir of Rothenburg, for Palestine in the year 1286.[32] There were also rumors of a Messiah who arose in Syria at that time.[33]

In Abulafia, as in the case of the pseudo-Messiahs of the seventh and eighth centuries, we find a recrudescence of anti-Rabbinism. He did not, however, abrogate any Rabbinic law, nor did he challenge the method or the authority of the Rabbis. He denounced the barrenness and the inadequacy of the Talmud. He bitterly criticized the Rabbis for ignoring the higher and holier study of Kabbala and the mysteries of the divine name. A passionate craving for prophetic freedom which he sought to discover in the world of theosophy and letter mysticism, as well as the relentless persecutions to which he was subjected at the hands of the Rabbis, led him to declare that the *Mishnah* is "the graveyard of law and judgment." The Rabbis are apes and only the Kabbalist can be called truly a man. "The difference between a Talmudist and one who knows the science of the Tetragrammaton is as vast as the difference between a Talmudic Jew and a learned non-Jew."[34] With Abulafia and the *Zohar*, which appeared about the same time and belongs to the same school of thought, the long-drawn out conflict between rigid legalism and fanciful, erratic mysticism begins.

4. The *Zohar* (c. 1290), the great textbook of medieval Kabbala, gives various Messianic dates, probably reflecting the age in which each successive part to the *Zohar* was written.

(1) The *Zohar*, Par. *Wayyera*,[35] basing itself on the

[32] Graetz, V, p. 166.

[33] See *ibid.*, p. 379.

[34] See J. Günzig, *R. Abraham Abulafia*, Cracow, 1904, pp. 24–25; and Graetz, V, p. 186.

[35] ספר הזהר, ed. Amsterdam, pp. 116b–119a.

mystic value of the Tetragrammaton, sets the date as 1300 C. E. When Israel was exiled the letters of God's name (יהוה) were separated; the *He* was separated from the *Waw*. As long as this separation lasts Israel will lie prostrate in the dust. The *He* means 5000 years, the *Waw* 6000 years. When the fifth millennium will end and the sixth begin (i. e. when the two will be joined), and that will take place in the 60th year of the sixth millennium (5060 A. M. = 1300 C. E.), the hour of Redemption will begin. The number 60 is arrived at by multiplying the letter *Waw* (6) by *Yod* (10), which is their highest common multiple. Every 60 years thereafter the letter *He* will ascend by degrees and gain in potency until the year 5600 A. M. = 1840 C. E. is reached, when the gates of wisdom will be opened from above and from below, and the world will be ready for the seventh millennium.

(2) Another calculation based on the mystic value of the letter *Waw* sets the date of the Messiah's coming as 1306 C. E. The *Waw* in the name יעקוב, in the sentence, "And I will remember my covenant with Jacob,"[36] is the key to this computation. The act of remembrance will occur in the year 60 of the sixth millennium (1300 C. E.). God will redeem his promise to the children of Jacob. "In the 66th year of the sixth millennium (1306 C. E.) the King Messian will appear in Galilee."[37] These two dates, 1300 and 1306, are probably the conjectures of the original compiler of the *Zohar* himself—Moses de Leon—who died in 1305.

(3) Still another calculation is found in Par. *Shemot*. The twelve tribes represent 1200 years. "Twelve hundred years after the destruction of the Temple (1268 C. E.) the night will darken on Israel." This night will last 66 years (until 1334 C. E.). At the end of that time the Messiah will appear and wage warfare; 66 years later (1400 C. E.) the letters in God's name will appear inscribed in the lower and the higher perfection; 132 years later, i. e. 1532

[36] Lev. 26.42.
[37] *Op. cit.*, p. 119a.

C. E., the dead of Palestine will arise; 144 years later, i. e. 1676 C. E., the dead of Israel in all other lands will arise.[38]

(4) The *Ra'ya Mehemna* gives a series of dates. There will in reality be four redemptions, just as there are four cups of wine prescribed for the Passover—the Feast of Redemption—celebrated by Israel scattered to the four corners of the earth. The twelve tribes represent 1200 years. The first redemption will take place 56 years later, i. e. in the 1256th year = 1324 C. E. (based on the numerical value of רנ"ו = 256, Jer. 31.7); the second in the 1260th year = 1328 C. E. (based on Gen. 46.26, כל נפש ששים, "all the souls were threescore); the third in the 1266th year = 1334 C. E. (ושש "and six"; *ibid.*); and the fourth in the 1272nd year = 1340 C. E. (based on Lev. 25.3, שש שנים תזרע שדך; "Six years thou shalt sow thy field."[39]

(5) The *Midrash ha-Ne'elam* gives still another date. "In the sixth millennium, in the 408th year thereof (1648 C. E.), all the dead will arise." He gives as his authority the Gematria of ח"ת, the children of "Heth,"[40] which is equal to 408, and that of זא"ת "this," which is equal to 408. "In *this* year of jubilee you shall return every man to his possession."[41] The Redemption will take place 40 years before the resurrection, i. e. in the year 1608 C. E. The righteous will be resurrected 210 years before all others, i. e. in 1438 C. E.[42] The date of the *Zohar*, 1648 C. E., was frequently quoted in the great Messianic movement which spread in the seventeenth century and culminated in Shabbetai Ẓebi.[43]

[38] פר' שמות, pp. 9b–10a.

[39] See פר' פנחס, pp. 251b–252a.

[40] Gen. 23.7.

[41] Lev. 25.13.

[42] פ' יצחק, pp. 139a–b.

[43] The *Midrash ha-Ne'elam* seems to attach great significance to the number 40. Forty years is a fixed period of suffering. Israel wandered in the wilderness 40 years; the rain of the Flood lasted 40 days; the time of the Redemption will be in the 40th year: זמן גאולת של ישראל בשנת הארבעים. Elijah Ha-Kohen (d. 1729), author of מדרש תלפיות, finds it difficult to explain the last statement, and conjectures that it must mean that beginning with the sixth millennium the Messiah may be expected either at the end of the first 40 years of each century, i. e. 5040 A. M., 5140, 5240, 5340, etc., or at the end of 40-year periods, i. e. 5080, 5120, etc. (*ibid., s. v.;* גאולה).

5. *Sefer ha-Temunah*, a Kabbalistic work of the thirteenth century, attributed to Neḥunia ben Ha-Ḳanah (1–2 c.), teacher of Ishmael ben Elisha, fountainhead of Kabbalistic thought, contains a Messianic calculation. This book gave great impetus to succeeding Messianic speculation along the lines of the mystic value of the letters of the Hebrew alphabet; for this pseudepigraph combines the whole Kabbalistic system of Sefirot with the mystic system of letters.

The secret of the Redemption is suggested in the letter *Samek* (ס): "In this letter all the redemptions are indicated."[44] In form this letter is made up of the two letters' *Kaf* (כ) and *Waw* (ו). The *Kaf* stands for כנסת ישראל, "the household of Israel"; the *Waw* (the sixth letter of the alphabet) stands for the sixth millennium. The Redemption will take place in the sixth millennium, i. e. after 1240 C. E. A more specific suggestion is contained in the phrase הר האלהים ("the mountain of God"),[45] where the revelation of the first redemption (from Egypt) took place. The *He* (ה') means 5,000; the *Raish* (ר') means 200; deduct the value of האלהים, which is equal to 91, from 200, and you get 109; add 60, which is the value of the redemptive letter *Samek*, and you have 169. The Messiah will come in the year 5,169 A. M., which is 1409 C. E. From that year until the year 5400 (which is 6000 minus 600, i. e. 1640 C. E.), all the soul-purifications and all "spiritual" redemptions will take place.[46]

The Yalḳuṭ Reubeni, written by Reuben Hoshke (d. 1673), quotes this Messianic prophecy of the *Sefer ha-Temunah* but gives another version. According to this version the value of האלהים, which is 91 = צ"א = 10(9+1), is to be deducted from the number 200, giving 190. The Messiah will come in 5190 A. M., which is 1430 C. E. The symbol for this date is ה'ק"ץ (the end), which is equal to 5190.[47]

[44] ספר התמונה, ed. Koretcz, 1784, p. 56b.
[45] Ex. 3.1.
[46] *Op. cit.*, p. 58a.
[47] ילקוט ראובני, ed. Amsterdam, 1700, p. 12c.

According to the author of the *Sefer ha-Temunah*, the exile lasts as long as it does in order that the souls of men may become thoroughly cleansed of all their sins before they appear before God.[48]

6. *Levi ben Gershon* (1288–1344), the philosopher, like Naḥmanides before him, takes the trouble to explain that Daniel alone was forbidden to reveal the secret of the end, lest its very distant date might dishearten the people. That prohibition, however, does not any longer apply to the men of these later times. Commenting on Dan. 12.4, "But thou, O Daniel, shut up the words and seal the book, even to the time of the end; many shall run to and fro, and knowledge shall be increased," he says that Daniel alone was commanded not to expound further on the matter, but others following him may (i. e. "many shall run to and fro in search of this truth until such time when the truth will be discovered). He explains why he could not agree with Ibn Ezra, who maintained that Daniel himself did not know the time of the end and that the date was unascertainable.

Gersonides maintains that there is clear reference to Rome, to the final Dispersion, and to the final Redemption in the closing chapter of Daniel. The definite date is given in chapter 12, verse 11. Twelve hundred and ninety years will elapse from the destruction to the Redemption; the destruction was in the year 3828 A. M.; the Redemption will therefore be in the year 5118 A. M=1358 C. E. The figure given in the following verse, 1335, which is 45 years later, refers to the end of the Messianic wars against Gog and Magog.

The calculation is quite simple, says Gersonides. The reason why previous calculators went astray was due to the fact that each one tried to bring the Messianic date as close to his own time as possible.[49]

7. *Baḥya ben Asher* (d. 1340), pupil of Solomon ben Adret, and Darshan at Saragossa, offers Messianic calculations both in his commentary on the Pentateuch and in

[48] *Op. cit.*, p. 57a.

[49] מפני שכל אחד מהם היה טורח להמציא חשבון יגיע בימיו

his *Kad ha-Ḳemaḥ*. He is more reserved in the *Kad ha-Ḳemaḥ*, which is a book of discourses and sermons intended for popular consumption. In the three dissertations on Redemption[50] he contents himself with the expression of steadfast faith in the coming of the Messiah. He interprets homiletically many Scriptural passages to reinforce this faith. The Messiah will appear when men most despair of his coming. The prescribed years of the exile are already over; nothing detains his coming but the want of universal repentance.[51] At the close of his third dissertation he intimates the subject of calculating the end. He is commenting on Is. 64.3: "And from of old they (the Gentiles) have not heard (of the wonder which God performed for Israel in the past). Neither hath the eye (of the Gentiles) seen . . . what he will do (at the latter end) for him (Israel) that waiteth for him." This refers to our future Redemption, concerning which it is written:[52] "Happy is he that waiteth and cometh to the thousand, three hundred and five and thirty days." And it is well known to all who understand that in the case of our present exile three dates were set for it, even as in the case of the Egyptian exile."[53]

In his Biblical commentary, which is intended for the learned, he goes further and indulges in outright Messianic computations. There are two such: one in Par. *Bereshit*[54] and one in Par. *Bo*.[55]

1. The calculation found in Par. *Bo*. is the simpler one. His reasoning is as follows: the Bible gives three figures for the duration of the Egyptian exile: 210, 400 and 430 years. The duration of the present exile will also have three terms. They are enumerated in the Book of Daniel: 1150,[56] 1290,[57] and 1335.[58] All three figures are correct.

[50] כד הקמח, ed. Warsaw, 1870, pp. 21b–23d.
[51] *Ibid*., p. 22a.
[52] Dan. 12.12.
[53] *Op. cit*., p. 23d.
[54] *Op. cit*., pp. 20b–21b.
[55] *Ibid*., p. 35a.
[56] Dan. 8.14. 2300 mornings and evenings, hence 1150 full days.
[57] Dan. 12.11.
[58] Dan. 12.12.

If found worthy, Israel would be redeemed after 1150 years, i. e. in the year 1218 C. E.; otherwise they would be redeemed in 1358 C. E., or if again proved unworthy, they would be redeemed in 1403 C. E. The exile under no circumstances would extend beyond this last date.[59] He gives as the authority for his reasoning Rabbi Hananeel ben Ḥushiel,[60] who is often quoted in his commentary.

2. In Par. *Bereshit* Baḥya's calculations are more extensive and are based largely on those of Naḥmanides commentary on Gen. 2.3. The seven days of Creation and of the heavenly rest are indicative of the seven millennia of the earth's existence and of the final destruction. The fifth day is symbolic of the fifth millennium, which will be entirely an era of exile. The sixth day (in which it was said "Let us make a man = Messiah") is symbolic of the sixth millennium, in which the Messiah will come. "We are now," says Baḥya, "in the 51st year of that millennium." He was therefore writing his commentary in the year 1291 C. E. "On the sixth day the animals were created first, and then man; hence the first part of the sixth millennium will be spent in exile before Man = the Messiah, will appear. But the Messiah will appear very early in the sixth millennium, shortly after its dawn, just as a man goes forth to his labors soon after sunrise."[61] To be more exact, at the end of the first tenth of the millennium (i. e. in the year 5100 A. M. = 1340 C. E.). To be still more exact, in the year 5118 A. M. = 1358 C. E., to conform with the prophecy of Daniel (12.11), 1290 days. The fifth millennium, which is the exile era, began 172 years after the destruction and lasted 1,000 years. The Messiah will come in the 118th year of the sixth millennium. Hence 172 plus 1000 plus 118 = 1290, which is the figure of Daniel. Baḥya is here following Naḥmanides closely.

The figure in Dan. 12.12, 1335 days, which is 45 day-years later, refers to the close of the period of the wars which the Messiah's coming will usher in.[62] The date

[59] אי אפשר שתתאחר הגאולה מן הקץ הקצוב האחרון ואילך.

[60] See *supra*, p. 65.

[61] Ps. 104.22–23.

[62] So also Bar Hiyya and Gersonides.

1335 = 1403 C. E. is the absolute ultimate date. The Messiah's coming cannot be delayed beyond this date.

He arrives at this last conclusion along another line of reasoning. The Messianic age must last 837 years. (The world will be destroyed at the close of the sixth millennium.) This figure—837—is suggested in the Gematria of Is. 9.6, לםרב"ה המשר"ה," that the government may be increased" = 837.[63] Already in Talmudic times this word with its closed *Mem* was regarded as holding Messianic meaning.[64] Furthermore, the years of rejoicing in the future must equal the years of rejoicing in the past.[65] These amounted to the 410 years of the first Temple, the 420 years of the second Temple and the seven happy years of the building of the first Temple, which give a total of 837 years; hence the Messiah must come not later than 6000 minus 837, which is equal to 5163 A. M. = 1403 C. E.

Again, the number 1335 is suggested in Dan. 7.25: "Until a time and times and half a time." The first "time" is not to be counted. The "times" refer to the period between the exodus from Egypt and the building of the first Temple, which is equal to 480 years, and the period of the first Temple, which is equal to 410 years; total, 890 years. The "half a time" is equal to 445 years. The sum total is therefore 1335 years.[66]

8. *Joshua ibn Shoeib* (first half of the 14 c.), another pupil of Solomon ibn Adret, in his book of sermons based on the Parashot of the week[67] presents a Messianic date in the sermon on the last day of Passover. He finds a Messianic reference in the Song of Songs, 6.10–8.14, which he paraphrases after the manner of *Mid. R. Shir ha-Shir.* VI. 16ff.: "Who is she that looketh forth as the dawn, fair as the moon?" The moon is the future reign of David. "I went down into the garden . . . to see whether the

[63] The *Mem* in לםרב"ה is "closed."

[64] See *supra*, p. 14, and *San.* 94a.

[65] Deut. 28.63. Here follows in modified form the reasoning of Bar Ḥiyya and of פענח רזא. See *supra*, pp. 71 and 86.

[66] Saadia's calculation.

[67] דרשות, ed. Cracow, 1573.

vine budded." The Shekinah went down into the exile to see whether Israel had repented and was ready for Redemption. "Return, return, O Shulammite, return, return." The four "returns" refer to the four kingdoms, Babylon, Persia, Greece and Rome, under whom the Jews at one time or another lived. "Thy neck is as a tower of ivory" refers to the Temple. "Thine eyes as the pools in Heshbon" refers to the prophets. "Thy nose is like the tower of Lebanon" refers to the high priest. "Thy head upon thee is like Carmel" refers to the King Messiah or King David. "The king is held captive in thy tresses" refers to the King Messiah who is in prison for our sins. "I adjure you, O daughters of Jerusalem, why should ye awaken or stir up love until it please." This is a warning not to hasten the end until it pleases God to bring it about. "Who is it that cometh up from the wilderness" refers to the resurrection in the days of the Messiah. "We have a little sister . . . what shall we do for our sister in the day when she shall be spoken for?" This is the cry of the ten tribes who will be the first to return to Palestine, inquiring whether their little sister—the tribes of Judah and Benjamin—is ready to return. "Solomon hath a vineyard in Baal-Hammon" refers to Israel in exile." Solomon, the man of peace, is God. Baal-Hammon (בעל המון) refers to the lands of the Gentiles where Israel is scattered. "My own vineyard is before Me." God will remember his vineyard. "Thou, O Solomon, shalt have the thousand" refers to the sixth millennium when the Messiah will come. "And those that keep the fruit thereof 200." Two hundred years later (5200 = 1440 C. E.) the resurrection will take place.

The Messiah will therefore come between 1240 and 1440 C. E.[68]

[68] *Op. cit.*, pp. 43b–44a. The Song of Songs was treated allegorically by the Rabbis as early as the second century. (At the Council of Yamnia toward the close of the first century the book's canonicity was still a subject of dispute.) In the Christian Church it was first intrepreted allegorically as celebrating the relations between Christ and the Church by Hippolytus of Rome and Origen in the third century. They followed the exegesis of the Rabbis.

9. We have also scattered references to numerous other calculators. 1. A Tosafist commentator of Genesis, quoted in *Da'at Zekenim*,[69] gives the year 1240 C. E. as the Messianic year. "And a certain man found him, and, behold, he was wandering (תע"ה) in the field."[70] Here the angel Gabriel revealed to him (Joseph) the three exiles: (1) Egypt, 400 years = ת'; (2) Babylon, 70 years = ע'; (3) Edom, 5000 years = ה'. At the close of the year 5000 (1240 C. E.) the exile will end. May it come soon in our lifetime. I received it from my father. A like statement I received from Rabbi Benjamin (נחל) concerning the verse: "And I stayed until now (ואחר עד ע'ת'ה')[71] This, too, refers to the three exiles: ע'=70, Babylon; ת'=400, Egypt; ה'=5000, the year of the final Redemption.

2. Abraham ben Alexander of Cologne, pupil of Eleazar of Worms, who lived in the middle of the thirteenth century, and author of a small Kabbalistic work, *Keter Shem Ṭob*, gives the year 1329 as the Messianic year.[72] The Messiah, according to Abraham of Cologne, will reveal the hidden meanings of the Torah, and the secret of the twenty-two letters of the alphabet, which are the foundations of all creation.[73]

3. Zunz brings the Messianic speculation of an Italian Rabbi, Isaac Ha-Kohen, who found in Ruth 4.6 the key to the Messianic year: "And the 'redeemer' said, I cannot redeem it for myself lest I mar mine own inheritance. Take thou my right of Redemption on thee" (גא"ל ל"ך את"ה א"ת גאלת"י). The Gematria of these five words is 1335. The Messiah is therefore to be anticipated in the year 1403.[74]

4. Zunz also quotes a manuscript in which Moses ben Judah (13 c.) announced 1260 as the Messianic year.[75]

5. Levi ben Abraham (France c. 1240–c. 1315) gives

[69] דעת זקנים, ed. Livorno, 1783, p. 19a.

[70] Gen. 37.15.

[71] Gen. 32.5.

[72] See Zunz, *Erlösungsjahre*, *Ges. Schr.*, III, p. 227.

[73] כתר שם טוב, in Jellinek, *Auswahl kabb. Mystik.*, p. 43.

[74] *Op. cit.* III, p. 228.

[75] *Ibid.*, p. 227.

the year 1345 as the Messianic year. Geiger[76] quotes a München manuscript of Levi ben Abraham's *Liwyat Ḥen* in which this date is given.[77]

C. Pseudo-Messiahs

We have previously spoken of the Messianic pretensions of Abulafia. Two of his disciples, one, Samuel, called the Prophet, in the city of Ayllon, in the Spanish province of Segovia, and the other, Abraham, in Avila, in Old Castile, continued his Messianic prophecies and pretensions. Abraham, concerning whose activities Solomon ben Adret was consulted, announced that the Messiah would appear on the last day of the fourth month (Tebet or Tammuz) in the year 1295.[78] The mystic-minded community of Avila believed him and awaited the appointed day with eagerness. The people assembled in the synagogue on the designated day and great confusion and distress ensued when the prophecy failed of fulfilment.[79]

Adret availed himself of this affair of Abraham of Avila to read the people a lesson in the proper precautions which should be taken by Jews when confronted with a Messianic pretender. He urges upon the people not to be easily misled by miracle-mongers and by freaks of nature. "Even Baalam's ass saw an angel."[80] Every case should be most thoroughly investigated by scholars and competent men.[81] The prophecies of a would-be Messiah must be severely tested, and his character, conduct and motives carefully scrutinized.[82]

Graetz believes it very likely that the Kabbalist Joseph ben Abraham Gikatilla (1248–after 1305), known as Baal Ha-Nissim, the "Miracle Worker," a pupil of Abulafia, also belonged to this group of false prophets.[83]

[76] החלוץ 1853, II, p. 21.

[77] ומחשב שנת הקץ לשנת הק'ה היא י'ג ממחזור רס'ט = the year 5105, the 13th year of the 269th cycle = 1345 C. E.

[78] Gematria of הנ'ה (Mal. 3.23).

[79] Graetz, V, pp. 186–187, and *J. E.*, I, p. 98.

[80] שאפילו אתון בלעם ראתה המלאך

[81] עד שיחקרו חקירה רבה, חקירה אחר חקירה.

[82] See his *Responsum*, No. 548.

[83] *Op. cit.*, pp. 187–188.

Shemariah ben Elijah Iḳriṭi, of Negropont, (c. 1275–c. 1352), Italian exegete, philosopher and Payyetan, who endeavored to harmonize Rabbinism and Karaism, announced himself as the Messiah prior to the year 1358. This is the testimony of the apostate Moses ben Samuel de Requemaure. There is nothing, however, to substantiate his testimony, and it has been seriously questioned.[84]

[84] See Vogelstein und Rieger, *Gesch der Juden in Rom.*, I, p. 449.

CHAPTER V

THE YEARS 1350 TO 1492

A. The Background

From the middle of the fourteenth century to the close of the fifteenth century, a period of almost 150 years, we have very few Messianic calculations. The failure of the Messiah to appear around the year 1358, the date so confidently predicted by outstanding leaders of thought such as Rashi, Naḥmanides, Levi ben Abraham, Abraham bar Ḥiyya, Gersonides, Baḥya and others, as well as his failure to appear in 1403 when he was similarly predicted by great authorities, was a terrible blow to the Messianic speculators and discouraged for a long time to come further essays in this field. In place of Redemption, the middle of the fourteenth century brought with it the devastating Black Death and frightful tragedies in the camp of Israel.

Baḥya died in 1340; Gersonides in 1344. Following them and in the succeeding 150 years we have but the calculations of (1) The *Yalḳuṭ Reùbeni* version of the calculations of the *Sefer ha-Temunah,*[1] (2) *The Book of the Alphabet*, (3) *The Sefer ha-Peli'ah, we-ha-Ḳanah*, and (4) Simeon ben Ẓemaḥ Duran. The latter quite deliberately projects the Messianic year into the nineteenth century. Whenever such a long range date is given the purpose of the author is quite clear; he desires to discourage the hope of an early Redemption and of all impatient anticipations.

This period seems to yield but one pseudo-Messiah—Moses Botarel—although the age did not lack in great tragedies, such as the expulsion of the Jews from France (1394) and the bloody persecutions in Christian Spain (1391).

[1] See *supra*, p. 93.

This is quite in keeping with historic precedents. We have seen that following the failure of the Messiah to appear at the close of the fifth century, speculation halted for nigh unto a century and a half. Similarly, following the failure of such hopes in the eighth century, speculation likewise disappears for almost 150 years. Such reactions are constant and may be anticipated. Messianic interest did not, of course, disappear, but among the leaders of thought speculation concerning the time of the coming of the Messiah was held in disfavor.

Menaḥem ben Aaron ibn Zeraḥ (d. 1385), writing after 1358, still clings to the hope that the calculations pointing to that year may have erred only in basing themselves on the figure 1290 instead of 1335.[2] The latter would yield 1403 C. E. as the Messianic year, which year is still in the offing: "And if great men and scholars like Saadia and Rashi and Naḥmanides fixed the time of the end, it was because their age and the men of their age forced them to it in order to strengthen the heart of the rash. And although many criticized them when their predicted year 5118 passed (without the Messiah), yet the matter is not so. For their calculation rested on the figure 1290 in Dan. 12.11, but Daniel gives another figure in the following verse, i. e. 1335, as Rashi explains in his commentary on Daniel. This would give us the year 263 in the fifth millennium in which we now are (5263 = 1403 C. E.). And as it is written "it (the end) will surely come, it will not delay."[3] But although he devotes considerable space to prove that all the prophetic promises of restoration were not fulfilled in the first exile and must therefore refer to the restoration at the end of the second exile, he nevertheless speaks disparagingly of calculations.

The author of the *Nizzaḥon* speaks of a belief popularly held by the masses that the Messiah would come about the year 1410, but it is significant that the author himself doubts its authenticity. The leaders generally refrain from indulging in speculation. This period, too, witnessed

[2] Dan. 12.11–12.

[3] Hab. 2.3. See his צידה לדרך, ed. Warsaw, 1880, p. 298a.

a determined attack upon the whole enterprise of Messiah speculation by many writers, among whom may be found Albo, Galipapa and Arama.[4]

B. The Calculators

1. *The Book on The Alphabet*, a mystic treatise on the chirography of the Hebrew alphabet, is found at the close of the *Sefer Baruk She-Amar*, a work on the correct method of writing phylacteries, by the German scribe Samson ben Eliezer (14–15 c.). *The Book on The Alphabet* is here attributed to the author of the *Sefer ha-Eshkol*. Samson Sachs has demonstrated that this author is none other than Lipmann-Mühlhausen, author of the *Nizzaḥon*.[5] In this treatise the Messianic year 1430 C. E. is given. The author of the *Nizzaḥon*, however, was strongly opposed to Messianic calculations[6] and mentions in his book without approval the popularly accepted Messianic year 1410 C. E., but nowhere does he mention the year 1430. It is not likely therefore that Lipmann-Mühlhausen is the author of the fifth part of this treatise on the alphabet which contains the Messianic calculation and which is clearly a later addition.[7] The tract definitely closes with a prayer and the author's signature at the end of the fourth part.[8] The fifth part[9] is the work of another hand and is closely modeled after the *Sefer ha-Temunah*[10]

The author, like the *Sefer ha-Temunah*, employs the letters *Mem* and *Samek* in his Messianic calculation. He finds his key in Deut. 32.34–5: הלא הוא כמס עמדי חתום באוצרתי לי נקם

[4] See *infra*, "Opposition to Messianic Speculation."

[5] See כרם חמד, VIII, 1854; also Judah Kaufman, ר' יום טוב ליפמן מיהלהויזן, New York, 1926, pp. 71–74 and 117–118.

[6] See *infra*, pp. 220 ff.

[7] Zunz had already pointed this out (*Nachtrag zur Literaturgesch*, Berlin, 1867, p. 46).

[8] ספר ברוך שאמר, ed. Shklov, 1804, p. 24a.

[9] *Ibid.*, pp. 24–32.

[10] Kaufman errs when he attributes this part and the Messianic year 1430 to Lipmann-Mühlhausen as well as an earlier year 1405, and when he attempts to explain these two conflicting dates, (*op. cit.*, p. 74.) Lipmann-Mühlhausen never indulged in Messianic calculations and was opposed to them.

("Is not this laid up in store with Me, sealed up in My treasuries? Vengeance is mine"). The word כמס inverted (on the basis of תשר"ק) is סמך. By means of the letter *Samek*, which is the seal of God, will the day of vengeance (נקם) come. The Gematria of נ'ק'ם' is 190, which is also the Gematria of ק'ץ' (the end). The Messiah will therefore come in the year 1430 C. E.[11]

This is the date and, in a measure, also the reasoning of the *Yalkuṭ Reubeni*[12]. The year 1430 seems also to have been arrived at by means of astrological calculations. This is the testimony of Aaron ben Gershon Abulrabi (d. after 1430).[13]

2. *Sefer ha-Peli'ah we-ha-Ḳanah* is an anonymous mystic commentary on the Parasha *Bereshit*, composed in the fifteenth century by a Sephardic Kabbalist. It is in the nature of a compendium of much of the mystic speculation of the day. The author is especially addicted to Notarikon and Gematria, believing that the essence of Kabbala is the mystery of the ten Sefirot and the twenty-two letters of the alphabet: "And I wish to inform you, my son, that the science of Kabbala consists in knowing the secret and content of the alphabet."[14] He arrives at the Messianic date by means of this favorite device. He bases his calculations on the mystic significance of the letter *Waw*.[15]

[11] ברוך שאמר, p. 29c.

[12] See *supra*, p. 93.

[13] See Zunz, *Zur Geschichte*, p. 518; Perles, R.E.J., XXI, p. 246., also Zunz, *Gesammelte Schriften*, III, p. 95.

[14] ואודיעך בני כי ידיעת הקבלה היא ידיעת סוד האלפא ביתא ועניינה (See ספר הפליאה והקנה, ed. Przemysl, 1883, p. 17b).

[15] This letter plays an important rôle in Kabbalisitc Gematria speculation. Philo regarded the number 6 as a perfect number. "Six is the product of the first female number 2 and the first male number 3. Indeed, the first three numbers, 1, 2 and 3, whether added or multiplied, give 6" (see Thorndike's *History of Magic and Experimental Science*," I, p. 356). The *Sefer ha-Temunah* calls the *Waw* the "pillar of earth" (הוא עמוד לעולמא. See ספר התמונה, ed. Koretcz, 1784, p. 14a.) The number 6 when squared (=36) is one-half of the 72-lettered name of the Ineffable One (*ibid.*, 13b). According to the *Zohar*, the *Waw* is the sword of God; the other two letters of the Tetragrammaton are the head and the two edges of the sword (Ra'ya Mehemna, פר' שופטים, p. 274b). The sixth Sefirah is Tiferet and its divine cognomen is Elohim. It is the Sefirah of Mercy. Abraham ha-Yakini wrote a book to establish the Messiaship of Shabbetai Ẓebi and called it ו"ו העמודים, *The*

The author of the *Sefer ha-Peli'ah we-ha-Ḳanah* sets out first to establish the fact that the *Waw* has redemptive value. By a process of permutation and combination of letters, he shows that the *Waw* is equal to ג'א'ל = Redemption. The value of the five final letters ך'ם'ן'ף'ץ',[16] integrated and taken in their major numerical value (חשבון הגדול) plus the value of the letter *Taw*, equals 6,000. The sixth millennium is the Messianic millennium. The first half of it, i. e. 500 years, is under the dominion of the Sefirah Keṭer-Crown, and in one-half of that period, i. e. 250 years = 5250 A. M. = 1490 C. E., "the children of Israel will go forth from exile."[17] In another connection the author states that the time prophesied by Jesus for the destruction of the world is really the time of the destruction of his followers and the beginning of the reign of the blessed one (the Messiah), and this will take place in the year 5250 A. M. = 1490 C. E.[18] It is likely that the author had in mind the defeat of Christendom at the hands of the Turks in 1453, when Constantinople was conquered.

He seems to find support for his calculations in Job 38.7: בר'ן' יחד כוכבי בקר ("When the morning stars sang together"). The value of בר'ן' is 250 = 1490 C. E.[19] Zunz mentions the Messianic calculation of Abigdor Ḳara, Bohemian Kabbalist and Payyetan (d. 1439) who also gave the year 1490 C. E. as the year of Redemption.[20]

[16] The Rabbis had already connected these final letters with the various redemptions from exile (see *Lev. R.* 18.17).

[17] *Op. cit.*, pp. 12c–13a., see also p. 76d.

[18] *Ibid.*, p. 12c.

[19] Still another figure is given, in the *Sefer ha-Peli'ah*, quoted undoubtedly from an earlier source (*ibid.* p. 76c): "The number of its years (the exile) will be 1222 years" (1290 C.E.). This is Abulafia's year based on Lev. 25.10: "And ye shall hallow the fiftieth year (of the sixth millennium = 5050 = 1290 C. E.) and ye shall proclaim freedom in the land." The author here seems to be strongly influenced in thought and style by Abulafia. The Christians will be destroyed in the 1290th year = 1358 C.E.

[20] *Ges. Schr.*, III, p. 228.

Pillars of the Waw (literally the hooks of the pillars), and he builds his argument around the letter *Waw* (see David Cahana, אבן התועים, App. III, p. 142. Shabbetai Ẓebi claimed to be this sixth Sefirah, which was also called God (see *ibid.*, "Letter of Abraham Michael Cordosa," pp. 144–148).

The author seems also to have been a firm believer in astrology.[21]

3. *Simeon ben Ẓemaḥ Duran* (1361–1444), author of "*Oheb Mishpat*," a commentary on the Book of Job, gives the year 1850 C. E. as the Messianic year. Having first given his own critical comments on chapters 40 to 42 of Job, which contain references to the Behemot and the Leviathan, he is tempted to present also the older allegorical interpretation of these passages. The two chapters 40 and 41 are in reality an allegory on the epic of Abraham, his experiences with Pharaoh (the Leviathan of Job), the sacrifice of Isaac, Lot, etc.: "God revealed to Abraham the hardness of the exile."[22] The sword mentioned in Job. 41.18 refers to the sword of Rome which will not prevail against Israel. The arrow (verse 20) refers to Ishmael. The key sentence, which gives the means of calculating the end, is verse 24: אחריו יאיר נתיב יחשב תהום לשיבה ("He (the Leviathan) maketh a path to shine after him. One would think the deep to be hoary"). This sentence should be taken to read: "He who wishes to understand this and to know the light of God's ways, let him calculate (יחשב) Tehom = the abyss = the years during which Israel sinned against God, to be equal to 70 (שבעים = שיבה). Thus Moses prophesied, "Your sins will be equal to 70."[23] This, too, is the meaning of Daniel's prophecy:[24] The "season"—מועד—is 70 years, which is the length of a man's life. This verse in Daniel, therefore, states that when מועד is taken to mean 70 years (כי למועד), then the Redemption will come at the end of 70 times 35 (מועדים וחצי, חצי being one-half of 70), or after 2,450 years.[25]

This figure is also hinted at in Ezek. 4.4 ff. Ezekiel is commanded by God to lie on his left side 390 days for the sins of Israel, and 40 days on his right side for the sins of Judah. The days, of course, are years. Deduct the 40 years of Judah's sins from the 390 of Israel's, for both

[21] *Ibid.*, II, pp. 57 ff.

[22] Job. 41.13: בצוארו ילין עז = הראה לו עז הגלות.

[23] Lev. 26.21: שבע כחטאתיכם.

[24] 12.7.

[25] אוהב משפט, ed. Venice, 1589, pp. 201b–202a.

Judah and Israel will be redeemed at the same time, and you have 350 years = 35x10 = 35x10x7 (the author maintains that each unit of ten is equal to seven: והקם חשבונך אחד לשבעה) = 2450 years.

It is difficult to establish the *terminus a quo* which the author had in mind. His chronology is somewhat confused. He seems to think that 150 years elapsed from the expulsion of some of the tribes of the northern kingdom,[26] under Tiglath-Pileser (c. 734), to the final expulsion under Sennacherib (c. 722), thereby accounting for the discrepancy in the two revelations of Dan. 12.7 and Dan. 8.14, the first, according to Duran, giving the figure 2,450, and the second, 2,300. If we assume Duran's starting point to have been the final destruction of the kingdom of Israel, which, according to the old chronology, was around the year 450 B. C. E.,[27] then the Redemption would take place 2300 years later, or in the year 1850 C. E.

The figure given in Dan. 12.11, "from the time of the removal of the continual burnt offering . . . there shall be a thousand two hundred and ninety days," refers to the conquest of Jerusalem by the Mohammedans. According to the author, the end of Mohammedan rule would occur 1290 years after the rise of Mohammed (1290+622 = 1912 C. E.); the beginning of the end would be sixty years earlier, i. e. c. 1850 C. E

C. Pseudo-Messiahs

This period of 150 years seems to offer but one pseudo-Messiah—Moses Botarel—Spanish scholar and Kabbalist. Moses Botarel wrote a commentary on the *Sefer Yeẓira* in which he shows his complete familiarity with the Kabbala. He even boasts of this fact: "By my head I swear that I did not leave any book treating of this science without first studying it thoroughly."[28] He announced

[26] *Cf.* II K. 15.29; I K. 5.6.

[27] Gedalia ibn Yaḥya gives the date as 3206 A. M., which would be 446 B. C. E.

[28] כי חיי ראשי לא הנחתי שום ספר מזאת החכמה שלא חקרתיו ספר יצירה (ed. Mantua, 1562, p. 15b).

himself as the Messiah in Cisneros in the year 1393, soon after the terrible persecutions in Spain (1391). These sufferings were widely interpreted as the birth-throes of the Messiah. Abraham of Granada writes in his *Berit Menuḥa*: "And this is an indication of the approach of Redemption. When it is near, the sufferings of the exile will increase, and many of the faithful ones will stumble when they see the terrible confusion of the exile and the great sufferings, and many will leave the faith in order to escape the sword of the destroyer . . . but blessed is the man who will cling to his faith and walk in the right path. Perhaps he will be saved from the tribulations which are called the pangs of the Messiah."[29]

From letters said to have been sent to friends by Ḥasdai Crescas (1340–1410) this great philosopher is thought to have believed in the Messiaship of Botarel as well as in the miracles which he was reported to have performed. Reports had it that Botarel once demonstrated his physical immunity to the flames of a burning furnace into which he had been cast, in order to convince the king of Spain that he was in very truth a prophet.[30] It is very doubtful, however, whether Crescas actually lent himself to such preposterous beliefs. Not even the terrible sufferings of 1391, which Crescas witnessed, and the martyrdom of his own son, could have affected his mind to such an extent as to prompt him to subscribe to the vagaries of this thaumaturge. It is hardly likely that a man of such clear and independent thought, who in his systematic theology even refused to give the Messianic belief the position of a basic doctrine in Judaism, and who bitterly opposed all Messianic calculations, would lend himself to such miracle-mongering and Messianic phantasies. It may well be that the use of Crescas's name is entirely spurious.

[29] ברית מנוחה, ed. Amsterdam, 1648, p.16c.

[30] Jellinek, *B.H.*, VI, pp. 141–143.

CHAPTER VI

THE SIXTEENTH CENTURY

A. The Background

The sixteenth century is an outstanding century of Messianic interest, speculation and adventure. It follows the catastrophic expulsions from Spain (1492) and Portugal (1498), and the extensive expulsions of Jews from Germanic provinces in the last decade of the fifteenth century. In Italy, too, the conditions of the Jews changed for the worse as the sixteenth century advanced. The first ghetto was established in Venice; Jewish economic activities were restricted; and a rigorous censorship of Hebrew books was instituted.

The exiles from the Pyrenean peninsula scattered themselves along the Mediterranean littoral and settled in Italy, Northern Africa, Turkey and Palestine. They spread Kabbalistic teachings wherever they went and inoculated the Jewish communities with their own perfervid Messianic expectations. In Italy the Abarbanel family established a center of mystic thought. Abraham Zacuto, his brother-in-law, Abraham Halevi and Moses Alashkar, established another such center in Northern Africa. Joseph Ṭaiṭazaḳ, Jacob Tam ibn Yaḥya and Judah Benveniste established still another in Turkey. The Spanish immigrants fairly dominated the intellectual life of the communities in which they settled.

In Palestine Solomon Alḳabeẓ, Moses Cordovero, Isaac Luria, Ḥayyim Vital, Joseph Caro, Joseph Saragossi and their disciples gave a new and more intensive bent to practical Kabbala. Safed became the capital of the Jewish mystic world. Kabbala was no longer the handmaid of Rabbinic Judaism, modest and deferential. It became imperious and aggressive. It threatened to eclipse Rabbinic Judaism. It held the field victorious. And it fast degenerated into a miracle-mongering, weirdly superstitious affair, in which demonology, necromancy, spiritism and all forms of magic played the chief rôles. It was also a joyless mysticism, gloomy and austere, leading men to excessive discipline, penance and asceticism. Its focal point was national Redemption. Its dominant interest was in the coming of the Messiah. Nowhere was theosophy so completely steeped in nationalism.

The age was one of unrest and confusion. The exiles from Spain and Portugal, uprooted and impoverished, crushed and humiliated, moved in a world of physical and spiritual confusion. In the midst of the overwhelming catastrophe, paralleled only by the tragedy of the expulsion from Palestine, their intellectual life, which at no time in the last two hundred years had been very vigorous, was completely submerged. The uncertainty of their lives and fortunes, the wanderings through many lands to find a place of refuge, and their complete emotional prostration made them put their faith in any rumor of hope, however fantastic, which promised sudden and certain relief.

These unsettled conditions prevailed throughout the sixteenth century. In Italy, after a period of comparative quiet, persecutions flamed out anew in 1554. Jeḥiel ben Samuel of Pisa, writing in 1539, gives evidence of the breakdown of thought in his generation. In his *Minḥat Kanaot*[1] he writes: "And if by chance there will be found inaccuracies in this book, they should be attributed to me and to the limitations of my knowledge, but also to the worries which now press us down, and the storm which is now sweeping over us fiercely, breaking the branches and tearing up the roots and blinding the eyes of our intellectual judgments."

Many of these exiles were persuaded that the terrible persecutions which they had experienced were the birth pangs of the Messianic times. Thus Judah Ḥayyat, a

[1] מנחת קנאות, ed. Berlin, 1898, pp. 2–3.

Spanish émigré, who so graphically recounts his own tragic experiences as an exile in his commentary on the Kabbalistic classic *Ma'areket ha-Elohut*, was convinced that his was the last generation before the Messianic times.[2]

The political conditions of Europe also contributed to the Messianic complex. The period was one of Turkish ascendancy. From the conquest of Constantinople in 1453 to the conquest of Hungary, almost one hundred years later (1547), the power of the Turk in Europe had been steadily increasing. It was the age of Mohammed the Conquerer, and Suleiman the Magnificent. "At the time of his death (Suleiman, d. 1566) the Turkish Empire extended from near the frontiers of Germany to the frontiers of Persia. The Venetians had been driven from the Morea and the islands of the Archipelago; and except a strip of the Dalmatian coast and the little mountain state of Montenegro, the whole of the Balkan peninsula was in Turkish hands. The northern coast of Africa from Egypt to Morocco acknowledged the supremacy of the sultan, whose sea power in the Mediterranean had become a factor to be reckoned with in European politics, threatening not only the islands, but the very heart of Christendom, Italy itself."[3] The Turk was crashing at the battlements of Europe, and Christendom stood in awe of him. This condition could not but kindle the apocalyptic dreams of an harassed and suffering people. Many Jews, especially those living in Christian lands, had long regarded the downfall of Rome as preliminary to their deliverance. The Rabbis had declared that one of the signs of "the latter end" would be the conquest of Rome by Persia,[4] and it was generally accepted at this time that Persia was Turkey.[5] Moses ben Joseph di Trani (1505–1585) states that the date of the fall of Constantinople was indicated in

[2] See his מנחת יהודה, a commentary on the ספר מערכת האלהות, ed. Ferrara, 1557, Intro. p. 2b.

[3] *Encyclopedia Britannica*, XXVII, p. 448.

[4] עתידה רומי שתפול ביד פרס (*Yoma* 10a).

[5] וכבר אמרו רבים שהפרסיים הם היום טורקאש (Abarbanel in ישועות משיחו, ed. Königsberg, 1861, p. 35a).

Lam. 4.21,[6] and that the Messianic prognostications contained in the *Pirḳe de Rabbi Eliezer* refer to the conquest of Constantinople and Rhodes.[7]

The rift in Christendom, too, fed these Messianic illusions. The Reformation cleft the heart of Christendom in twain. Wars and confusions set in. Vast millennial hopes swept over the Christian world. The same "enthusiastic" tendencies which predominated in the primitive Church now made their appearance in the new reformed Church. There was the same emphasis on the freedom of the soul in Christ, on the gift of illumination and prophecy as within reach of the faithful, on pacifism and communism, and the same intense expectation of the Second Coming. The Anabaptist movement, which spread through Germany Switzerland, Italy and Holland immediately after the rise of Protestantism, aimed at the reestablishment of primitive Christianity in doctrine and practice, and was steeped in mysticism and in millenerian dreams.

The Protestant communities were anticipating the fall of Papal Rome—the fourth Beast—Babylon—as the prelude to the drama of the Second Coming and the Thousand Years' Reign of Christ. The leaders of the Reformation in the sixteenth century—Luther, Zwingli, Calvin, Knox, Tyndale and numerous others—regarded the Pope as the Antichrist, the "man of sin" of the Apocalypse, and the Roman Church as Babylon. The overthrow of Papacy and the Catholic Church, which they regarded as imminent, would usher in the glorious millennium.[8] Of the wild excesses of the early Anabaptists, whose millennial orgies took place about the same time as the Messianic exploits

[6] The Gematria of 'ב'ת' א'ד'ו'ם' is 1453. This was already noted by the author of the *Yoḥasin*, Abraham Zacuto (d. 1515). (See ספר יוחסין השלם, ed. London, 1857, p. 226).

[7]

ולכידת קושטנטינה בשנת רי״ג נתייעד בפסוק שישי ושמחי בת אדום יושבת בארץ עוץ וגו׳ כפי התרגומים. וכמו שהבאתי באגרת גאולת עולם פ״ג שחברתיה בשנת הרצ״ה. וכן ממה שאמרו בפרקי רבי אליעזר על פסוק כי מפני חרבות נדדו וגו׳ שלשה מלחמות של מהומה עתידין בני ישראל לעשות באחרית הימים שמורה על לכידת קושטנטינה ורודאס.

(ספר בית אלהים, ed. Venice, 1576, p. 102b.)

[8] See Guinness, *Romanism and the Reformation from the Standpoint of Prophecy*, Sect. VI.

of Molko and Reubeni, Motley writes in his *Rise of the Dutch Republic:* "The turbulence of the sect was alarming to constituted authorities, its bestiality disgraceful to the cause of religious reformation. . . . The Germans, Muncer and Hoffman, had been succeeded by a Dutch baker, named Matthiszoon, of Haarlem, who announced himself as Enoch. Chief of this man's disciples was the notorious John Boccold, of Leyden. Under the government of this prophet, the anabaptists mastered the city of Munster. Here they confiscated property, plundered churches, violated females, murdered men who refused to join the gang, and, in brief, practiced all the enormities which humanity alone can conceive or perpetrate. The prophet proclaimed himself King of Sion. . . . The prophet made many fruitless efforts to seize Amsterdam and Leyden. The armed invasion of the anabaptists was repelled, but their contagious madness spread. The plague broke forth in Amsterdam. On a cold winter's night (February, 1535) seven men and five women, inspired by the Holy Ghost, threw off their clothes and rushed naked and raving through the streets, shrieking, "Woe, woe, woe! the wrath of God, the wrath of God." . . . The numbers of the sect increased with the martyrdom to which they were exposed, and the disorder spread to every part of the Netherlands. . . ."[9]

The repercussions of the great struggle in the Christian world were felt in the ghettoes of Israel. Thus Joseph d'Arles, follower of Molko, entertained great hope that the Protestant Reformation would dismember Christendom and destroy Rome.[10] The seeming break-up of Christendom, the decline in the power of the Papacy, added to the victorious advance of the Turk, led many to feel that they were actually living in the period of the great denouement of the Messianic drama.

The discovery of the New World, too, inflamed the imagination of men. Columbus himself believed that his

[9] *Op. cit.*, Hist. Intro., xii. See also Belfort Bax, *Rise and Fall of the Anabaptists*, Chap. VII.

[10] See S. D. Luzzato, *Hebräische Bibliographie*, V, p. 45.

discoveries were the fulfilment of prophecy.[11] The successful explorations in the new continent and the accounts brought home by travelers and Conquistadores gave rise to the most fantastic rumors. The Jews quite naturally looked to the newly discovered lands as the possible home of the long Lost Ten Tribes, whose existence no one doubted, concerning whose whereabouts vague reports had drifted in through the centuries since the dispersion, and whose return to Palestine was, in the minds of the people, preliminary to the complete restoration of the whole of Israel.

The renewed interest in the Ten Tribes is evinced in the Biblical commentary of Isaac Caro, uncle of Joseph Caro, called *Toldot Yiẓḥaḳ*. Caro was a Spanish refugee, and wrote his book in haste on the way to Palestine (1518).[12] He follows Naḥmanides in the main, though his book is singularly free from excessive Kabbalism and Gematria—legerdemain. In his commentary on Deut. 30 he takes pains to point out that the chapter refers not alone to the Judean exiles but to the Lost Ten Tribes as well. Here the word שב is mentioned twice in verse 3: "Then the Lord, thy God, will turn (ושב) thy captivity and have compassion upon thee, and will return (ושב) and gather thee from all the peoples." The first שב refers to the Ten Tribes; the second to Judah and Benjamin.[13]

Judging from the *Letter of Joshua Lorki*, the belief in the existence of the Ten Tribes somewhere in the distant East was widespread in the fifteenth and sixteenth centuries. He points to the numerous reports brought back by travelers and merchants concerning the happy and prosperous conditions of the Ten Tribes, whose number is "like the sands of the sea," and implies that no one doubts this

[11] Bishop Agostino Giustiniani, in his suppressed Polyglot *Psalter* (Genoa, 1516), in which appears the first biographical account of Christopher Columbus, writes: "At vero quoniam Columbus frequenter predicabat se a Deo electum ut peri ipsum adimpleretur haec prophetia, non alienum existimavi vitam ipsius hoc loco inferere" (commentary on Psalm 19.4).

[12] תולדות יצחק, ed. Warsaw, 1877, p. 163b.

[13] *Ibid.*, p. 156a.

fact.[14] The discoveries in the New World undoubtedly colored and intensified these hopes. Neubauer correctly states: "The sixteenth and seventeenth centuries produced the richest material and the wildest fictions concerning the lost tribes."[15]

These notions fed the pretensions of the adventurer David Reubeni, and assured them an eager and favorable reception.

The Messianic expectations of this century, which are given classic expression in the writings of Abarbanel, rise in successive up-thrusts through the succeeding 150 years, until they reach their climax, and, in a sense, their final defeat in the Shabbetai Ẓebi movement.

B. The Calculators

The Messianic calculators of this period are (1) Isaac Abarbanel, (2) Abraham Halevi, (3) Solomon Molko, (4) Mordecai Dato, (5) Daniel ben Peraḥia, (6) Isaac Luria, (7) Naphtali Herz, (8) Eliezer Ashkenazi, (9) Gedalia ibn Yaḥya, (10) David ben Solomon ibn Abi Zimra, (11) Joseph ibn Yaḥya and (12) Samuel Velerio.

1. The outstanding Messianic writer of this period whose works had a far-reaching influence on the Messianic movements of the 16c is *Isaac Abarbanel* (1447–1508). He composed three books on this theme: (1) *The Wells of Salvation* (1496), (2) *The Salvation of his Annointed* (1497), and (3) *Announcing Salvation* (1498). They are, respectively: (1) a discussion of the prophecies in the Book of Daniel, (2) a compendium of all Talmudic Messianic passages, and (3) a compendium of all Biblical Messianic prophecies (other than those of Daniel). Abarbanel is encyclopedic in his grasp of the Messianic material, and his works are the most complete and thoroughgoing of their kind in the whole field of Jewish adventist literature.

Abarbanel regarded the belief in the coming of the

[14] וזה דבר שאין בו שום ספק (see אגרת יהושע לורקי ed. Landau, Antwerp, 1906, p. 3).

[15] See *J. Q. R.*, I, p. 201.

Messiah as an indispensable dogma of the Jewish faith.[16] He viciously attacks Albo for presuming to say that the Messianic belief is not a dogma and that it has no Biblical authority. He calls Albo's book, ספר העיקרים, *The Book of Roots*, ספר העוקרים, "The Book of Uprooters."[17]

Isaac Abarbanel wrote his *Wells of Salvation* in exile, in Naples. "My entire purpose and aim in writing this book, so dear to me," he writes, "is to strengthen the feeble hands and to uplift the stumbling feet."[18] It was to comfort his people in "their night of darkness, to slake their thirst when their spirits grew faint," that he wrote his book and called it the *Wells of Salvation*.[19]

The *Wells of Salvation*, composed of twelve "Wells" and seventy "Palms," is an elaborate treatise on the Book of Daniel. The first Well apologizes for the author's temerity in undertaking a task clearly proscribed by the Rabbis. This prohibition, argues the author, applies only to those who calculate by means of astrological phenomena, and not to those who seek to read the riddle of Scriptural prophecies and intimations.[20] He quotes precedents—Saadia, Rashi, Abraham bar Ḥiyya and Naḥmanides: "Our life is so hard and our fortunes so unhappy that we are constrained to inquire after the hour of our release and Redemption. Furthermore, the end is not far off, and it is now proper to reveal it."[21] Here Abarbanel is one with Naḥmanides and Gersonides. He does not claim absolute truth for his statements; he did not receive his information by way of tradition or revelation; it has come to him from his studies of the Book of Daniel.

Abarbanel devotes the next four Wells to a systematic discussion of the content, form, object and authorship of the Book of Daniel.[22]

[16] היות ביאת המשיח עיקר מעיקר הדת in his ישועות משיחו, ed. Königsberg, 1861, p. 25b.

[17] י"ם, p. 27b.

[18] מעיני הישועה, ed. Amsterdam, 1647, p. 91b.

[19] *Ibid.*, Intro. p. 8a.

[20] *Ibid.*, p. 12a.

[21] *Ibid.*, p. 12b.

[22] *Ibid.*, p. 22a.

The content of the book focuses itself in the Vision of the Four Kingdoms. In Well 2 Abarbanel establishes the fact that the fourth kingdom mentioned in Daniel is Rome, and that the Merkabah chapter of Ezekiel is Messianic in character and not metaphysical; that "the four living creatures and the four wheels" refer to the four kingdoms. He also explains why only the four kingdoms (Babylon, Persia, Greece and Rome) are mentioned and no others.

The form of the Book of Daniel is prophetic. In Well 3 Abarbanel sets out to prove at great length that, contrary to the opinion of Maimonides, Daniel was a prophet of the first rank.

In Well 4 Abarbanel lays bare the reasons for Messianic prophecies. They were made in order to proclaim the power of a retributive God, and to urge men to repentance, else punishment is certain to overtake them. Suffering is the certain punishment which God visits upon sinners, and salvation is the certain reward of the righteous. They are not accidental or unpremeditated. The prophet, therefore, foretells the doom which will befall the people because of their sins, but lest they despair utterly and lose hope, he also announces the ultimate Redemption which will follow repentance. Hence, while prophesying exile, he also prophesied Redemption.

In Well 5 Abarbanel speaks of Daniel himself, the author of the book, and of the three supreme prefections which may be attributed to him: (1) exalted ancestry and position; (2) piety and holiness, and, (3) wisdom and prophetic excellence. Abarbanel raises Daniel to the rank of a prophet, contrary to the traditional view.[23] He is compelled to do it by the fact that his major Messianic calculations are based on the prophecies in Daniel. He is at one here with Christian calculators.

He then proceeds to write a running commentary on the book itself. In Well 6 he discusses Nebuchadnezzar's dream of the image and Daniel's interpretation of it. The

[23] *Pesiḳ.* 128b.

head of gold is Babylon; the breast and arms of silver are Persia; the belly and thighs of brass are Greece; the legs of iron are Rome; the feet, part iron and part clay, refer to the Christians and the Mohammedans who have divided the Roman world. The fifth kingdom is Israel, and the one which shatters the feet of iron is the Messiah.[24] This is followed by a verbose dissertaion on the episodes of the image of gold which Nebuchadnezzar set up, the burning furnace, and the second dream of Nebuchadnezzar—the dream of the Tree.

Well 7 takes up the banquet scene of Belshazzar, the writing on the palace wall and the story of Daniel in the lions' den. The author sees in these experiences of Daniel analogies to the experiences of the people of Israel.[25]

It is in Well 8, discussing Daniel's first dream[26] that Abarbanel sets out upon his calculations. The contention of Albo and others that this vision of Daniel applies to events and kingdoms antedating the destruction of the second Temple, he regards as stupid and senseless.[27] Abarbanel's animus is undoubtedly heightened by the fact that Jewish apostates, like Solomon Halevi and Joshua Lorki, had made similar claims, but to a different end, of course. He maintains that the first beast, which is likened to a lion, is Babylon. Its eagle's wings are symbolic of its swiftness to conquer and of its vaunting pride. Its wings were plucked by the king of Persia; its dominion was "lifted up from the earth"; and its people were reduced to cowardly flight ("made to stand upon two feet, as a man, and a man's heart (i. e. not a lion's) was given to it" (verse 4). The second beast, likened to a bear, is Persia. She was not as great as the lion, Babylon. She will rule only in one direction ("it raised up itself on one side"; verse 5), and will comprise three kingdoms, Media, Persia, Babylon ("it had three ribs in its mouth between its teeth"; verse 5.) The third beast, likened to a leopard, is Greece. She was

[24] *Op. cit.*, p. 27b, c.
[25] *Ibid.*, p. 38b, c.
[26] Dan. 7.
[27] *Op. cit.*, p. 39b.

swifter than Persia and conquered more territory; hence the "four wings of a fowl" (verse 6.). The four heads of the beast are the four divisions of the kingdoms of Alexander the Great, which took place after his death. The fourth beast, "dreadful and terrible and strong exceedingly," is Rome. Its "feet" are the kings of Rome; the "great iron teeth" are the Roman consuls; the "horns" are the emperors. The ten horns are the ten emperors who ruled over Rome up to the destruction of the Temple.[28] The "little horn" is the papacy, which was established in Rome after the Destruction. This interpretation was generally accepted by Protestant interpreters after the Reformation. The three horns which were plucked out by the roots were the three emperors who preceded the birth of Christianity. The "eyes" which the "little horn" had is symbolic of its wisdom, and the "mouth speaking great things" is symbolic of the power of its speech (oratory) and of its commands and the harm which its words will do.[29]

After dwelling at length on the judgment day mentioned in Dan. 7.9–10, he returns to the account of the fourth beast. Rome will be destroyed because of the teachings of the "little horn" = papacy (verse 11). Then the Messiah will come (verse 13). He will come after a period of great suffering ("There came with him clouds of heaven"), humbly ("like unto a son of man"), through the will and favor of God ("and he came even to the Ancient of days"). Israel will then have the three things of which the exile deprived it: power ("dominion"), honor ("glory"), and independence ("and kingdom"). Israel's kingdom will endure forever (verse 14).[30]

The duration of the fourth kingdom will be for "a time and times a half a time" (verse 25). Abarbanel rejects ibn Ezra's interpretation of this chapter and points out that the calculations of Saadia, Rashi, Naḥmanides and others

[28] *Ibid.*, pp. 42d–43a.
[29] *Ibid.*, p. 43d.
[30] *Ibid.*, pp. 49c–51a.

have been historically proved false.[31] He gives his own interpretation. "A time" (עדן) is the period of the duration of the first Temple, which is 410 years. Three and a half times (time and times a half a time) are 1435 years. Add this to the year 68 C. E., the year of the destruction, and you get the year 1503 C. E. as the Messianic year.[32]

Then follows a discussion of Daniel's second vision.[33] The ram which Daniel saw is Persia, the two horns of the ram are Persia and Media, or Darius the Mede and Cyrus the Persian; the he-goat which smote the ram is Greece, and the conspicuous horn which was between his eyes was Alexander. The four horns are the four parts into which Alexander's empire was divided. The little horn which came out of one is Antiochus Epiphanes. The host in whose hands the continual burnt offering was given over on account of the transgression of the people is Titus of Rome. The two holy ones are the angels Michael and Gabriel; the 2,300 evenings and mornings, which are the duration of the Exile, are 2,300 years. They are to be counted from the division of the kingdom which took place in the year 2965 A. M. Add these two figures and you have 5265 A. M., or 1504 C. E., or approximately 1503 C. E.[34]

Well 10 interprets Daniel's third vision:[35] "The 70 weeks" (verse 24) means 70 times 7, which is 490 years. This is the time between the destruction of the first and the second Temples.[36] Abarbanel here follows Saadia. The later figures, found in verses 25–27, are subdivisions of this figure. "Seven weeks" (verse 25) means 7 times 7, which is 49 years. Forty-nine years after the destruction of the first Temple, Cyrus granted the Jews permission to rebuild it. "The three-score and two weeks" is equal to 62 times 7, which is 434 years. This is the period from Darius to the second destruction. The "week" mentioned in verse 27 refers to the 7 years during which

[31] *Ibid.*, 51b, c.
[32] *Ibid.*, p. 51c.
[33] Dan. 8.
[34] *Op. cit.*, pp. 56d–57a.
[35] Dan. 9.
[36] *Op. cit.*, pp. 62d–63a.

the Emperor Vespatian offered peace to Jerusalem. The three figures, then, 49 plus 434 plus 7, equal 490 years. The half week mentioned in verse 27, during which he shall cause the sacrifice and the burnt offering to cease, is included in the week.[37]

Well 11 tells of Daniel's fourth and last vision.[38] The man clothed in linen is the angel Gabriel; the fourth king of Persia whom Greece will overthrow is Darius; the mighty king who will then arise is Alexander. Abarbanel has difficulty in interpreting the wars between the kings of the South and the kings of the North, mentioned in chapter 11. He accordingly presents the interpretations of Rashi, Gersonides and Abraham bar Hiyya, as well as the Christian interpretation[39] concerning Dan. 11.31: "And arms shall stand up on his part" refers to Rome. "Who shall profane the sanctuary" and "such as do wickedly" refer to Titus, and "they that are wise among the people shall cause the many to understand" refers to the martyrs of the destruction. The king who "will do according to his will" is Constantine, who accepted Christianity. "Neither shall he regard the desire of women" refers to the celibacy of pope and priest. The Gematria of אלוה נכר (verse 39) = 316 is equal to that of י'ש'ו' = Jesus.[40] Dan. 11.40 ff. tells of the wars of the Christians and the Mohammedans during the period of the Crusades, which will terminate in the complete defeat of the Christians.[41] Abarbanel believed that the Turks, who conquered Constantinople, the eastern stronghold of Christendom, in 1453, will also conquer Rome.[42]

[37] *Ibid.*, p. 64d.

[38] Dan. 10–12.

[39] *Op. cit.*, p. 70c.

[40] *Ibid.*, p. 75d.

[41] *Ibid.*, p. 76a.

[42] *Ibid.*, p. 79d. It was generally believed that the struggles between Mohammedan Turkey and Christian Europe in the 15th and 16th centuries had Messianic significance. A Gematria was found for it. The numerical value of ח'ב'ל'י' מ'ש'י'ח' (birth-throes of the Messiah) is equal to י'ש'ו', מ'ח'מ'ד' (see S. D. Luzzato, *Heb. Bibl.*, V, p. 46). The Christian world regarded the Turk as the Antichrist. Luther wrote: "Anti-Christ is the pope and the Turk together . . . the spirit or soul of Anti-Christ is the pope, his flesh or body

The Messiah will then appear, deliverance will come to Israel, to be followed by the resurrection.[43] The righteous and wicked alike will be resurrected, not only that they may stand in judgment, but that the faithful Jews who died in exile amidst suffering and martyrdom may now enjoy the glory of Redemption, and that the wicked who persecuted Israel during the years of exile may now receive punishment. Resurrection will follow soon after the Redemption.[44] After resurrection the true faith will be universally acknowledged.[45]

The "other two" whom Daniel saw,[46] are Edom and Ishmael; the river on whose banks they stood is the land of Israel. These two asked the angel Gabriel (the man clothed in linen): "How long shall it be to the end of wonders?" That is, how long shall it be to the time of the resurrection. The angel replies that the resurrection will take place at the time of the redemption of Israel, i. e. and for a time, times and a half. Daniel understands this allusion, for he had received a similar revelation in his earlier vision.[47] It refers to the year 1503 C. E. Daniel is furthermore informed that the first defeat of Edom which will precede the final defeat of Rome will be the conquest of Constantinople by the Turks in the year 1453. This is the meaning of verse 11: "And from the time that the continual burnt offering shall be taken away (i. e. three and a half years before the destruction = 64 C. E.) until (the time when) the detestable thing that causeth appallment (was taken over by the Mohammedans) there shall be 1390 years, i. e. c. 1453 C. E. Abarbanel takes the

[43] Dan. 12.2.
[44] *Op. cit.*, p. 77c, d.
[45] *Ibid.*, p. 78a.
[46] 12.5.
[47] Dan. 7.25.

the Turk" (*Table Talk*, ed. Hazlitt, CCCCXXVI). Luther expressed the thought that Christ might come in 1558, or 105 years after the conquest of Constantinople by the Turks. He calculated "time" to be the age of Christ (30 years). Hence "time, times and half a time" = 105 years (*ibid.*, CCCC-XXVII). It is of interest that Isaac Ḥayyim Cantarini (1644–1723) also interpreted מועד to be the term of a man's life = 120 years (עת קץ, ed. Amsterdam, 1710, p. 49d).

Gematria of ימים "days," which equals a hundred, and adds it to the 1290 mentioned in verse 11.[48] Fifty years will elapse between the time of the conquest of Constantinople and the final Redemption, just as during the Babylonian exile 50 years elapsed before Cyrus gave the Jews permission to return.

The figure 1335 given in verse 12 refers to the time which must elapse from the destruction, or, in other words, 1335 + 100 + 68 = 1503 C. E. In that year either the Messiah himself will come or the preliminary events, the destruction of Rome and the punishment of the Gentiles, will take place.

His conclusions are summarized as follows: There are six Messianic dates found in Daniel. 1. "Until a time and times and half a time" (7 v. 25) = 1435 years; 1435 years after the destruction = 1503 C. E., the end of the Roman dominion over Israel will take place.

2. "Unto 2300 evening and mornings" (8.14), 2300 years after the division of the kingdom under Rehoboam, which took place in 2964 A. M., or, in other words, in the year c. 1501 C. E. the Messiah is to be expected.

3. "Seventy weeks are decreed" (9.24) = 490 years, the number of years between the first and second Temple.

4. "It shall be for a time, times and a half" (12, v. 7) = the same as 1.

5. "There shall be 1290 days" (12. v. 11) = 1290 years plus 100 years (Gematria of ימים) = 1390 years after the destruction, i. e. 1458 C. E., minus 4 (see *supra*) which equals c. 1453 C. E., the year of the fall of Constantinople—the beginning of the end.

6. "To the 1335 days" (12 v. 12) = 1335 + 100 = 1435 years, after destruction—the final end.

In the final Well, Abarbanel endeavors to adduce corroborations for his calculations from astrology. The conjunction of Saturn and Jupiter is especially significant for world affairs. It is the most potent when it occurs in Pisces and has a special significance for Israel[49] This

[48] *Op. cit.*, p. 80a.

[49] *Op. cit.*, p. 84b.

was the belief also of Bar Ḥiyya, to whom Abarbanel is greatly indebted throughout his works. Abarbanel makes it clear elsewhere that Israel is not subject to the control of heavenly bodies, but is directly under the providence of God.[50] "It is clear from this second introduction," he writes, "that Israel is subject to no star or guardian, but to God alone."[51] But the motions of the heavenly bodies, while not causative are yet indicative. This ominous conjunction first occurred in the year 2365 A. M., three years before Moses was born, and indicated the deliverance of Israel from Egypt.[52] The second conjunction in Pisces took place in the year 5224 A. M., or 1464 C. E., and likewise pointed to the deliverance of Israel.[53] The Egyptian deliverance did not actually take place until 83 years after the conjunction. The final deliverance from this exile cannot therefore exceed the time limit of 1464 plus 83, or 1547 C. E. It is probable, says Abarbanel, that God will hasten the day.

Abarbanel is certain that the Messiah was born before the expulsion of the Jews from Spain.[54]

Abarbanel's second work, *The Salvation of His Annointed*, written in 1497, is frankly polemical in character. Its chief aim is to refute "the men who contend against us," principally those Jewish apostates who quoted in public disputations Talmudic authority to prove that the Messiah had already come.[55] Abarbanel pays particular attention to the convert Joshua Lorki, of the Tortosa-disputation fame (1413–1414).[56]

The Talmud seems to contain Messianic calculations which clearly point to a date long since past. Besides, there are certain opinions expressed there implying that the Messiah will never come. Abarbanel sets himself the task of interpreting these passages to show that the Rabbis

[50] See Chap. XII of his עטרת זקנים, ed. Warsaw, 1899.
[51] *Ibid.*, p. 44.
[52] *Op. cit.*, p. 84d.
[53] *Ibid.*, p. 86c.
[54] *Ibid.*, p. 88a.
[55] See ישועות משיחו, pp. 4b–5a; 16a.
[56] המופקר הגדול שמו בישראל לפנים לודקו (לורקי) יש"ו ראש הפוקרים (*ibid.*, p. 5a).

did not deny the ultimate appearance of the Messiah, nor did the Talmudic dates imply that the Messiah has already come. *The Salvation of His Annointed* is divided into two parts. The first is a discussion of chapter 39 of *Pirḳe de Rabbi Eliezer*, and the second is an analysis of numerous Talmudic and Midrashic Messianic passages. The second part is divided into four themes.

The *P. R. E.* states that the rule of the four kingdoms would last one day of God, or a thousand years. Assuming that the "day" began with Nebuchadnezzar's reign (1319 A. M.) the Messiah would appear in the year 4319 A. M., or 559 C. E.—a date long since past. Abarbanel resolves this difficulty by pointing out that the day which is equal to a thousand years is the "daylight day" made up of twelve hours.[57] Hence a full day, which is clearly the meaning of chapter 29, and which contains twenty-four hours, is equal to 2000 years. The rule of the four kingdoms would therefore end in the year 1559 C. E. When you deduct two-thirds of an hour[58] which is equal to 56 years, from this date, you will get the year 1503 C. E., the very year established in the Wells.[59]

In the second part of his book Abarbanel takes up the passages found in *San.* 97a, b, which seem to indicate that the Messiah would appear in the fifth century. He meets the situation by laying down a general rule that in all Messianic calculations there are three possible terminals: (1) The period during which the Messiah cannot come; זמן המנעות ביאת המשיח; (2) the period during which he may come, contingent upon the merit of the people, זמן אפשרות בואו; and (3) the period when he must come, זמן המחויב וההכרחי.[60]

The first period ended 400 years after the destruction. Prior to that time the Messiah could not come. The exile had to last at least 400 years. This was in the mind of the Rabbis when they pointed to the fifth century as the Messianic age. It marked the beginning of the age during

[57] *Cf. P. R. E.*, Chaps. 7 and 48.
[58] *Ibid.*
[59] יש' משיח, pp. 12b–13a.
[60] *Ibid.*, pp. 11b, 18b, 19a.

which the Messiah *could* come. The period when he must come is indicated in the story of the mysterious scroll found in the archives of Rome, which declared that the world would come to an end in the year 4291 A. M., or 539 C. E.[61] Abarbanel accepts as an emendation the reading of Rabbi Aḥa son of Raba, "after 5000 years."[62] This gives 5291, or 1591 C. E., which is Abarbanel's *ultimate* Messianic year.[63]

Abarbanel devotes considerable space to the startling dictum of Hillel, namely, that there is no longer a Messiah for Israel, for he had already been consumed in the days of Hezekiah. He offers two explanations. The first is that the true intention of Hillel was that the Messiah can no longer come in the "contingent era," by the merit of the people, for all such merit had already been "consumed" in days of Hezekiah.[64] The second explanation is that Hillel did not deny the ultimate Redemption at the hands of a Redeemer, but insisted that his name would not be Messiah (אין משיח לישראל). The future Redeemer will not be *annointed*, for he will not be king over Israel. God alone will be king; the Redeemer will only be their prince (נשיא); "And my servant David will be prince (נשיא) over them forever."[65]

Abarbanel also explains Akiba's belief that Bar Kochba was the Messiah, and his statement that the Lost Ten Tribes would never return. Akiba may have believed that God had repented Him of his decree and hastened the day, even though Israel was still living in the period when the Messiah could not come, just as God had reduced the 400 years of the Egyptian bondage to 210 years. Or Akiba may never have regarded Bar Kochba as the true Messiah, for the latter was not of the house of David, nor was he a judge. Bar Kochba was only the instrument of God to punish Rome. Such messengers of God are frequently called Messiah (e. g. Cyrus), and only in this sense did

[61] *San.* 97b.
[62] *Ibid.*
[63] *Op. cit.*, p. 21b.
[64] *Ibid.*, 25b–26a. See also his Intro. to מש' ישועה, p. 2c, and ראש אמונה, p. 18b.
[65] Ezek. 37.25,. 26b–28a.

Akiba regard Bar Kochba as the Messiah. As regards the Lost Ten Tribes, Akiba had reference only to those of the Ten Tribes who never returned to Judea and to the neighboring provinces, and were therefore never absorbed by the people of Judea. Those who did return are, of course, counted among the Judeans, and they will return with the return of Judea. The former, however, Akiba maintained, will never return, and Akiba was entitled to his opinion, for he could find many Biblical texts to substantiate it. Abarbanel himself was inclined to believe in the return of the Lost Ten Tribes in the traditional sense.[66]

The first theme closes with a polemic against Joshua Lorki's Christian interpretation of the passage in *'Ab. Zar.* 8b: "Forty years before the destruction of the Temple the Sanhedrin was driven from the chamber of the Hewn Stone in the Temple (Lishkat ha-Gazit) and met in the market." According to Lorki this event coincided with the year of the crucifixion of Jesus.

Abarbanel also contradicts Lorki's deduction from *Yeb.* 82b and *Nidah* 46b: "Rabbi Jose said the Bible reads, 'and the Lord thy God will bring thee into a land which your fathers possessed, and thou shalt possess it.'[67] From this you may learn that they will have a first and a second possession (restoration, i. e. from Egypt and Babylon), but not a third." Lorki maintained that this meant that the Jews would never return to Palestine. Abarbanel answers that the second possession refers to the *ultimate* restoration; for the return from Babylon to Palestine was not in the true sense of the word a possession: "Cyrus gave them persmission to return. The land was not conquered by Israel."[68]

The second theme is devoted to Talmudic passages, which imply that the Messiah was already born, especially to the famous passages in *Ekah R.* 1.57 and *Jer. Ber.* 4a, in which the lowing of an ox announces the destruction

[66] *Op. cit.*, p. 33b.
[67] Deut. 30.5.
[68] *Op. cit.*, pp. 37b–39a.

of the Temple and the birth of the Messiah. Lorki interpreted these passages to refer to Jesus. The apostate Pablo Christiani made similar use of them in his disputation with Naḥmanides and forced Naḥmanides to declare that he was not bound to accept the individual opinion of a Rabbi in matters Aggadic. Abarbanel says that both the literal and allegorical reading of this passage contradict the conclusions of Lorki.[69]

The third theme is devoted to an anti-Christian exposition of the character of the Messiah to prove that the Messiah is man, not God, and to bring Talmudic passages into accord with this thought.

In the fourth theme Abarbanel sets out to prove that with the advent of the Messiah the Torah, in part or in full, will not be abrogated. The apostate Pablo de Santa Maria (c. 1351–1435) devoted the eighth chapter of his *Dialogus Pauli et Sauli* to establish the very opposite thesis.[70]

Abarbanel's purpose in writing his third work, *Announcing Salvation,* was to refute those among his people and others who construed the Messianic prophecies of the Bible to apply to the first restoration. He also sets himself to contradict the belief that the coming of the Messiah is only a tradition of the Elders (הבלת הואשונ'ם) and has no Biblical authority. Among those whom he specifically singles out for criticism are Judah ibn Balaam of Toledo, Moses ibn Gikatilla of Cordova and Ḥayyim Galipapa, whose epistle on Redemption is mentioned approvingly by Albo. Abraham ibn Ezra, too, according to Abarbanel, is somewhat tainted with this heresy.[71]

Abarbanel undertakes to investigate each and every passage in the Scriptures containing a Messianic prophecy, in order to establish that in each case the reference is to

[69] *Ibid.*, pp. 39a–43a.

[70] "In primo capitulo (Distinctio Octava) ostenditur ut legi mosaice posset aliquid addi vel diminui . . . In secundo capitulo ostenditur ut deus promisit dare populo Israhelitico novam legem aliam a lege mosaica . . ." (ed. Mantua, 1475).

[71] משמיע ישועה, ed. Offenbach, 1767., Intro., p. 2b.

the ultimate Redemption.[72] According to Abarbanel there are seventeen announcers of the Messiah mentioned in the Bible, from Balaam to Daniel, sixteen of whom he discusses in this book; the seventeenth (Daniel) he had already discussed in full in the *Wells*. All together, sixty-three prophecies are analyzed in detail: Balaam, 1; Moses, 4; Isaiah, 15; Jeremiah, 7; Ezekiel, 10; Hosea, 1; Joel, 1; Amos, 1; Obadiah, 1; Micah, 2; Habakkuk, 1; Zephaniah, 1; Haggai, 1; Zechariah, 4; Malachi, 1; and Psalms, 12.

2. *Abraham Halevi* (early 16c.), Spanish exile and Kabbalist, calculated the Messianic year to be 1530 C. E. His treatise on Daniel which contains his calculations was written in 1508 in Seres, Greece, and was published two years later in Constantinople, under the title *Mashre Ḳiṭrin*—"The Loosener of Knots."

At the outset Halevi craves indulgence for embarking upon calculation. He is not a prophet and his conclusions are not the results of prophetic insight, but rather the simple findings of logical deduction. If time will prove them false—why, greater men than he have erred. Witness the great authorities who pointed to 1358 as the Messianic year! Again, only such as would despair of the Messiah, if his predicted advent at a given time were not to materialize, are enjoined from calculating. Others may. Further, the injunction was valid in earlier times, but not now when the Messianic period had actually begun.[73] It began with the conquest of Constantinople by the Turks in 1453, and this conquest will be followed by the fall of Rome.[74] He quotes as his authority the Targum of Jonathan ben Uzziel on Lam. 4.21.[75] as well as *Obad.* 1.20: "And the captivity of this host of the children of Israel that are among the Canaanites unto Zarephath (עד צרפת = unto France, i. e. there will be no Jews in France at the time of the Redemption) and the captivity of Jerusalem

[72] *Ibid.*, Intro. p. 3a.

[73] משרא קיטרין, p. 4b.

[74] ולדעתי כי מעת שנכבשה קוסטאנטינ' על ידי המלך הגדול התוגרמי מאז התחילה עת קץ. *ibid.*, p. 5a.

[75] See *supra*, pp. 112-13.

that is in Sepharad (אשר בספרד=Spain, i. e. the Redemption will come in the days of the Spanish Jewish exiles) shall possess the cities of the South," i. e. Palestine. We are now living in the closing hour—the Ne'ilah hour—of the exile.[76]

The key to the discovery of the date is found in Dan. 12.11: "And from the time that the continual burnt offering shall be taken away, and the detestable thing that causeth appallment set up, there shall be 1290 days." Abraham Halevi is quite original in his calculations. These 1290 day-years are to be reckoned not from the destruction, which occurred in 3828 A. M., but from the year 4000 A. M. It was not intended that any years of the fourth millennium should be included in the figure 1290. Accordingly we should add 172 years (4000–3828) to 1290=1462. To be exact we should add 175 years, for the continual burnt offering was actually taken away 3½ years before the destruction,[77] or in the year 3825 A. M. This would give 1465 years (1290+175) as the duration of the exile. In other words, the Messiah may be expected in the year 1530 C. E. (65+1465).[78]

The "time, times and half a time"[79] according to Halevi, yields the same figure 1465. The first "time" refers to the Egyptian exile which lasted 430 years.[80] The second "time" refers to the duration of the first Temple, which was 410 years. Hence "times" (plural) equals 820 years. The third "time" refers again to the Egyptian exile. Hence "half a time" equals 215 years. Total 1465 years.[81]

[76] *Op. cit.*, p. 18a.

[77] Dan. 9.27: "And for half of the week (=3½ years) he shall cause the sacrifice and the offering to cease."

[78] כללן של דברים שהאלף שחרב בו הבית אין בו אפילו שנה אחת מן האלף מאתים ותשעים.... ושיעור דברי הכתוב כך הוא כי מעת הוסר התמיד ועד שיעקר השיקוץ ויהיה שומם יעברו ימים ועוד יעברו אלף שנים והוא האלף החמישי ועוד מאתים ותשעים שנה.....ויש משהוסר התמיד עד שנת מאתים ותשעים לאלף ששי אלף ות'ס'ה שנים. *Op. cit.*, pp. 8b–9a.

[79] Dan. 7.25

[80] Ex. 12.40.

[81] *Op. cit.*, pp. 9b–10a.

The figure "2300 evenings and mornings"[82] is to be interpreted in the same sense as the figure 1290. The 2000 years refers to the fourth and fifth millennia and the 300 years to the first 300 years of the sixth millennium. At that time (i. e. 5300 or 1540 C. E.) the last act in the Messianic drama of restoration—the rebuilding of the Temple—will be accomplished. Therefore, Scriptures says: "then shall the sanctuary be victorious."[83]

The figure 1335[84] should likewise be interpreted in the same sense as the foregoing, namely, 1335 years after the completion of the fourth millennium, i. e. 5335 or 1575 C. E. This will probably be the year of the Resurrection.[85]

Having established his calculation on an adequate and "scientific" interpretion of Scriptures, Halevi now feels free to indulge himself in some Gematriot, which while not decisive are yet as "dessert to a meal." The first Gematria is אהיה אשר אהיה ("I am that I am").[86] The first א'ה'י'ה' indicates that the length of the Egyptian exile would be 210 years.[87] The second א'ה'י'ה' gives the length of the last exile, 1465 years.[88] He also found Gematriot in Ex. 17.15 (where יהוה נסי yields the number 1460) and in Is. 34.6 (כי זבח יהוה בבָצְרָה where בצרה=5292 or 1532 C. E.).

Halevi adduces the astrological calculations of his brother-in-law, Abraham Zacuto, to substantiate his calculations. According to Zacuto, a major conjunction of the planets Saturn and Jupiter occurred just prior to the birth of Moses. Fourteen hundred and sixty-one years elapsed

[82] Dan. 8.14.

[83] *Op. cit.*, pp. 12b–13b. Halevi finds a Gematria for the year 1540 in the last two words of the Book of Daniel: ק'ץ' ה'י'מ'ין=5300=1540 C. E. (p. 136).

[84] Dan. 12.12.

[85] *Op. cit.*, p. 14 a-b.

[86] Ex. 3.14.

[87] This is arrived at on the basis of the permutation איבכ, א=10; ה=50; י=100; ה=50; total 210.

[86] This is arrived at first by taking the normal numerical value of א'ה'י'ה', which is 21. Add to this the value of the letters according to the permutation of איבכ = 210; total 231. Add to this the value of א'ה'י'ה' where the א equals 1000, the ה equals 50, the י equals 100 and the ה equals 50=1200; total 1431. Add again the value of אהיה according to the permutation אבגד or 34. Grand total 1465. (*Op. cit.*, p. 15b.)

from that time until the destruction of the second Temple. A period equal in length will lapse before the beginning of the final Redemption, i. e. 1529 C. E.[89]

Abraham Halevi also wrote a commentary on the *Nebuat ha-Yeled,*—"The Prophecy of the Child," an Aramaic apocalypse of unknown date and origin in which five Messianic prognostications are put into the mouth of a prodigy child named Naḥman Katofa.[90]

On the threshold of this eventful decade—1530–1540—vested with such rich Messianic hopes by Halevi, Zacuto and, to a degree, also by Abarbanel, the two amazing figures of the 16c.—Reubeni and Molko—appeared.

3. *Solomon Molko* (c. 1500–1532), the Marano Kabbalist, mystic and pseudo-Messiah, whose career was contemporaneous with that of David Reubeni, applies himself in some of his sermons, which were published in 1529 under the title of *Sefer ha-Mefoar*, to Messianic calculations.

According to Molko, Job is the prototype of Israel. The Gematria of א'י'ו'ב' is equal to י'ש'ר'א'ל' in its minor value (19=19). His three friends are Edom, Ishmael and Amon. The phrase, "And the Lord returned the captivity of Job" (42.10), really refers to the captivity of Israel.[91] In Job, 38.1 and 40.6, the letter *Nun* in the word מנ is written short and not final. This is intended to inform us that the proclamation which the Lord will make out of the storm of the exile will concern the inverted letters of the *Nun* in the Torah.[92] These *Nuns* are found in con-

[89] *Op. cit.*, pp. 14b–15a

[90] In the third prophecy two dates are given: "From the South he (the Arabs) will increase and greatly will he multiply, and in the year 125 (Sel. Era 813-4) will he multiply, and in 1100 (Sel. Era 788-9) will he shine forth." Steinschneider mentions a manuscript of the *Nebuat ha-Yeled* in the Bodleian library, which contains the Messianic date of 1530 (*Die Geschichtslit. der Juden*, I, p. 170, No. 314). Halevi may have edited this Prophecy.

[91] ספר המפואר, ed. Amsterdam, 1709, pp. 17a, b.

[92] Num. 10.34, 36. The inverted *Nuns* of Numbers must have been employed as Messianic data by others also in the sixteenth century; for Abraham Halevi in his *Mashre Ḳitrin* alludes to such a practice and warns his readers against evident attempts to ascribe such interpretations to the *Zohar* (see p. 5b).

nection with two sentences which concern the coming of the Messiah: "Rise, O Lord, and let thine enemies be scattered"; "Return, O Lord, unto the ten thousand of the families of Israel."[93]

When the two short *Nuns* of Job are combined with the two inverted *Nuns* of Numbers, thus [] and [], they form two final *Mems*. These *Mems* really belong at the end of the words בחיין (Job. 24.23, should be בחיים) and הימין (Dan. 12.13, should be הימים). The final *Nuns* of these two words belong to the above two מנ. Just as these *Nuns* were torn from their rightful place, so Israel was torn from its home, and just as these return to their proper place, so Israel will return to its home, when Elijah will announce the blessed Redemption. Just as Elihu, in the story of Job, appears suddenly, just so suddenly will Elijah appear in Rome. Elihu, whose name has the same letters as that of Elijah (אֵלִיָהוּ = אֱלִיהוּ), is mentioned seven times in Job[94] referring to the 7,000 years of the world's duration. Five times the name Elihu is written with an *Aleph* (אֱלִיהוּא), pointing to the fifth millennium, at the close of which Elijah will appear. When you take the value of the two inverted *Nuns* and add to it the value of the two small *Nuns* of מנ plus the two *Nuns* of Numbers, which are out of their place, which together equal 300 (50x6 = 300), and add the sum to 5,000 A. M. = 5.300 A. M. = 1540 C. E., you will have discovered the Messianic year. Molko ends his calculations by saying: "I have no permission to reveal that which is hidden, but our deliverance is near at hand and will be revealed to all soon in our own days."[95]

In a letter to his friends Molko paraphrases Prov. 3.2–18, "A time to be born and a time to die, etc.," as prophetic of the whole history of Israel, and concludes that the present time is the עת לאהב—the period of divine

[93] This passage in Numbers was already regarded as especially significant by the Rabbis, who looked upon it as a holy book in itself (*Yad.* 3.5). See also Abarbanel, יש' משיחו, p. 21a: שבאותה הפרשה נכללה קדושה רבה וסוד עולם.

[94] 32.2, 4, 5, 6; 35.1; 36.1.

[95] *Op. cit.*, p. 31b.

love—in which the Lord is about to fulfil his promise of Redemption, suggested in Jer. 31.3: "I have loved thee with an everlasting love; therefore with affection will I draw thee to me again."[96]

4. *Mordecai ben Judah Dato* (1527–1585), Italian rabbi and Kabbalist, author of *Migdal David* (still in manuscript), expressed the conviction that the Messiah would appear in the year 1575. His Messianic prognostications are quoted by his contemporary, Azariah dei Rossi:[97] "And more particularly do we know that a famed Kabbalist and scholar, Mordecai Dato, wrote a special book named after his brother, *Migdal David*, in which he convincingly proved that the great hope of Israel for the beginning of Redemption and the rebuilding of the Temple will be fulfilled in the year 1575." Dei Rossi adduces two of Dato's methods of calculations. In the one, Dato bases his figure on the Messianic prophecy found in the *Pirḳe de Rabbi Eliezer*, chapter 28,[98] and in the other on the *Midrash ha-Ne'elam* in the *Zohar*.[99]

The passage in *P. R. E.* reads: "The rule of these four kingdoms will only last one day, according to the day of the Holy One . . . except for two-thirds of an hour (of God)."

[96] See אגרת שלמה מולכו quoted from Joseph Cohen's דברי הימים למלכי צרפת ומלכי בית אוטומאן II, p. 106. Abraham Abulafia already spoke of the mystic significance of these inverted Nuns employed by Molko (see שבע נתיבות התורה Jellinek's in *Philosophie und Kabbala*, I, p. 3).

The number 50 seems to have had a great mystic significance, based, probably, on the "50 gates of understanding" (נ' שערי בנה) already found in the Talmud. Philo, who was much given to number mysticism, called the number 50 "the most holy and natural of number" (*De Vita Contemplativa*, chap. viii). The *Zohar* declares that the Redemption from Egypt occurred in the "jubilee group" (מסטרא דיובלא). The exodus from Egypt is mentioned 50 times in the Bible; 50 days elapsed from the exodus to the giving of the Torah on Mount Sinai, and the jubilee period is composed of 50 years (פ' יתרו, II, p. 85b).

In later generations this belief in the redemptive quality of the letter *Nun*, and especially of the inverted *Nuns*, was still held. Moses ben Menaḥem, writing at the close of the 17c., declared: "All redemption and all emancipation emanated from these two *Nuns*" (כל הגאולה והחירות יוצאים מאלו הב' נונין). See ויקהל משה, ed. Dessau, 1699, p. 49c.

[97] מאור עינים, ed Wilna, 1865, Chap. XLIII.

[98] See *supra*, p. 38.

[99] See *supra*, p. 92.

Dato reasons that inasmuch as a day of God is equal to 2000 years, two-thirds of an hour will equal 55 years, 6 months and 20 days. In other words, the rule of the four kingdoms will last 1944 years, 5 months and 10 days. The rule of Persia began in the year 370 B. C. E.; the rule of the last kingdom will therefore end on the tenth of Adar, 1575 C. E.; the actual Redemption will take place in the year 1608, and the resurrection in 1648.[100]

Judging from the writings of dei Rossi, the year 1575 was generally regarded by his contemporaries as the Messianic year. "I am aware," he writes, "of a whole group of the 'sons of prophets' who are waiting for the year 1575 as the day of God, in which God will lead forth his people in joy to everlasting salvation." Their calculations were largely based on Dan. 12.12. The 1335 day-years were counted from the year 4,000 A. M., when, according to Talmudic tradition, the 2,000 years of the Messianic epoch were to begin,[101] giving the year 5335 A. M., or 1575 C. E.[102] It was also found that the Gematria of the last two verses of Daniel was 5335, that of ל׳ק׳ץ׳ ה׳י׳מ׳י׳ן in the last verse was 335, and that of ה׳ס׳ת׳ר׳ א׳ס׳ת׳י׳ר׳[102] was also c. 1335. The "time, times and half a time" was interpreted to mean 1335 years.[103] This number is also found in the death-bed prophecy of Jacob:[104] "The scepter shall not depart from Judah, nor the ruler's staff from between his feet, until he shall come to Shiloh." ש(י)לה = 335.

That the Gematria of Shilo, as well as of ה׳ס׳ת׳ר׳ א׳ס׳ת׳י׳ר, yields the Messianic figure 1335 was already suggested by Tobiah ben Eliezer, author of the *Midrash Leḳaḥ Ṭob* (c. 1100 C. E.), who states, however, that he does not know the *terminus a quo*.[105]

[100] See also Gedalia ibn Yaḥya's שלשלת הקבלה, ed. Lemberg, 1864, p. 34b.

[101] *San.* 97a, b. Abraham Halevi also employed the year 4000 A. M. for his starting point (see *supra*, p. 131). He added the figure 1290 instead of 1335 and obtained 1530 C. E. as the Messianic year.

[102] Deut. 31.18.

[103] This according to Saadia, Hananeel, Baḥya and others.

[104] Gen. 49.10.

[105] מדרש לקח טוב, ed. Buber, Wilna, 1924, I, p. 236; and IV, p. 107.

5. *Daniel ben Peraḥiah,* who edited Joseph ben Shem-Ṭob ben Joshua Ḥay's *She'erit Yosef,* also places the Messianic year in 1575.[106]

Daniel ben Peraḥiah disclaims any desire to calculate the end. His sole wish is "to strengthen the weak hands and make firm the tottering knees, and not, God forbid, to calculate the end. He, too, reckons the 1335 day-years from the beginning of the fifth millennium; hence 5335 = 1575 C. E.[107]

6. *Isaac Luria* (1534–1572), father of modern "practical" Kabbala, left none of his teachings in writing, so that we have no record of his Messianic calculations. It is clear, however, from the legends which have survived him that he entertained the hope that the year 1575 was the appointed year for the Redemption, and that perhaps he himself would bring it about. He is quoted as having declared that, although the earlier Kabbalists like Naḥmanides and Neḥunia ben Ha-Ḳanah did not reveal anything of the science of parẓufim (physiognomy), it is permitted to do so now for the day of the Messiah is near at hand.[108]

Solomon Shelemiel ben Ḥayyim, in his "*Shibḥe Ho-Ari,* written in the year 1609, narrates (quoting Vital): "At one time near to the hour of his death, we stood with our master Luria by the tomb of Shemaya and Abtalion in Giscala, which is three miles distant from Safed, and he said to us that Shemaya and Abtalion had told him that we should pray that the Messiah ben Joseph should not die. But we did not understand and we did not inquire further. . . . It was not long before our master was summoned on high. . . . It was then that we understood that he spoke of himself, and that he was the Messiah ben Joseph, whose sole mission on earth was to bring about

[106] Zunz wrongly attributes this date to Joseph ben Shem-Ṭob, who died in 1480. The author of the Messianic passage in *She'erit Yosef* is writing in 1568 (שארית יוסף.עד השנה הזאת השכ"ח ליצירה, ed. Salonica, 1568, gate 8). It is clear that Joseph ben Shem-Ṭob could not have been the author of this passage.

[107] הכוונה כי חשבון זה של של"ה שנים מתחיל מהאלף החמישי שהוא בשנת השל"ה ליצירה.

[108] ספר עץ חיים, ed. Shklov, 1800, Intro. p. 5c.

the Redemption and fill the whole earth with the Messianic kingdom.[109] The followers of Shabbetai Ẓebi regarded Luria as the Messiah Zedekiah.[110]

At another time, on the eve of Sabbath, he asked his disciples whether they would go with him to Jerusalem to celebrate the Sabbath. Upon their failure promptly to accede to his proposal, he exclaimed in great trepidation of spirit: "Woe unto us that we have not proved worthy to be redeemed. Had you promptly and unanimously replied that you were ready to go, Israel would have then and there been redeemed. For the hour had come, but you were not ready."[111]

A later version of the *Shibḥe Ho-Ari*[112] adds the following account: "At his death Rabbi Joseph Ha-Cohen was present, and the Master said to him that had the generation merited it, that very year would have been the year of Redemption and the true end . . . the Master then quoted the verse, 'And she again bore a son and called his name Shelah.'"[113] In Gematria Shelah is the year 1575. Evidently there is some confusion here. Luria died in 1572. But the tradition persisted. Moses ben Menaḥem, too, quotes the tradition that Luria predicted the Messianic era would begin in 1575.[114]

7. *Naphtali Herz ben Jacob Elḥanan* (end of 16 c.), German Kabbalist and disciple of Luria, author of *'Emeḳ ha-Melek*, a treatise on the elements of Kabbala and on the *Zohar*, repeats in full the Lurianic legend. Isaac Luria was the Messiah ben Joseph. Had he lived three years longer, (i. e. to 1575) he would have brought about the deliverance. But the age was not worthy and so he died after two years' sojourn in Palestine. The year 1575 was the time of grace for that generation. It is implied in Daniel's figure of 1335.

[109] See ספרות ההסטוריה הישראלית, ed. Warsaw, 1923, II, p. 231.

[110] See "Letter of Nathan of Gaza," in Kahana's אבן התועים, ed. 1913, p. 69.

[111] ספרות ה"ה, p. 212.

[112] Found in סדר לידת האריין ושבחיו, Constantinople, 1720.

[113] שֵׁלָה (Gen. 38.5.)

[114] ויקהל משה, p. 8c, d.

Since that year God raises up a righteous man in every generation who may become the Messiah, if the people merit Redemption by their repentance. We are still waiting for his coming. The year 1648 will be another one of these Messianic periods of grace which began with the fall of Constantinople in 1453.

Rabbi Naphtali quotes the *Zohar* and the customary Biblical passages which allude to the year 1648, especially Lev. 25.13 and Psalm 132.14: ז'א'ת' מנוחתי עדי עד "(This [=1648] is my resting place forever"). In Gematria ה'מ'ש'י'ח' = ז'א'ת' (the ה taken as 50) = 408. But whether the Messiah will come that year or not will again depend upon the people's merit, for God hath sworn that the people shall not be redeemed unless they repent.[115]

It is of interest that the *'Emeḳ ha-Melek* was printed in Amsterdam in the year 1648, and carries on the title page the chronogram, בשנת היובל ה'ז'א'ת' תשבו איש אל אחוזתו.[116] ("In this year of jubilee ye shall return every man unto his possession").[117]

8. *Eliezer Ashkenazi ben Eli Rofe,* (d. 1586) author of an homiletical commentary on the Pentateuch, called *Ma'ase Adonai,* which contains both in the chronogram on the title page and in the colophon, Messianic verses, offers the year 1594 as the Messianic year.

He, too, does not wish to be accused of calculating the end. "But it is apparent," he writes, "that the prophecies in Daniel show that we are very near to the Messianic times."[118]

There are two Messianic dates given in Dan. 12.12–13. The one—that of 1335 day-years—points to the year 1404 C. E. (1335 years after the destruction, which, according to the author, took place in the year 69 C. E.). The other is found in the word ק'ץ' (verse 13) and points to a date 190

[115] עמק המלך, ed. Amsterdam, 1648, pp. 33a, b.

[116] Lev. 25.13.

[117] On the mystic significance of the word זאת see Joseph Gikatilla's (13 c.) ספר שערי אורה, ed. Offenbach, 1715, p. 16a, b; and תקוני הזהר, ed. Amsterdam, 1719, pp. 17b and 39a, b (ופורקנא דישראל לא יתי אלא בזאת).

[118] ולא לחשב קיצין אני אומר׃ אמנם לפי המשך הכתובים בדניאל יראה היותנו קרובים אל ישועת יהוה (see מעשי יהוה, Venice, 1583, p. 181b).

years later=1594 c. e. He finds his Gematria in Deut. 31.10: "In the set time of the release (שנת ה'ש'מ'ט'ה=5354 c. e.=1594 c. e.), in the feast of the Tabernacles, when all Israel will come to appear before the Lord thy God in the place which he hath chosen.[119] The author is writing in 1580. He is therefore fourteen years removed from his Messianic year. He finds a pleasing Gematria for that, too: "May God say unto our sufferings, it is enough." דַי=14.[120]

9. *Gedalia ibn Yaḥya* (1515-c. 1587), in his *Sefer Shalshelet ha-Kabbala*, after reviewing many Messianic calculations, suggests the year 1598 as his own Messianic year. "But I, though young," he writes, "have bethought me to tell you in connection with this matter (the Messianic calculation) what occurred to me, and I swear to you that my words are true. On the night of the seventh day of Passover in the year 1555, being unable to sleep, I began to reflect on how long it will be to the end of the wonders. After a long time I fell asleep, but in the morning, behold, there was an olive leaf in my mouth.[121] (An idea occurred to him which gave him a promise of a solution.) The verse אראנו ולא עתה ('I see him but now)[122] came to my mind. I found that the numerical value of the entire verse was 5358. Actually the value of the verse is 5312, which is equal to the Gematria of ה'ש'י'ב, suggesting the verse, השיב את חמתי מעל בני ישראל ('He hath turned My wrath away from the children of Israel').[123] Add to this figure the number of letters in the verse Num. 24.17 from the words דרך כוכב to the end of the verse (omitting the *Waw*, which is silent)=46 (which incidentally suggests 'אל'י'ה'—Elijah), and you have the year 5358, or 1598 c. e."[124] Yaḥya finds support in Targum Onkelos. The latter, too, finds in this verse a Messianic reference.[125]

[119] *Op. cit.*, p. 181c.
[120] *Ibid.*, p. 181d.
[121] Gen. 8.11.
[122] Num. 24.17.
[123] Num. 25.11.
[124] See ספר שלשלת הקבלה, ed. Amsterdam, 1697, p. 36b.
[125] ויתרבא משיחא מישראל (*Loc. cit.*).

Gen. 49.1 also yields Yaḥya the figure 5358. "Gather yourselves together that I may tell you that which shall befall you in the end of days" (ה'י'מ'י'ם'). The *He* means 5000. The numerical value of ימים taken simply and integrated (100+200) is 300. The vowels and the *Dagesh* of the word (הַיָּמִים) give you the two *Waws* and three *Yods* = 12+30 = 42. Add to this the number of letters in the word הימים (=5) with the number of letters of the same word when integrated (11) = 16, and you will have the number 358 (300+42+16).

Yaḥya adduces also the verses in Ex. 15.2, 15, which, by the device of Gematria, yield him the number 5358. He also brings Num. 25.48, 49, where the five forms of גאולה—Redemption—are used, which lead him to discover in them a Messianic allusion, as well as the Messianic year 5358. In this he finds support in Jacob ben Asher, who also believes that these verses are Messianic in character.

10. *David ben Solomon ibn Abi Zimra* (1479–1589) wrote a mystic interpretation of the alphabet under the title *Magen David*, which Moses ibn Jacob Ḥagiz (1671–1750) edited in Amsterdam, 1713. He is strongly under the influence of the *Sefer ha-Temunah*. He, too, attached redemptive virtue to the letter *Nun*. The letter *Nun* is the jubille letter, "the place of all redemptions, celestial and mundane."[126] It is the "mistress of Redemption." The letter *Samek* specifically represents Israel in exile. It upholds (סמך) them when they fall, and raises them up when their time of Redemption is come.[127] The letter ס is a combination of כ, and ו. The *Kaf* represents the congregation of Israel, כ'נסת ישראל; the *Waw* is the channel through which the redemptive potency of the *Nun* descends and enters into the *Samek*. In this letter is hidden the time of the Redemption and in the future it will redeem them.[128] He quotes the *Sefer ha-Temunah*, which likewise

[126] מגן דוד, ed. Amsterdam, 1713, p. 35a.

[127] See Ps. 145.14 *Cf.* מדרש אותיות דרבי עקיבא, on the letter *Samek*, ed Wertheimer, I Version, pp. 44 ff., also *supra*, pp. 93 and 104-5.

[128] והנה הסמ'ך סומכת את ישראל בגלות. ובהסתום זמן הגלות ולעתיד היא גואלת אותם (*op. cit.*, p. 38b).

maintains that the letter *Samek* alludes to the Redemption, and that the *Kaf* refers to Israel and the *Waw* to the sixth millennium. The final Redemption will transpire 600 years before the close of the sixth millennium = 5400 A. M. = 1640 C. E. David Zimra accepts this figure and justifies it. The Messiah will undoubtedly come in the fourth century of the fifth millennium (1540 to 1640). We do not know exactly in what year of that century. The people's sins may delay his coming, but the Messiah must come within that century.[129]

He defends the practice of calculating the end. The Rabbinic imprecation upon calculators applies only to the men of the type of Elisha ben Abuya, who despaired and left the fold when their calculations proved false, but not to those who remain faithful unto the end, whether their calculations come true or not, the men who would remain steadfast even *if there were no Messiah.* Calculating the end does not necessarily mean "forcing the hour." It helps to strengthen those who grow weary of the long exile.[130]

11. *Joseph ben David ibn Yaḥya* (the fourth, 1494–1539), in his commentary on Daniel, advances the Messianic year to 1931 C. E. Like Ẓemaḥ Duran, he projects the date to a far distant future, in order to discourage early anticipations, thereby sparing the people sad disillusionment. He holds cheap all calculations, his included: "We chatter like a swallow or a crane."[131] Nevertheless he would essay a calculation even if it is only guess-work. He finds the key in Dan. 8.14: "Until 2300 evenings and mornings shall the sanctuary be victorious." The prophecy was delivered in the reign of Cyrus, which was in the year 3391 A. M. The Redemption will take place 2300 years later = 5691 A. M. = 1931 C. E. This would give the children of Israel about 300 years of Messianic times in which to dwell in joy before the end of the world, which would be

[129] David Zimra's teacher, Joseph Saragossi, announced in Safed that the Messiah was to appear in 1512 (see Zunz, *Ges. Schr.*, III, p. 229).

[130] *Op. cit.*, p. 39b.

[131] Is. 38.14.

ushered in with the seventh millennium. This date, too, is contained in "time, times and half a time."[132] עדן=יום=1000 years. עדנין=2000 years; half of עדן=500 years. The total is approximately 2300 years.[133]

12. *Samuel ben Judah Velerio* (second half of 16 c.), physician and Biblical commentator, who lived in the Greek archipelago, wrote a commentary on the Book of Daniel called *Ḥazon la-Mo'ed*, which was printed in Venice in 1586. After giving the current explanation as to why the hour of Redemption was not revealed to Daniel, the author, with profuse apologies, proceeds to suggest a date. The "time" is 400 years (the length of the Egyptian exile), "times" is 800 years; total, 1200 years. "Half a times" is 600 years $\left(\frac{1200}{2}=600\right)$; hence the full length of the exile will be 1800 years. The second Temple was destroyed in the year 3828 A. M. The end of the present exile will therefore be in the year 5628 A. M. = 1868 C. E.[134] He wishes his readers to know that it is not his intention to claim that the Messiah will without fail come on that date. Only that the verses in Daniel would be understood as he understands them if the Messiah would come on that date.[135] Like Joseph ibn Yaḥya, he too sets the date in the distant future, and for the same reason.

C. Pseudo-Messiahs

1. *Asher Lämmlein*, a German Jew, the first of the pseudo-Messiahs or forerunners of the Messiah whom the catastrophies of the last decade of the fifteenth century projected into Jewish life, appeared in Istria near Venice in 1502. He announced that the Messiah would come that year. Abarbanel's Messianic year was 1503. Lämmlein was undoubtedly swayed by the Messianic writings of Abarbanel, which first made their appearance in Venice

[132] Dan. 7.25.
[133] See his commentary on Daniel, ed. Bologna, 1538, pp. 109b–110a.
[134] חזון למועד, ed. Venice, p. 110a.
[135] אבל כוונתי היא לאמר שאם יבוא באותו זמן יבוארו הפסוקים על האופן ההוא (*ibid.*, p. 110b).

in 1496–97. Perhaps, too, Abarbanel's suggestion that the Messiah would appear in the West, in a Christian country, did not pass unnoticed by Lämmlein.[136] Lämmlein may have also been aware of the Messianic prophecy of Bonet de Lates (15–16c.) who in his *Prognosticum*, published in Rome in 1498, predicted the coming of the Messiah in the year 1505.[137]

Lämmlein was the first Ashkenazi Jew to pose as the Messiah.

David Gans (1541–1613), in his chronicle *Ẓemaḥ David*, throws some light on the Lämmlein affair. He recounts some personal reminiscences: "In the year 1502 Rabbi Lämmlein announced the advent of the Messiah, and throughout the dispersion of Israel his words were credited. Even among the Gentiles the news spread, and many believed him. My grandfather Seligman Ganz smashed his oven in which he baked his matẓẓot, being firmly convinced that the next year he would bake his matẓẓot in the Holy Land. And I heard from my old teacher, Rabbi Eliezer Trivash, of Frankfurt, that the matter was not without basis, and that he (Lämmlein) had shown signs and proofs, but that perhaps because of our sins was the coming of the Messiah delayed.[138]

The historian Joseph Ha-Cohen (1496–1575) adds the information that even leaders in Israel believed in him, and that they had decreed fast days and days of penitence in preparation for the great day.[139] Tobias Cohn adds that that year (1502) came to be known as the "Year of Repentance."[140]

Sebastian Münster (1489–1552), Christian Hebraist and disciple of Elijah Levita, in a work called *Ha-Wikkuaḥ*, written in 1530, which is cast in the form of a dialogue between a Jew and a Christian on the subject of the

136 ונלו בזה שני דברים נדולים עתידים האחד שיולד המלך המשיח בארצות הנוצרים אשר במערב הנמשכים לדת רומי (see 'יש' משיחו, p. 23b).

137 Zunz, *Ges. Schr.*, III, p. 228, and *J. E.*, III, p. 305.

138 צמח דוד, ed. Warsaw, 1859, p. 29b.

139 עמק הבכא, ed. Letteris, pp. 109–110; see also his דברי הימים, ed. Amsterdam, p. 53b.

140 מעשי טוביה, ed. Venice, 1707, p. 26a.

Messiah, makes the Christian say: "And it happened in the year 1502 that the Jews did penance in all their dwelling places and in all the lands of exile in order that the Messiah might come. Almost a whole year, young and old, children and women (did penance) in those days, the like of which had never been seen before. And in spite of it all there appeared neither sign nor vestige, not to speak of the reality itself (i. e. the Messiah)."[141]

The author of *Shalshelet ha-Kabbala* adds that numerous conversions followed the death of this pseudo-Messiah.[142]

2. *David Reubeni*, (c. 1490-d. after 1535), possibly kindled by the writings of Abarbanel, Abraham Halevi and others, capitalized the Messianic interest of his day in a most remarkable fashion. He appears upon the scene in Nubia, Egypt, in the year 1522, hailing from Khaibar in Arabia. He curries favor with Christian, Jew and Mohammedan alike.

To the Mohammedan he is a descendant of the prophet, newly come from Mecca, bringing blessing, absolution and the promise of a place in Paradise to his Mohammedan hosts.[143]

To the Jew he is the brother of King Joseph, who reigns in Khaibar over 300,000 members of the tribes of Reuben, Gad, and half of the tribe of Manasseh, engaged in a secret mission to effect the emancipation of the Jews in the Diaspora and their restoration to Palestine.[144]

141 וזה היה מעשה בשנת רס״ב לפ״ק שעשו היהודיים תשובה בכל מושבותם ובכל הארצות בכל הגולה איך משיח יבא. כמעט שנה תמימה נער וזקן טף ונשים אשר לא נעשה מעולם תשובה זו שעשו בימים ההם. אפילו הכי לא נתגלה להן אפילו אות אחת או רמיזה אחת כ״ש ממשות הויכוח, ed. Basel, 1539, p. 19a, b.

142 וימות האיש ולא בא משיח ונלגל המרות נדולות כי בראות הפתאים שמשיח לא בא מיד המירו p. 34b. See also Graetz, *Geschichte*, Leipsig, 1897; IX, p. 506, note 3.

143 See his Memoirs, ספור דוד הראובני, in Newbauer's *Med. Jew. Chron.*, II, pp. 134 ff.

144 *Ibid.*, p. 133. לא אמות מזה החולי עד אשר אקבץ ירושלים ואבנה המזבח ואקריב הקרבן (p. 154); see also pp. 179 and 187: ובאתי ממזרח למערב בעבור עבודת יתברך שמו ובעבור ישראל לקבצם מכל המקומות להביאם לארץ נושבת בירושלים עיר הקדש.

Dr. Mann has published (*R. E. J.*, LXXIV, pp. 148 ff.) a Genizah fragment telling of the mythical army of this king Joseph ben Solomon, which, according to the author, was already encamped at Ancona, Italy, ready to march on Rome. Dr. Mann says this fragment is perhaps one of several false epistles broadcast by Reubeni and his henchmen as part of their propaganda.

To the Christian he comes as an ambassador to pope and king to offer the assistance of his brother's armies in fighting the Mohammedans and in expelling the Turks from Palestine.

He traveled through Egypt and Palestine on his way to Rome to see the Pope. He rode into Rome on a white charger. He was received by Pope Clement VII, to whom he presented his credentials and his cause (1524).[145] From there he went to Portugal (1525) to the court of King John III, of whom he requested ships and cannon for his brother's armies. The king promised him eight ships and four thousand cannon, which promise he later rescinded. Everywhere Reubeni was royally received and entertained. The Portuguese Maranos especially were deeply stirred by Reubeni's mission, around which he deliberately cast a veil of mystic glamor. Solomon Molko, mystic and dreamer, was completely captivated by this man, by his mission, and by the marvelous expectations which he aroused.

Reubeni never publicly claimed to be the Messiah, nor the messenger of the Messiah, nor a prophet. That would have interfered with his plans, which were known to him alone. He strongly denied any and all Messianic attributes. When he was told that the Jews and Mohammedans in Fez regarded him as a prophet and as the Messiah, he exclaimed: "God forbid! I am a sinful man, more sinful than any other man. I have in my lifetime killed many men. On one occasion I slew forty of my enemies. I am not a wise man, a Kabbalist, a prophet or the son of a prophet—just an officer in the army, son of King Solomon of the House of David, son of Jesse, and

[145] It was generally believed that one of the first acts of the Messiah would be to call upon the Pope and seek his conversion and the emancipation of Jewry. In his disputation with Pablo Christiani, Naḥmanides declared: וכן המשיח כשיגיע את הקץ אז יבא אל האפיפיור במצוות השם ויאמר שלח את עמי ויעבדוני, ואז הוא בא ועד אותו זמן לא נאמר עליו ביאה ואינו משיח· ("Disputatio R. Naḥmanides" in Wagenseil's *Tela Ignea Satanae*, p. 32). Abulafia was the first among the pseudo-Messiahs to visit the Pope in pursuance of this mission.

brother of King Joseph, ruler over 300,000 men in the wilderness of Khaibar."[146]

He did not even promise that his mission would bring immediate deliverance to the Jews. To a group of waiting and imploring Maranos he said: "Trust in God, for you will be privileged to behold the rebuilding of Jerusalem, and do not fear. But I did not come this time to the king to take you and bring you to Jerusalem, because we must first wage great battles around Jerusalem before you can come there and before the land will be ours, and before we can offer sacrifices there. After that is done we will return to you and take you there, but at this time I only came to announce to you that the time of deliverance is near at hand."[147]

But he cunningly stirred the people's interest and curiosity. Jewry was profoundly agitated. The affair ended as all such affairs must end—in bitter disillusionment. The king of Portugal soon tired of his Jewish ambassador. Reubeni returned to Italy, where he again met Molko, now in the high tide of his own Messianic adventure, and traveled with him to Ratisbon to meet the Emperor Charles V. This was in the year 1532, the year prophesied by the *Zohar* in which the dead of Palestine would arise.[148] Both Reubeni and Molko were arrested and tried before the Inquisition in Mantua. Molko was sentenced to death for having returned to his ancestral faith. Reubeni was sent prisoner to Spain—and there his story ends.

3. *Solomon Molko* (c. 1500–1532) was perhaps the most guileless and the least designing of all his confreres in the long line of Messianic adventurers. There is an air of true romance about him—the lovable and Quixotic qualities of a Galahad. The ring of sincerity in his words reaches the heart. His is the pathos of the dreamer who is crushed by his dream. He seems borne along swiftly

[146] *Op. cit.*, p. 179.
[147] *Ibid.*, p. 199.
[148] See *supra*, pp. 91-2.

through a few crowded years on the waves of an ecstatic religious fervor to an inevitable martyrdom.

Molko (Diego Pires) was a Portuguese Marano, born a Christian. He occupied the post of a secretary in a court of justice. The desperate plight of his people moved him. The widespread Messianic anticipations fired his imagination, and the mission of David Reubeni seemed to confirm and strengthen these hopes. Strange and prophetic dreams disturbed him. He sought counsel of Reubeni, who spurned the proffered discipleship of Molko. Hoping to win the favor of Reubeni, Molko circumcized himself. Reubeni, fearing lest this rash act of Molko, reaching the ear of the court, might incriminate him and endanger his entire mission, reproached Molko, who now grew even more confused and troubled. His nightly visions increased in frequency and intensity. The whole world of Kabbala and the mystery of the holy alphabet were revealed to him, and the voice of God himself commanded him to leave Portugal and travel to Turkey on a strange and mysterious mission (1525–6).

He visited Salonica. Here he made the acquaintance of the mystic Joseph Ṭaiṭazaḳ and of Joseph Caro. The latter seems to have been guided through life by a mentor angel, the spirit of the Mishnah, who visited him in his dreams. Caro found in Molko a kindred spirit and became attached to him. He frequently calls him "My beloved, my dearest Solomon."[149]

Molko then visited Turkey and Palestine. Palestine was in the throes of a Messianic fever. In 1522 Joseph del Riena of Safed and his five pupils undertook to effect the coming of the Messiah by means of "practical" Kabbala, fasting, prayer, self-castigation and the employment of the Holy Name. They proceeded to the grave of Simeon ben Yoḥai, where they engaged in the rite of letter-magic and other mystic practices. When their mighty effort failed, del Riena left for Sidon, where he turned apostate.[150]

[149] See his מגיד מישרים, ed. Vilna, 1879, pp. 8b, 16a, *et al.*

[150] See Kahana's אבן נגף, pp. 4–5, and App. I, p. 49.

In 1521 an inquiry was sent to Jerusalem from Rome asking whether the signs of the approaching Messiah had not already appeared there.[151]

The vividness and intensity of the Messianic hope of that period voice themselves in the superb hymn "Lekah Dodi" of Solomon Halevi Alkabeẓ (Safed, first half of 16 c.): "Arouse thyself, arouse thyself, for thy light is come: Arise, shine, awake, awake. Give forth a song. The glory of the Lord is revealed upon thee."

These high hopes of the first half of the sixteenth century reflect themselves also in Jacob Berab's attempt, made in Safed, to reintroduce the old Semikah (Ordination) and to reorganize the old Sanhedrin. These efforts at the reëstablishment in Palestine of the central spiritual authority in Israel found their justification in the belief that the restoration of the Jewish state was imminent.

In 1529 Molko published in Hebrew a number of sermons under the title of *Sefer ha-Mefo'ar*, in one of which he announced that the Messiah would appear in the year 1540.[152] That same year (1529) he visited Italy, where he met Reubeni for the second time. He was received by Pope Clement VII. His fame spread. It may be that the rôle of Messiah or that of his precursor was thrust upon him by popular acclaim. It is clear that he gladly accepted it. Rome was then being overrun by the forces of Charles V, and threatened with destruction. The city was sacked, churches were destroyed and the Pope himself was held prisoner. This invasion lent fuel to the Messianic hopes of the day. Molko's successful prognostication of the great Tiber flood of October 8, 1530, also won him tremendous prestige.

In 1532, in the company of Reubeni, he set out for Ratisbon, carrying with him on his journey a flag with the word מכבי inscribed upon it, to give a semblance of a diplomatic character to his mission. His object was to meet Emperor Charles V and to solicit his aid in fighting the Turks. The missions of Molko and Reubeni now merged into one.

[151] See Zunz, *Ges. Schr.* III, p. 229; and הלבנון, V, p. 406.
[152] See *supra*, p. 134.

The Turk was to be driven from the Holy Land with the aid of the Christian powers, preparatory to the return of the Jews to their land. His mission failed. Molko was arrested, tried by the Inquisition for conversion to Judaism, and burnt at the stake at Mantua. Just before he was cast into the flames he was offered a pardon on condition that he return to Christianity. He refused. He died as he had wished—a martyr.

Many believed that Molko saved himself from the flames. One even testified that Molko stayed at his house for eight days after his supposed burning at the stake and then disappeared.[153] Thus popular fancy saves its heroes from the flames and bestows upon them immortality!....

[153] עמק הבכא, p. 117.

CHAPTER VII

THE SEVENTEENTH CENTURY

A. The Background

Messianic speculation suffered no abatement in the seventeenth century. This century also witnessed its most tragic consequences.

As the year 1648 approached—the *Anno Mirabile*—the great year heralded by the *Zohar* and many subsequent teachers, the national fever mounted. Fantastic hopes engulfed the whole of Israel, from Safed to London, from Morocco to Poland. The Rabbis of Palestine sent an encyclical prayer to be recited at dawn and in the evening in all the lands of the Diaspora, the recitation to be accompanied by lamentation and penance, asking for the restoration of the Kingdom of David and for the remission of the travail-pangs of the Messianic times.[1] Another pastoral letter was dispatched from Palestine to the Diaspora, urging upon all men to forego strife and dissension and to cultivate peace and good will, in preparation for the imminent advent of the Messiah.[2] Numerous pamphlets on the correct practice of repentance, based on the tradition of Luria, were widely circulated and read.[3] Men prayed and castigated themselves, knowing that the great day was at hand.

In Amsterdam, Manasseh ben Israel, believing that the end was nigh, petitioned Cromwell to permit the return of the Jews to England, in order that their universal dis-

[1] See Kahana, אבן נגף, p. 46, first printed by R. Aaron Beraḥia, of Modena, אנה ה׳ כתבנו לנאלה..כתבנו לישועה והקל חבלי משיח מעלינו (see מעבר יבק, ed. Wilna 1922, pp. 122–124).

[2] See קב הישר, ed. Frankfurt, a. M., 1709, Chap. XV, pp. 33b–34a.

[3] אבן נגף (*ibid.*). See the של״ה under הלכות תשובה.

persion might thereby be accomplished—a condition precedent to their Redemption.

The *Zohar* was assiduously studied, for the merit of such study hastened the end. Vital wrote in the introduction to his *'Eẓ Ḥayyim* that in these days it is a religious duty and a great joy to God to have Kabbala widely made known, for through the merit of such study the Messiah will come.[4] Abraham Azulai, a contemporary (d. 1643), writing in Gaza, likewise declared: "This book (the *Zohar*) will be revealed in the days of King Messiah in order to give support to the Shekinah, and all those who will be favored by this revelation will also merit Redemption. Verily this service (the study of the *Zohar*) which is all too rare in our day is more important than all "the rams of Nebaioth"[5] which were sacrificed in the days when the Temple existed."[6] The Hebrew presses were busily engaged in turning out numerous commentaries on this work which had now taken its place alongside of the Bible and the Talmud.

In the seventeenth century the stage was set for a great Messianic movement. Politically the conditions were propitious for such a movement. Mystically the people had been prepared for it. Even the Christian world was in the grip of a millennial frenzy.

I. The Political Situation

The outstanding political events of the century were the Thirty Years' War, which closed in 1648, and the Cossack Rebellion, which began in 1648; the former unsettled the life of German Jewry and impoverished it; the latter crushed and decimated Polish Jewry in one of the most horrible tragedies in history.

[4] אבל בדורות הללו מצוה ושמחה גדולה לפני הקב"ה שיתגלה החכמה הזאת שבזכותו יבא משיח (see ספר עץ חיים, ed. Shklov, Intro. p. 3b). The origin of the belief is in the *Zohar* itself; *cf.* פ' נשא p. 124b:
דעתידין ישראל למטעם מאילנא דחיי דאיהו האי ספר הזהר ויפקון ביה מן גלותא ברחמי
Failure to study Zoharitic Kabbala delays the coming of the Messiah (see תקוני הזהר, p. 76b).

[5] Is. 60.7.

[6] חסד לאברהם, ed. Lemberg, 1860, p. 6b.

The first half of the seventeenth century is a tragic and bloody period in the annals of German history. It begins in seething unrest, religious conflicts, political rivalries and economic decline and terminates in the Dance of Death—the Thirty Years' War (1618–1648). The Hanseatic League had begun to disintegrate, commerce was fast decaying and the monetary system of the country was depreciating to an appalling degree. The Thirty Years' War, which was the culmination of a century of bitter religious struggles and hatreds, brought unutterable ruin and devastation upon the Empire, and left it broken and bleeding. Out of an estimated population of sixteen million only six million were left when the Treaty of Westphalia was finally signed. Five-sixths of all the towns and villages were destroyed. In Bohemia alone, where the war first broke out, only 6000 villages out of 35,000 remained. The successive invasions of the country and the endless sieges and occupations disorganized the social and economic life of the country, disturbed trade, ruined agriculture, impoverished peasant and burgher and left disease, desolation and anarchy in their wake. The Jews could not but feel the effects of such a prolonged struggle and such an economic upheaval. It is true that they fared no worse than their German neighbors. In many instances they fared even better. They were not involved in the religious disputes, and the contending forces relied upon Jewish capital to help finance their military expeditions. In the hope of obtaining loans, the warring governments occasionally furnished protection to the Jews. It may be assumed that some Jews profited financially from the war; but the rank and file could not but be effected unfavorably by the general disorganization and impoverishment of the land. Throughout the first half of the seventeenth century the Jews of Germany were subjected to all the irksome and humiliating restrictions of the dark ages of Europe. The Middle Ages were still on. The Reformation had availed them little. The German Jews were still huddled in ghettoes, branded with the yellow badge, victimized by excessive taxation and subjected to the menace of frequent popular outbursts and riots.

A bitter economic struggle between German merchant and craft guilds and the Jews marked this period. The Jews of course were not admitted to membership in these guilds. They therefore carried on their trades and crafts without regard to the standards and traditions of these guilds, and perhaps with greater skill and aggressiveness.

The Jewish communities of Frankfort-on-the-Main and Worms suffered most from this economic rivalry. In Frankfort an infuriated mob, led by the baker, Vincent Fettmilch, broke into the ghetto on the eleventh of September, 1614, and plundered, robbed and destroyed. Close onto 1400 Jews were compelled to flee the city. The Jews of Worms, too, were compelled by the menace of a mob, led by the lawyer Chemnitz, to flee the city (April 20, 1615). Upon their departure the mob destroyed the ancient synagogue of the city and desecrated the cemetery. It was nine months before the Jews of Worms were permitted to return, and more than a year before their co-religionists of Frankfort enjoyed a similar privilege.

Ruppin summarizes the period accurately when he states: "The period of the Thirty Years' War marks the time when Judaism had reached its lowest ebb."[7] Hence the nigh incredible eagerness with which they received the Messianic reports of Shabbetai Ẓebi. Glückel von Hameln (1645–1719) wrote in her *Memoirs:* "It is difficult to describe the joy with which the letters (from the East telling of Shabbetai Ẓebi) were received in Hamburg. Most of these letters were received by the Sephardim, who thereupon went to their synagogue and had them read. There they were joined by the Ashkenazim, young and old. The young Portuguese would dress themselves in their best garments. Each one wore a wide green band of silk (the livery of Shabbetai Ẓebi), and dancing and singing as if it were the Feast of the Drawing of the Water, they would go to their synagogue to read those letters. Some of them,

[7] Arthur Ruppin, *The Jews of Today*, Eng. trans. Margery Bentwich, New York, 1913, p. 32.

unfortunately, sold all they had—house, land and possessions—hoping to be redeemed any day."[8] She narrates further that her own stepfather, who lived in Hommel, departed for Hildesheim, leaving everything he had behind him except some possessions which he sent on ahead to Hamburg, expecting any day the Messianic summons which would take him from Hamburg to the Holy Land.[9]

The Cossack uprisings in the middle of the seventeenth century broke the back of Polish Jewry. A contemporary, Shabbetai Sheftel Horowitz, son of the author of the *Shelah*, in his ethical testament, speaks of this catastrophe and calls it "The Third Destruction," alike in enormity to the earlier two.[10]

With the seventeenth century Poland entered upon a period of swift decline. The close of the Yaghello Dynasty (1386–1572) terminated the era of Polish national unity and inaugurated the age of Shlakhta rivalries and animosities, which culminated in the tragic events of 1648 and in the ensuing partitions. With Polish decadence came Jewish decadence. The internal strife and the hostile invasions which brought ruin and desolation upon Poland undermined the economic, political and cultural life of Polish Jewry almost beyond repair.

In the sixteenth century Polish Jewry had reached its high-water mark of autonomous development and cultural achievements. Comparative security, economic affluence and strong internal organization gave to Polish Jewry an almost unique and enviable position among the Jewries of the Diaspora.

The Jews of Poland enjoyed almost complete social autonomy in the sixteenth century. The Kahal was the unit of communal organization. By the Charter of Sigismund Augustus (August 13, 1551) the Jewish communities were confirmed in their autonomy and self-government.

[8] *Die Memoiren der Glückel von Hameln*, ed. Kaufmann, Frankfurt, a. M. 1896, pp. 81–82.

[9] *Ibid.*, p. 82.

[10] היות כי ידוע החורבן השלישי שנעשה בימים בשנת ת״ח לאלף הששי...ממש היה דומה לחורבן הראשון והשני (see ברית אברהם, ed. Warsaw, 1878, App., p. 31).

Along with economic prosperity and social self-determination went a strong intellectual activity, which, though circumscribed as to content and medieval in technique, was yet vigorous and in its field comprehensive. Schools were everywhere established—elementary schools and academies for higher education.[11]. In the sixteenth century and in the early part of the seventeenth century Poland contributed to the galaxy of renowned Rabbinic scholars the names of R. Shalom Shakhna (1500–1558), Moses Isserles (1520–1572), Solomon Luria (c. 1500–1573), Mordecai Jaffe (d. 1612), Joshua Falk Cohen (d. 1616), Meir of Lublin (1554–1666), Samuel Edels (d. 1631), Joel Sirkis (d. 1640) and Shabbetai Kohen (1621–1662).

As a result of the favorable social, economic and cultural conditions enjoyed by Polish Jewry, Messianism is little in evidence in Poland up to the seventeenth century, and no pseudo-Messiah hails from that country. Kabbala was, of course, during the sixteenth century, studied extensively in Poland as elsewhere,[12] but the Polish Kabbalists, like Mattathiah Delakruta (c. 1550), were under the influence of the speculative Sephardic Kabbala, brought into Poland from Palestine by way of Italy. It was more theosophic in character than "practical," and less given to Messianic romancing.

The decline in the fortunes of Polish Jews began with the new Swedish Vasa Dynasty in the reign of the fanatic, church-dominated Sigismund III (1588–1632), and reached its nadir in the closing days of the reign of Vladislav IV (1632–1648). The Jesuits invaded Poland during the reign of Stephen Báthory (1578–1586), and the Catholic reaction was on. The Jesuits succeeded in having the Academy of Wilna placed in their charge. They soon gained control of the entire school system of Poland, and

[11] See Nathan Hannover, יון מצולה, ed. Petrokov, 1902, pp. 42–43.

[12] Moses Isserles writes: "Many among the masses of the people pounce upon the study of Kabbala . . . even ordinary burghers, who cannot distinguish between their right hand and their left, who walk in darkness and who cannot explain a simple Talmudic argument or a section of the Bible, even with the aid of Rashi, rush to study Kabbala" (see S. A. Horodezky, תורת הקבלה של רבי משה קורדובירו, ed. Berlin, 1924, p. 15).

with thoroughness and implacability they began to inculcate in the minds of the rising generation hatred of everything and everyone not Roman Catholic.

The Jews became the particular object of the studied malice and fanatical attacks of the Jesuits. The seeds sown by them soon bore fruit. A wave of furious intolerance swept over the country. All the medieval forms of persecution, blood accusations, host-desecration charges and inflammatory pamphleteering were revived.

And then came the cataclysm of 1648. The Cossack hordes, led by the cunning and ruthless Bogdan Khmielnitzki, aided by Tartars sent by the Khan of Crimea, with whom Khmielnitzki had formed an alliance, swept over the whole of the Ukraine, bringing death and destruction with them. Volhynia and Podolia were soon engulfed in the onrushing tides of the ruthless bands who were bent upon the extermination of Poles and Jews, and who executed their purposes in most terrible and savage ways. For nearly two years (1648–1649) the terror reigned. It is estimated that 300 Jewish communities were destroyed, and that 300,000 Jews were massacred. The ghastly experiences of these two years left a scar on the soul of Polish Jewry. Five years later the Russian and Swedish invasions took place, adding new disasters to the already long catalog of national catastrophies. These invasions reached, in their destructive sweep, the distant communities of Lithuania.

II. The Jewish Mystic Background

The seventeenth century was therefore very favorable to the spread of vivid Messianic hopes among the Jews of Poland, even as it was for all the Jews of Western Europe. With the change for the worse in their condition there followed also a shifting of interest from theosophic and speculative to practical Kabbala. The life of uncertainty and persecution led to an avid and intense interest in the Ashkenazic Kabbala of the school of Luria and Vital, the Kabbala whose central theme was Messianism, whose practice was asceticism, whose chief literary foci were gilgul (transmigration of souls), ‘ibbur (syzygy) tiḳḳun (soul-consummation), and whose method was alphabetic and numeric mysticism.

Everyone studied Kabbala. It engulfed Polish Jewry. A contemporary, Jacob Temerls (d. 1667), commented upon the great avidity of his generation for this study: "Nearly all of them, lay and clerical, young and old, are eager to study the divine mystic teachings and to fulfil them.[13] The eminent Polish Rabbi, Samuel Eliezer Edels who was himself a student of the Kabbala, complained bitterly of the many people who waste their lifetime studying it, and especially of the very young who are allowed to study it.[14] The Italian, Simeon Luzzato, speaks of Poland as one of the two great centers of Kabbalistic study.[15]

The seventeenth century saw the three great Kabbalists whom Poland produced—Isaiah Horowitz, Nathan Spira and Samson of Ostropole—whose works bearing the Lurianic stamp filled the minds of the people with great Messianic hopes.

The Polish refugees who fled from the Cossack persecutions to Turkey and the near East came in direct contact with the highly developed Messianic thought of the Orient and were captivated by it.[16] There had been such contact previously through commercial intercourse. It was now multiplied manifold. The channel of mystic communication between Poland and Turkey was thereby widened. Heretofore Kabbala had found its way into Poland largely by way of Italy.

The Shabbetai Ẓebi movement found Polish Jewry bleeding, broken, intellectually and spiritually exhausted, steeped in Messianic lore, eager to receive any message which promised swift and miraculous surcease from its suffering. No anti-nomist sentiment was responsible for

[13] Quoted by S. A. Horodezky in החסידות והחסידים, ed. Berlin, 1922, I, Intr. p. xlvi.

[14] See S. A. Horodezky, ספר שם משמואל, ed. Drohobycz, 1895, p. 16.

[15] *Discorso circa il Stato de gl'Hebrei*, ed. Venice, 1638, pp. 79–80.

[16] See A. Kraushaar, פראנק ועדתו, ed. Warsaw, 1895, p. 45.

the favorable reception of Shabbetinism in Poland. The Shabbetian movement was not in its inception anti-Rabbinic or anti-legalistic. If the Shabbetians abrogated a few fast days or a few ritualistic observances, it was only to establish more vividly in the minds of the people their belief that Shabbetai Ẓebi was in truth the Messiah; for tradition had it that the ritual law would be nullified at the coming of the Messiah.[17] It is quite easy, however, to trace the development of antinomism from these few simple acts of the early Shabbetians to the unrestrained license of the out-and-out religious "anarchists" of later times.

When the Shabbetai Ẓebi movement failed, it did not disappear in Poland. It went underground and reappeared again in the eighteenth century in the Frankist movement. Whereas formerly no Messianic movement originated among them, Polish Jews, now came to look upon Poland as the appointed starting point for the Redemption. Writing toward the close of the seventeenth century, Ẓebi Hirsch Kaidanover, native of Wilna, stated categorically that "when the Redemption will come it will take place first in the North, in Poland and Lithuania."[18]

It is of interest, too, to note that Messianic calculation held its own in Poland and in Russia long after it had disappeared elsewhere; in fact, up to the close of the nineteenth century. As late as 1861 the Malbim (1809–1879) calculated that the beginning of the Redemption would take place in 1913, and that the period would extend to 1928.[19]

It is therefore not surprising that while the Messiahs up to the sixteenth century were almost exclusively Sephardic, from Oriental or Mediterranean countries, those of the sixteenth and seventeenth centuries were largely Ash-

[17] See Jacob Sasportas, קיצור ציצת נבל צבי, ed. Odessa, 1867, p. 39: וכולם הוראת שעה על דבר ישועה; also interesting explanation of Caro in מגיד מישרים, p. 51b.

[18] ולכן כשיבא הגאולה יהיה הגאולה תחילה במדינת צפון שהוא פולין ליט״א כמש״ה עורה צפון ,בואי תימן (See קב הישר, ed., Frankfurt, a. M., 1709, Chap. CII, p. 83b).

[19] See his commentary on Dan. 7.25, ויגיע זמן הקץ בשנת תרע״ג; also 12.11–12.

kenazic and Northern European. Molko was, of course, Sephardic, but Reubeni was probably Germanic; so was Lämmlein. Shabbetai Ẓebi himself was of Sephardic descent. But the evil genius of the movement, its prophet and chief engineer, was Nathan of Gaza, an Ashkenazi. So were many of the other "prophets" and propagandists—Mordecai Ḥasid, Mattathiah Bloch, and Nehemiah Ha-Kohen. Shabbetai Ẓebi's wife, Sarah, who tremendously influenced him and his followers, was Polish. According to Shabbetai Ẓebi himself, the Messiah ben Joseph, who preceded him, was the Polish Jew, Abraham Zalman, who was killed in the Cossack Rebellion. Shabbetai Ẓebi made a tremendous effort to win over Polish and German Jewry to his cause; hence his gifts to the Polish delegation and his eagerness to welcome the prophet who hailed from Poland, Nehemiah Ha-Kohen. Shabbetai let it be known that he came especially to avenge the sufferings of the Jews of Poland and Germany.

The Shabbetian movement appealed particularly to the Jewish communities of Germany and Poland, whose tribulations were greater than those of all other Jewish communities, though it was widely heralded in the Sephardic communities as well. Jacob Sasportas, the courageous opponent and chronicler of the movement, refers to the preponderance of Shabbetian sentiment among the Ashkenazic communities as against the Sephardic: "In particular those who believed (in Shabbetai Ẓebi), most of whom were Ashkenazim."[20] The German-Polish Jews were the last to relinquish belief in Shabbetai Ẓebi, when the movement collapsed following his conversion to Islam. Long after the collapse, the Shabbetian agitation continued in Germany and in Poland. Up to the middle of the eighteenth century pseudo-prophets and Messiahs such as Ḥayyim Mal'ak, Mordecai Mokiaḥ of Eisenstadt (d. 1729), Löbele Prossnitz (d. 1750) and Judah Ḥasid continued Shabbetian propaganda. Both Ḥayyim Mal'ak and Judah Ḥasid headed groups of disciples fleeing from

[20] המון המאמינים ורובם אשכנזים (see ק'צ'נ'צ, p. 90). וקצת מהאשכנזים שהיו יותר אדוקים היו ממאנים להאמין ולא לשמוע דבר רע כנגדו (*ibid.*, p. 64).

Rabbinic persecution on simultaneous pilgrimages to Palestine to meet the Messiah (1699). The Shabbetian movement in the Slavic countries found its last and grossest expression in the Frankist agitation (1726–1816).

Northern Africa, too, became a stronghold of Shabbetian sentiment as a result of the unfortunate political conditions which prevailed there in the latter half of the seventeenth century. Civil war and the cruelties of the fanatic, Muley Arshid, brought misery upon the Jews of Morocco, Fez and Tafilet. Jacob Sasportas, writing in 1669 to the communities of Northern Africa, warning them of the spread of the Shabbetian heresy among them, referred to the wars and misfortunes which have come upon them, and to their tribulations which he stated are double those of Jewry elsewhere.[21]

III. The Christian Mystic Background

As far as Christendom is concerned, the seventeenth century was one of vast confusion and conflict. Mystic sects increased in number and in volume and superstition was rampant throughout Europe among Catholics and Protestants alike. The Thirty Years' War disorganized the whole intellectual life of Europe. "Yet it was not till the period (1580–1620) that the growth of superstition and of delusions . . . became epidemic in Germany. . . . Among the princes of the age we find every kind of fixed delusion, from the visions of Christian of Denmark to the ravings of John Frederick of Weimar. Nor should the inveterate endurance and rank growth of countless petty superstitions be overlooked, which seemed to place life and death under the control of dealers in astrological certificates and magical charms."[22] The Thirty Years' War did not improve matters. "Terror, suffering, the loss of all effective spiritual guidance and the absence of all controlling mental discipline, drove the population at large . . . headlong into the wildest and most irrational

[21] ובפרט גלילות המערב אשר גלותם כיפול ומכופל בערך אחרים (see קיצור צ'נ'צ', pp. 96 and 100).

[22] A. W. Ward, *The Cambridge Modern History*, IV, p. 6.

varieties of misbelieving. . . . Within the years 1627–8 the Bishop of Würzburg is stated to have put to death nine thousand witches and wizards, and between 1640–1 nearly one thousand of these unfortunates are said to have been sent to the stake in the single Silesian principality of Neisse."[23]

The mystic movements which began in Western Europe simultaneously with the Reformation, continued throughout the seventeenth century, and they were all filled with apocalyptic intoxication. A contemporary, Friedrich Brekling, enumerates one hundred and eighty visionaries of that century, men and women, who were millenarian dreamers and eschatologists.[24] This magico-scientific age was on the threshold of revolutionary movements in science and philosophy, but as yet the mind of man had not emancipated itself from its mystic vagaries. Chemistry, astronomy and medicine were still steeped in alchemy, astrology and magic. In a similar manner were the spiritual movements of the age beset with theosophic fabulism and strange occult doctrines.

(*a*) *In Germany.* The outstanding leader of the spiritual reformers of the seventeenth century was, of course, Jacob Boehme, "the shoemaker theosophist of the Renaissance." Boehme was overwhelmed with the consciousness that the age was on the threshold of the Great Visitation and the New Kingdom. "It was a time which all the prophets have prophesied of . . . the fierce anger of God is at hand, the Last Judgment is at the door. God will purge the earth with fire and give every man his wages. The Harvest comes, this garment will remain no longer, everything will be gathered into the barn."[25]

In his *Mysterium Magnum* (1623) he writes: "Also it (Gen. 22.5) intimates very presumably that He (Jesus) . . . will certainly come again to us from the place whither

[23] *Ibid.*, p. 423.

[24] See Gottfrid Arnold's *Kirchen und Ketzer Historie*, Frankfurt a. M., 1715, IV, Chap. XIX.

[25] *The Threefold Life of Man*, 1619, ed. William Law, II, 15.3, 16; see also 12.34.

he has gone . . . which times is now near; and his voice to prepare the Bride has already sounded; and therefore hold not this for an uncertain fiction; the Morning Star and Messenger of Annunciation has appeared."[26] In answer to the Thirty-eighth of the Forty Theological Questions propounded to him, "What are the things that shall come to pass at the end of the world?" he writes: "You know well what Daniel, Ezekiel and David say in their prophecy, especially the Revelation of Jesus Christ. In them lies all that shall heretofore come to pass, and they also spoke magically (mystically) of things to come. But in our writings, you have them more clearly, for the time is now neared the end; and therefore it appears the more plainly what shall be done at the end."[27]

Boehme, believing in the impending advent, was also concerned about the Jews. He urged them to accept the Christ as a preliminary act to their Redemption. He believed that the time of the "recalling" of the Jews was near at hand. "Therefore we admonish the Jews that they learn to know their Messiah, for the time of their visitation is at hand, wherein they shall be redeemed from the captivity of their misery and be made over again."[28] And again: "Therefore do the Jews in vain hope for another Master or Ruler, although, indeed, he will come to them also in the time of his revelation, manifestation or appearing, which time is near, wherein the kingdom of Christ will be manifested to all people.[29]

Boehme's faith was shared by most of the mystic dissenters and sectarians of the age, many of whom were exceedingly friendly to the Jews. The return of the Jews to the Holy Land and their conversion to the faith in Christ was dogmatically inseparable from the Second Coming of Jesus and the establishment of the Kingdom. Convinced of the millennial approach these mystic sectarians therefore urged upon the Jews to accept Jesus so as to be

[26] *Op. cit.*, 48.13; see also 69.13; 76.50; 77.69–70.
[27] *The Forty Questions*, II, p. 112.
[28] Mysterium Magnum, 37.36; also see verse 59 and 51.42.
[29] *Ibid.*, 76.50.

prepared for their promised restoration. Again the dissenters spent most of their theologic odium upon Rome, the Beast of the Apocalypse, the Antichrist, and the Jews were accordingly spared.

In the seventeenth century the Christian scholarly world was very much taken up with the study of Hebrew and Hebrew literature. This movement, which began seriously with Reuchlin in the early sixteenth century, now reached its crest in Scaliger, the Buxtorfs and their disciples.[30] Many contacts were thereby established between Jewish and Christian scholars, who now freely exchange their mystic and apocalyptic hopes. At least three German scholars of adventist tendencies are known to have communicated their Messianic hopes to the great Jewish Messianist of the seventeenth century, Manasseh ben Israel—Abraham Franckenberg of Silesia (1593–1652), John Mochinger of Danzig (1603–1652) and Paul Felgenhauer of Bohemia.

This last mystic and chiliast (1593 after 1660) was convinced of the swift approach of the Judgment Day. In 1620 he wrote his *Chronologie,* in which he maintains that the world is in reality 235 years older than is generally assumed, and that Jesus was born in 4235 A. M. This being the case, the world has only 145 years more to last, since it must terminate in the year 6000. Men may therefore expect the early unfoldment of the great drama of the End of Days.[31]

Felgenhauer dedicated his *Bonum Nuncium Israeli,* written in Latin, in 1655, to Manasseh ben Israel. In this work the writer sets forth his reasons for expecting the immediate advent of the Messiah and the restoration of the Jews. He bases his arguments upon Scripture and

[30] Steinschneider has enumerated a great many sixteenth-century Christian scholars who were interested in Hebrew literature and who translated Hebrew books. See his "Christliche Hebraisten," *Zeitschrift für Hebräische Bibliographie,* I–V. Translations were made from the works of Gikatilla, Cordovero, Vital and from the *Zohar,* and the Messianic works of Abarbanel were frequently translated. Translations were also made of the נצחון and of Isaac of Troki's חזוק אמונה.

[31] See Michaud, *Biographie Universelle,* XIII, p. 491.

upon esoteric knowledge which had been prophetically revealed to him. He points to the three signs of the Messiah's coming—universal disorders, the coming of Elijah and a universal outpouring of the prophetic spirit. He intimates that he himself is the Elijah sent to announce the Messiah. He writes: "For he comes whom you greatly desire, the Messiah whom Jehovah announces to you, who is the true and only Elias, the Lord God, who hath sent me in His Spirit to announce to you the nativity of that child and son, whose name is Adonai, Wonderful Counselor, the mighty Zabaoth, Everlasting Father, Prince of Peace. With the birth of this son who is given to you and of this child who is born to us, there comes and is manifested the throne of the true David, who is no other than that Adonai promised to us.[32] Wherefore now a great light shall shine for that people, which has hitherto walked in darkness, upon those who dwell in the land of the shadow of death hath the light shined; while Jehovah hath multiplied the nation, He hath increased the joy of Israel and Judah."[33]

Felgenhauer seems to have been tremendously impressed by the comets which appeared in 1618[34] and 1652 and regarded them as portents of the Great Judgment. The wars in Poland likewise fed his apocalyptic dreams. "We accordingly announce to you Jews," he writes, "what we have seen in a divine vision, that is to say (what) Jehovah and the Spirit of the Messiah, and the Messiah whom God hath sent[35] in order to announce and proclaim to you Jews and Israelites the Good Tidings of Israel; and in order that you may be able to recognize the time of the Seventh Trumpet,[36] whether it falls or has fallen in the year 1618, in which that great comet appeared, which announced to us the Seventh Trumpet and the first judgment which ended in the year 1648. Further, that

[32] Jer. 23, 33.

[33] Is. 9.1–2. See *Bonum Nuncium Israeli*, ed. Amsterdam, 1655, p. 61.

[34] Another German mystic, Ludwig Gifftheil, was also moved to prophesy by the appearance of this comet (see Arnold, *Kirchen, etc.*, IV, p. 1032a.

[35] Is. 48.16.

[36] Rev. 8–9.

comet which appeared in 1652 and the star or comet which followed it announced a second judgment, which is near at hand and begins in the war in the Kingdom of Poland, which in the year which is approaching (1655) will be very savage and beyond measure bloody; for before war broke out in Poland, I saw in a vision a very great fiery sword, naked or unsheathed, over Poland, the point of which looked toward Germany.[37]

But along with his good tidings to Israel went the inevitable hope of the conversion of the Jews to Christianity. Manasseh ben Israel is therefore cautious in his reply to Felgenhauer. He deftly pricks Felgenhauer's pretension to the rôle of Elijah by pointing out that Elijah must be of the race of Israel. He also indicates that a primary condition of the Messianic times is Israel's supremacy over all peoples and pointedly ignores all of Felgenhauer's allusions to the conversion of the Jews. In his reply to Felgenhauer, Manasseh ben Israel writes:

> Manasseh ben Israel prays for health and blessing for Paul Felgenhauer from the God of Israel. That good news brought by you, O most respected Sir, to the people of Israel in these recent times of affliction, was the more welcome to my mind since, after the sorrows of so many ages and the long deferring of our hopes, I have not ceased to desire the same most ardently, if only, in view of the importance of the matter, your words can prove true. So then, O worthy messenger of good things, is the arrival of our God at hand, who pities us, and will he send in a short time to us the desire of so many ages, the Messiah as our Head? Do you then declare that the time is at hand when

[37] *Op. cit.*, p. 32. See also his *Postilion, or a New Almanacke and Astrologicke, prophetical, Prognostication*, trans. from the Dutch, London, 1655, p. 4: "The Great blazing star anno 1618 hath sounded the seventh trumpett for an alarme to all the world, which you cannot gainesay, and foretold the ruin of all Kingdoms and Kings of the earth and the Judgment over the world and the coming of the Lord." In this work Felgenhauer also expresses the thought that the defeat of the Turk will pave the way for the Millennium: "Now whether Christ's prophesie will be accomplished will appeare, when first that great and bloody Battaile is passed in which the Turke perisheth" (p. 6). The Turk was defeated before Vienna in 1653.

God, hitherto offended with and turned away from us, will again console his people and redeem them not only from a captivity worse than the Babylonian, from bondage worse than the Egyptian, in which they have grown faint from delay, but also from their iniquities, whereby they are as it were consumed? Would that it should prove as true as your good news and that I could believe you as much as I would desire! However, I gladly accept the signs of the arrival of the Messiah (to acknowledge what is the fact) which you produce from the writings of the prophets to confirm our joy, and the more I consider them, the more hope from them seems to shine upon me.

As for the first sign, it is acknowledged among our rabbis; for since it must needs be that all the Kingdoms of this world be overthrown, before Kingdom and power and the greatness of the Kingdom be given to the people of the holy ones of the Most High, whom all Kings ought to serve and obey, it is clear that immediately before that arrival of the Messiah and the restoration of his Kingdom great disturbance, tumults, seditions, internal and most cruel wars, followed by the devastation of Kingdoms and peoples, are bound to occur; and judging from the present appearance of the empires of the world it seems not unlikely that this will occur within a short time.

As for what you say concerning Elias, the second sign of the coming of our Messiah, we do not deny it, nay, we specially rejoice, because in it we Jews are of one and the same opinion with chosen men of the Christian faith that he shall be born from our race. But since that Elias has not yet appeared to us, our hope must be held in suspense until this happens; wherefore, until God has revealed him to us, it would appear unsafe to lay down anything as certain and beyond a doubt in regard to the coming of the Messiah. As for what you say about the third sign of the coming of the Messiah, concerning this prediction of a Kingdom of Israel throughout the world, that not only appears probable to me but we see something of the kind already coming to light and producing its effect; nay, no inconsiderable number of prognosticators

(*Praedicatorum*) has become known to myself by means of letters, who have come forth from different parts of the world to console Zion; among such distinguished for nobility and learning, who are at hand, we have from Silesia Abraham of Frankenberg; from Prussia, John Mochinger[38]; from France, the author of the little French work entitled "*Du Rappel des Juives.*" From England, Nathanael Homes, doctor of divinity, has brought a work in English on this very subject, and Henry Jesse has dedicated to us a book on the Glory of Judah and Israel, written in Belgian. I could mention several others who, like the little cloud I Kings 18 (which Elias saw rising from the sea and which suddenly grew to such great size that it covered the whole expanse of heaven) daily increase in number and virtue until they are likely to fill the whole circle of the world with their prophecy. In order, my dear Paul, to give you an example of this in confirmation of your testimony, I have selected several of their letters to me, which are in my possession and which you will be able to read and rejoice with me concerning those who say "we will go into the house of the Lord, our feet shall stand in thy courts, O Jerusalem," who speak to the heart of Jerusalem, preaching salvation and saying to Zion, "Thy God shall reign."

But beside this I also send you, most learned Sir, an autograph of a panegyric which Immanuel Bocarus Frances of Rosales, otherwise Jacobus Rosales, a Hebrew, mathematician and doctor of medicine, upon whom the Emperor has bestowed the insignia of nobility and the rank of Count Palatine, has dedicated to me; I am sending it chiefly with the intention that

[38] The letter of John Mochinger, written in Danzig in 1636, is printed on pp. 98–101 of *Bonum Nuncium Israeli.* Mochinger hails Manasseh as an unusual star whom men run to gaze at. His learning and more especially his knowledge of Latin single Manasseh out from among his Jewish contemporaries: "For to approach you seemed like not only gazing upon a star, but like approaching a spring from which it were well to drink (p. 100). He desires to open correspondence with Manasseh upon theologic subjects. He would like to know more about certain Talmudic references to Jesus, and he would be interested in further confirmations of Manasseh's Messianic calculations: "Quod, si poposceris, rationibus, quas, ipsa scrinia vestra, calculusque temporis suppeditant, confirmatum dare haud tergiversabor" (p. 100).

> you may see that some scions of the stock of David still exist and can be distinguished up to the present day.[39] Lastly, to satisfy your desire, I send you a catalogue of the books which I have either already published or have by me ready to publish, both in Latin or Spanish. Herewith I heartily commend you to the God of our fathers and to his grace and favour. Amsterdam, Feb. 1, 1655.[40]

Among the German chiliasts of the day may also be mentioned the noted Protestant divine, Johann Heinrich Alsted (1588–1638), who in 1627 dedicated a book, *De Mille Annis,* to Messianic calculations. On astrological evidence and on the text of Daniel he computes the Messianic year to be 1694.

"The twelfth chapter of Daniel ought to be our pole-star in explaining prophetic numbers, for there we are led, as by the hand, from the building of the second Temple to its destruction; and from the destruction thereof, which was Anno Christi 69, by a term of days he numbers first 1290, and then 1335; that is, in all (with the 69 years which were elapsed from Christ's birth, to the overthrow of the Temple) 2694 years; from which, if we deduct the 1000 years, Rev. XX. 2, we shall be brought to the year of our Lord 1694, whence we may gather that the seven vials are to be poured forth at or before that time, or their significations to continue no longer."[41]

(*b*) *In Holland.* Holland, notwithstanding the fact that it was the home of religious tolerance in the seventeenth century, witnessed a bitter religious conflict between the orthodox Calvinites and the Remonstrants and the formation of the Society of Collegiants, a sect having

[39] Manasseh ben Israel here alludes to the verse: "The scepter shall not depart from Judah, nor the ruler's staff from between his feet, until he will come to Shiloh" (Gen. 49.10). This had been the battleground of Christian and Jewish apologists for ages, the Christians maintaining that עד כי יבא שילה referred to Jesus and the proof was that the scepter *did* depart from Judah soon after the coming of Jesus. Manasseh, like many Rabbis before him, declared that the scepter has not departed, but that to this very day great leaders in Israel, scions of the House of David, exist.

[40] *Op. cit.*, pp. 87–91.

[41] Quoted from *Miraculous Prophecies and Predictions*, London, 1821, p. 23.

many of the features of the earlier Anabaptists. "From the first there was a decided strain of 'enthusiasm' evident in the movement and a pronounced tendency to encourage a ministry of 'prophetic openings.'"[42] The appeal of this society was not limited to the common people, but found adherents among the lettered and leaders of thought in Holland, many of whom were well versed in Hebrew. The Collegiants were in contact with the Jewish scholars in Holland. Peter Balling, a leader in this group, was a close friend of Baruch Spinoza, and in his religious mysticism was undoubtedly influenced by Spinoza. So was another Collegiant, John Rienwertsz, to whom Spinoza bequeathed all his unpublished manuscripts. The Collegiants, much like the Seekers in England, were waiting for a new apostolic age, a new epoch of miracle and prophecy, a new revelation bound up with the Second Coming of Jesus. Many of the Dutch mystics were in touch with Manasseh ben Israel in Amsterdam, the most celebrated of whom was Hugo Grotius.

(*c*) *In France*. The apocalyptic wave reached France. In 1643 Isaac La Peyrere (1594–1676) published his *Du Rappel des Juifs*, in which he summons the king of France and the French people to take the initiative in the conversion of the Jews to Christianity as the preliminary step to their restoration to Palestine.

In his Introduction he outlines the main theses of his book:

> My purpose is to show in this treatise that the Jews will be called to the knowledge of the Gospel; and in what I make their Recall which I lay down as spiritual to consist. By the same means I prove that the salvation of the Gentiles is contained in the Recall of the Jews, and that all men on earth will at the same time be converted to the Christian faith. This is the subject of the first book.
>
> I next show that from the Recall of the Jews which I laid down as spiritual there results the Recall of

[42] R. M. Jones, *Spiritual Reformers in the Sixteenth and Seventeenth Centuries*, London, 1914, p. 117.

the Jews, which I lay down as temporal. I show that the Jews, converted, will be recalled from all the places in the world where they are scattered, to be led and reëstablished temporally in the land which has been promised to them, which is the Holy Land and their heritage. I prove that this Recall and this temporal reëstablishment of the Jews will take place through the agency of a temporal King who shall summon the Jews to this holy zeal to know Jesus Christ, and to serve him. I show that this temporal King will be the universal king predicted by the holy prophets, to whom all the other Kings of the earth shall pay homage. And I show that this King will be a king of France. This is the subject of the second book.

The third book exhorts the Christians to do everything possible to induce the Jews to become Christians, to which the Christians are exhorted and entreated by the dictates of Christian charity, and by the consideration of their own interest.

The fourth book presents Jesus Christ to the Jews, and clearly shows them that Jesus Christ who came in the flesh for the Gentiles, must come in spirit for the Jews. This is proved by passages taken from the books of the ancient law which are the books of the Jews, and by arguments taken from their own faith. The fifth and last book sets forth reasonable and possible expedients to attract the Jews to us. And I show that among these expedients there are fit and plausible means for recalling and reuniting in the bosom of the church all the Christian sects, which have broken away from so holy a union.

This is the abstract of this entire treatise. What shall I do that will prove worthy of promises so great? The kindly reader shall be the judge.

La Peyrere is convinced that the French Jews will be the first to be converted and that France will be the place of the mobilization of all Jews for the conquest of the Holy Land.[43] His reasoning abounds in pretty conceits. For example, the Jews of Persia were delivered in Shushan (שושן) = The Lily = the emblem of the Royal House of

[43] *Op. cit.*, p. 137.

France), hence the Jews will now be delivered in the Royal city of France.[44]

Another Frenchman, Philippe Albert, published a booklet called *Traitte d' Observations sur Quelques Propheties, touchant la Fin du Monde et La venue de Nôtre Seigneur Iesus Christ Dont les temps predits semblent expirer dans le present Siecle.*"[45] He prognosticates the advent of the Messiah and the Redemption of the Jews to take place soon after the year 1672, and bases his calculations on the figures of Daniel, dating them from the time of Constantine the Great.

(*d*) *In England.* In the middle of the seventeenth century England was rent by religious and civil warfare. It was in the midst of a vast political and spiritual turmoil. A twofold struggle raged: Parliament against the King, Puritanism against the Established Church. The political and religious issues were not kept apart. Characteristic of nearly all the national struggles of the seventeenth century was the manner in which these two were invariably embroiled. In England the political conflict was envisaged as a great drama of spiritual salvation. When wars take on such a religious mood and bias they release an inordinate emotionalism and enkindle incredible Messianic hopes. For half a century a goodly section of English society was enthralled by this religio-political romanticism.

The Puritans were among the more conservative of the enthusiasts who were anticipating epochal changes. Numerous sects of extremists sprang up whose doctrines were quite like those of the Anabaptists, to whom the religious and political upheavals of the Reformation gave rise on the Continent a century before. A contemporary print which caricatures the diversity of religious sects in England toward the middle of the seventeenth century enumerates among them Adamites, Libertins, Anti-Scripturians, Soule-Sleepers, Anabaptists, Familists, Seekers and Divorcers.[46] Most of these sects were profoundly Messianic.

[44] *Ibid.*, p. 138.

[45] Cologne, 1674.

[46] See *Social England*, London, 1909, IV, Sect. I, p. 355.

All the Messianic speculation of the day was related in an essential way to Israel, for the Scriptural apocalypses upon which they were all based were *Jewish* apocalypses, in which the restoration of Israel to dominion and glory was a central motif. Thus the Messianic hope of Christian England in the seventeenth century and that of universal Israel converged. From it there devolved some very important historical events.

Interest in the fate of the Jewish people, which was correlated with adventism, began in England quite early. Toward the close of the sixteenth century a Protestant divine and traveling preacher, Edmund Bunny, wrote several books replete with deep affection for Israel and voicing the hope of their imminent restoration.[47] The same spirit animated the writings of Rev. Thomas Draxe,[48] and of Rev. Thomas Brightman, who guided, as he believed, by divine inspiration, wrote a commentary on Revelation, in which he affirms his strong convictions concerning Israel's restoration.[49]

In 1607 there appeared a tract called "Newes from Rome," which, in the form of a letter translated from the Italian, conveys the news "of a Hebrew people till this time not discovered, coming from the mountains of Caspy (Caspian) who pretend their war is to recover the Land of Promise and expel the Turks out of Christendom. . . . Also certain prophecies of a Jew serving to that army, called Caleb Shilocke, prognosticating many strange accidents which shall happen in the following year, 1607."[50]

In 1621 a Puritan, Sir Henry Finch, moved by apocalyptic study, wrote a book called *The World's Great Restauration. Or, The Calling of the Jewes*,[51] in which he predicted the early restoration of Israel to Palestine and the establish-

[47] *The Scepter of Iudah*, London, 1584; *The Coronation of David*, 1588; *The Head-Cornerstone*, 1611.

[48] *The Worlde's Resurrection, or The gener'all calling of the Jewes*, London, 1608.

[49] See N. Sokolow, *History of Zionism*, London, 1919, I, pp. 42–43.

[50] See reprint of this tract in *History of Zionism*, II, pp. 191–206.

[51] Published by William Gouge, B. of D. and Preacher of God's Word in Black-fryers, London, 1621.

ment by them of a world-wide empire. What prompted the writing of this book, for which both author and publisher were imprisoned by order of King James I, is indicated on the second title page: "The Lord give them grace, that they may returne and seeke Iehovah their God, and David their King, *in these latter dayes*."[52] The end was approaching. Israel will soon be converted and restored. Then the Scriptural prophecies of the Second Coming will be fulfilled.

But it is from 1640 on, that is, from the period of bitter conflict and revolution, which culminated in the overthrow of the monarchy, the execution of the King and the establishment of the Commonwealth, that we find a veritable literature devoted to this and cognate apocalyptic subjects. Among the Thomason tracts there are hundreds of such apocalyptic pamphlets.[53] From this time, too, dates the phenomenal growth of the many sects of independents and dissenters all steeped in Messianic lore, and impressed with the imminence of the end.

In 1641 a religious independent, Henry Burton, who was imprisoned for his seditious preaching and sentenced "to deprivation, degradation, fine, pillory, loss of ears and perpetual imprisonment," addressed an appeal from prison to the House of Commons: "So the sounding of the seven Trumpets is a speciall prophecie of things to come to passe in the very last times, on which we are now falne, and more especially the sixt Trumpet points to these very present times, and the seventh to the now approaching times, in the end whereof time shall have an end and so bee swallowed up of Eternitie."[54]

The Quakers organized in the middle of the seventeenth century. Their antecedents were the Seekers, whose main belief was that the visible church, its doctrines and organization were false and that men should "wait and seek" a new revelation which will suddenly usher in a new

[52] Hos. 3.5. See *History of Zionism*, II, pp. 207–9; also I, pp. 47–48.

[53] *Catalogue of the Thomason Tracts* (1640–1661), published by the British Museum, London, 1908.

[54] *The Sounding of the Two Last Trumpets*, London, 1641, p. 1.

apostolic age, together with new prophets and new miracles. They were eagerly awaiting a cataclysmic end of the present order and the early return of Christ to earth.

The Quakers adopted many of the Anabaptist doctrines. They were "The Friends of Truth," who believed in the Inward Light—the direct revelation of divinity in the soul of man—as the ultimate source of spiritual guidance and authority. They had no creed, no ordained ministry, no ritual and no sacraments. They were intense millenarians. They, too, awaited the early advent of Christ upon earth.

Thus the Quaker, John Harwood—"a servant of the Lord in outward bonds for the truth-sake, in scorn by the prophane world, called Quaker, whose name in the flesh is John Harwood"—writing from jail in 1655, admonishes his countrymen: "Therefore now be ye warned, and while you have time prize it; for the mighty terrible day of the Lord draweth nigh."[55]

One of their number, James Nayler, actually conceived of himself as the Christ, entered Bristol nude and on horseback, followed by his disciples, singing, "Hosanna, Holy, Holy, Lord God of Sabaoth" (October, 1655). Another fanatic, a Welshman, named Evins, was committed to Newgate about 1644 for saying that he was Christ.[56]

Another sect of religious mystics who shared the Quakers' millenarian hopes were the Fifth Monarchy Men. The Thirty Years' War on the Continent fanned the fires of their expectancy. They were convinced that the last days of Rome were at hand and that the approach of Christ at the head of the Fifth Monarchy Men was imminent. Writing of these Fifth Monarchy Men, L. F. Brown says:

> A sufficient number of writings of these enthusiasts (the Fifth Monarchy Men) has come down to us to give a pretty clear idea of the doctrines set forth at their meetings. The Book of Revelations and the

[55] *The Path of the Just Cleared*, London, 1655, p. 26.

[56] *Sathan Inthroned in His Chair of Pestilence, or Quakerism in its Exaltation*, London, 1656.

prophets Zechariah, Ezekiel and Malachi furnished them with a large number of their texts, but the book to which they had recourse most frequently was Daniel, and the favorite chapter of Daniel was the seventh. Although the interpretations given by different preachers to the vision of Daniel varied in detail, their general features were the same. The four beasts were the four great empires of history; the little horn which appeared upon the head of the fourth beast and made war upon the saints was explained as the papacy, William the Conqueror and the remnants of the Norman yoke, the Stuart line, or simply Charles I. The year 1648 had marked the beginning of the dissolution of the Roman power, and the High Court of Justice in that year was the throne of the Ancient of Days. After the destruction of anti-Christian forms in England the war would spread to the Continent, and the Pope would be driven from his throne. Meanwhile the Jews would return to their own country and make war on the Turk; the righteous alone would flourish, finishing the destruction of the fourth monarchy, and Christ's kingdom would be established, the saints ruling with him. The exact dates of these happenings varied with the individual interpetations of "a time, and times, and the dividing of time." The date of 1655 was given by one writer for the return of the Jews to Palestine, and 1660 for the final destruction of the "little horn." According to another, 1660 was the year when the Fifth Monarchy should extend to Rome, and in 1666 it was to be visible over the whole earth. It was to be inaugurated "gradually and mysteriously, yet suddenly." The methods of computation employed are perhaps worthy of attention. They were summarized by an unsympathetic contemporary as follows: "Some that have heard that the end of Paganism is placed in the year 395. . . will easily be induced to believe that the famous number 1260 ought to be added to it, and then . . . 1655 must be pointed out for an apocalyptical epoch. Others pitch upon the year 1656, because, having summed up the lives of the patriarchs in the fifth chapter of Genesis, they find 1656 years

> from the creation of the flood, and thence infer that the coming of Christ will be the next year, because it must be as in the days of Noah. To 325 (the Council of Nicea was in 325) add 1332, that is, twice 666, the sum will be 1657. Others will wait three or four years more, hoping that the 1260 years must be reckoned from the death of Theodosius. Nor need we wonder, if we find some confident that eleven years hence we shall see the fatal change, because of the number 666."[57]

Some Fifth Monarchy Men actually attempted insurrection to carry out their program and to "hasten the day."[58]

Some of the more prominent millenarians of the day were friends of Manasseh ben Israel and in sympathy with his efforts to effect the readmission of Jews to England. Grounded as all their thought was in Old Testament tradition, they could not but look with favor upon the People of the Book. The Christian millenarians were as desirous of having the Jews come to England as the Jews were to go there. Their missionary zeal intensified this desire. The Jews were to play a great rôle, after their conversion, in the setting up of Christ's Kingdom.

Henry Jessey, the Baptist preacher whose millennial hopes led him to a friendly interest in Israel, brought him in contact with Manasseh ben Israel and inspired him to collect money for the impoverished Jews of Jerusalem, gave frequent expression to his faith in the near approach of the end. In his Almanac for the year 1645 he speaks "of the four Monarchies having dominion and ruling over most of the knowne World, scattering, battering and trampling upon the Jewes and Saints of the most High, and of the Fifth shortly succeeding and farre surpassing them all."[59] On another occasion he writes of "the God of Heaven himselfe in his Son who *shortly* will bring down every high thing, and he alone will be exalted in the earth."[60]

[57] *Pell to Thurloe*, March, 1655; *Vaughan, Protectorate*, I, p. 155. See Louise Fargo Brown, *Baptists and Fifth Monarchy Men*, pp. 22–24.

[58] See "The Fifth Monarchy Insurrection," *Eng. Hist. Review*, XXV, 1910.

[59] *A Calculation for this Present Year 1645*," London, end.

[60] *The Exceeding Riches of Grace Advanced*, etc., London, 1647, Intro.

With the hope of the Second Coming went the hope of the speedy conversion of the Jews. Henry Jessey believed that the Jews would be converted before the year 1658.[61] This hope of the conversion of the Jews, coupled with a genuine sympathy for them, also inspried his book, *The Glory of Jehudah and Israel*, which Manasseh ben Israel employed in his *Humble Addresses* to Cromwell as Christian testimony to Jewish rectitude and nobility. This same high hope led George Fox, founder of the Quakers, to address a lengthy epistle to the Jews, in which he urges conversion upon them as a preliminary to their restoration.[62]

Another friend of Manasseh ben Israel who was an intense millenarian was Nathanael Homes. In *The New World, or The New Reformed Church* he enumerates various Messianic calculations, some placing the fall of Antichrist (the Papacy) in 1860, some in 1706 and others in 1639: "Others upon these principles lay downe by Saint John long concluded with much comfort that the time of Antichrists fall should beginne to good purpose 1639 which they expressed in their bookes some 40, some 60 yeares since. And what God hath done from that yeare and so on, you have eyes and eares to inform yourselves, perhaps better than I."[63]

John Sadler, town clerk of London, and friend of Cromwell, was also led by his millenarian views to champion the cause of Israel. In his *Rights of the Kingdom* (1649), he writes: "The more I think upon *the great change now coming on them* (the Jews) *and all the world*, the more I would be just and merciful to them, to all."[64] He quotes an old prophecy which fixed the time of the restoration in the year 1648.[65]

[61] See his Introduction to Mary Rande's *The Little Horn's Doom and Downfall*, London, 1651. The author of this tract in common with many other visionaries of that day reads into the prophecies of Daniel the entire political drama of seventeenth-century England. The "little horn" is King Charles, etc., etc.

[62] *A Visitation to the Jewes*, London, 1656.

[63] London, 1641, p. 37.

[64] *History of Zionism*, II, p. 176.

[65] *Ibid.*, I, p. 40.

In 1648 there appeared in London an anonymous romance, *Nova Solyma.* Rev. Walter Begley, who edited and translated it, calls it "The poetical expression of the restoration ideas of the seventeenth century." It assumes that the restoration had already taken place fifty years ago, and contains a description of the ideal state on Mount Zion.[66]

A pamphlet called *Doomes-Day,* printed in London in 1647, announced that the great day of the Lord's judgment was imminent and called attention to the fact that "even those people the Jewes, according to certaine and credible information, are at this time (under Josias Catzius and according to Letters from beyond the Seas, they are numerous, and shew themselves in great bodies in Illyria, Bethinia and Cappadocia) assembling themselves together into one body from out of all countreys, whereinto they have been driven with a resolution to regaine the holy land once more out of the hand of Ottaman.[67] The author asks, commenting on Dan. 12.1 ("And there shall be a time of trouble, such as never was since there was a nation, to that time"): and is not that time now? Is not the whole world involved in warres, was there ever such a time of trouble as there is now, since there was a nation upon the earth?[68] He concludes his tract with the following admonition: "We are sufficiently informed in the Scriptures, and next to them from others, that the day of Doome is even now at hand, and that the Second Coming of Christ is each day and houre to be expected; what remaineth then, but that we prepare ourselves to meet the Bridegroome, with the loynes of our minds girded, and oyl in our lamps, that when our Lord cometh, he may say, well done good and faithful servants, enter ye into your masters joy.[69]

Coupled with the thought of Israel's restoration went

[66] *Ibid.*, II, pp. 176–179.

[67] *Doomes-Day: or, The Great Day of the Lords Iudgement, proved by Scripture; and two other Prophecies, the one pointing at the yeare 1640, the other at this present yeare 1647, to be even now near at hand*, London, 1647, p. 2.

[68] *Ibid.*, p. 5.

[69] *Ibid.*, p. 3.

a growing interest in the Lost Ten Tribes, whose return was predicated in prophecy. Various theories were propounded, not the least intriguing of which was that the Indians were the Lost Ten Tribes. In 1648 Thomas Thorowgood wrote *The Jews in America* to demonstrate this theory. This was followed in 1649–50 by a book written by John Dury, who was in correspondence with Manasseh ben Israel, called *An Epistolical Discourse of Mr. John Dury to Mr. Thorowgood, concerning his conviction that the Americans are descended from the Israelites.*[70]

Preoccupation with apocalyptic calculations in England in the seventeenth century was not limited to divines and enthusiasts. Sir Isaac Newton, the great physicist and natural philosopher, was not above writing an interpretation of the Book of Daniel, and the eminent mathematician John Pell, on the basis of Daniel, prognosticated that the fall of Rome (papacy) would take place in 1670. He added the 1260 day-years found in Rev. 11.3 and 12.6 to 410, the year of Alaric's sack of Rome, and obtained 1670 as the year of the final collapse. It may be delayed a few years, he thinks, but 1688 is the utmost possible date: "This is the utmost or farthest day, beyond which no apocalypse account (reckoning from Alaric) can point out a time for the final destruction of the city of Rome."[71]

At times a voice was raised in England against this obsession of computing the end. Thus Robert Vilvain, a physician, writes in his tract, *A Compend of Chronography*, the following: "Seek not to wrest a connexion of sacred Chronology from Daniel's Vaticiny which the Holy Ghost never intended. Swim not against the stream, nor cast dust against the wind, lest it fly in thy face. 'Tis impossible to make points of a pig's tail, or to frame a clear concatenation of times past with those to come, when no such matter appeers."[72]

It is significant to note that in the middle of the seven-

[70] *History of Zionism*, II, p. 211.

[71] John Pell, "Day-Fatality of Rome," in Aubrey's *Miscellanies*, London, 1696, pp. 22–26.

[72] London, 1656, p. 14.

teenth century the Christian and Jewish Messianic years approximated. The year 1648 was generally regarded as the Jewish Messianic year; 1666 was the Christian Messianic year. The latter was based on Rev. 13.18: "Here is wisdom. Let him that hath understanding count the number of the beast; for it is the number of a man; and his number is six hundred, threescore and six."[73] It is very likely that Shabbetai Ẓebi knew of the great adventist expectations entertained in England for the year 1666. His father was an agent for an English exporting house, and English millenarians visited their home. Shabbetai Ẓebi undoubtedly heard the marvelous tales concerning this miracle year and must have been profoundly impressed. He had announced himself as the Messiah in 1648, but it was not until 1665–6 that he aggressively renewed his campaign, and his movement spread throughout the Jewish world.[74]

When the Shabbetai Ẓebi movement swept over Europe in the year 1666, it stirred England profoundly. Under date of February 12–20, 1666, Pepys writes in his *Diary:* "Here I am told for certain what I have heard once or twice already of a Jew in town, that in the name of the rest do offer to give any man £ 10 to be paid £ 100, if a certain person now at Smyrna be within these two years owned by all the princes of the East, and particularly the grand Signor as the King of the world, in the same manner we do the King of England here, and that this man is the true Messiah. One named a friend of his that had received ten pieces in gold upon this score, and says that the Jew hath disposed of £ 1100 in this manner, which is very strange; and certainly this year of 1666 will be a year of great action; but what the consequences of it will be, God knows."

[73] The Gematria, probably, of נרו'ן קס'ר=666. On the numerous Kabbalistic interpretations of the number 666, see Begley, *Biblia Cabalistica*, pp. 119–125; also Peter Bungus, *Numerorum Mysteria*, Paris, 1618, pp. 623–633, where various names such as Martin Luther, Mohammed, Titan, Latinus and others are suggested as the Antichrist whose mystic numbers are 666.

[74] See Graetz, *Geschichte*, Leipsig, 1897, X, p. 426, note 3. The author has in preparation a study of the Shabbetai Ẓebi movement, a full account of which is therefore not included in this volume.

Again, under date of November 10, 1666, he writes: "Read an hour to make an end of Potter's Discourse of the Number 666,[75] which I like all along, but his close is most excellent, and, whether it be right or wrong, is mighty ingenious. Then to supper and to bed. This is the fatal day that everybody hath discoursed for a long time to be the day that the Papists, or I know not who, had designed to commit a massacre upon; but, however, I trust in God we shall rise tomorrow morning as well as ever. . . . What the meaning of all these sad signs is, the Lord knows; but every day things look worse and worse. God fit us for the worst."

In the *Calendar of State Papers* for 1665–6[76] we find six separate references to the Shabbetai Ẓebi affair:

> *Under date of November 10, 1665:* H.O. to Williamson: "Thinks the report of the Jewish King's turning Turk is false. Letters from Smyrna import that the King was gone from Gallipoli to the Grand Seignior at Adrianople, but being taken with fear by the way, turned Turk to escape danger. The Jews do not believe this, but are confident the work will go on. It was before thought that it would cost him his life if he went to the Grand Seignior, but as he has been received with all honor, some consider he must be turned Turk."
>
> *Under February 5, 1666:* Petition of Jean d'Illan, Jew of Amsterdam, to the King, for a pass for a Holland ship to transport himself and fifty families of Jews from Amsterdam to Palestine. God has at length begun to gather in his scattered people, having raised up a prophet for them; they will pray for His Majesty when they arrive at Jerusalem (French).

[75] *An Interpretation of the Number 666*, Francis Potter, Oxford, 1642. This book "supposeth this number 666 to be an image and typicall representation of the whole body of Antichrist (Intro. p. 4). The interpretation depends upon the extraction of the root of the number 666, which is 25+, —"an unfortunate number in itself, and that it hath been branded for an evill and unluckie number, both by prophane and sacred writer" (p. 77). The number 25 applies to Papacy, the Church of Rome, Antichrist, etc. (p. 176).

[76] Ed. Mary Anne Everett Green, Domestic Series, London, 1864.

Under date of March 15, 1666: "The Jews hurry from Amsterdam with great expectation of their Messias, who is said to be a silly fellow, a baker's son."

Under May 15, 1666: "The New Messias of the Jews was hanged in chains at Stamboul, having first confessed, after some blows on the feet, that he was persuaded by some Jews."

Under July 12, 1666: Thos. Chapell writes to James Fitton Chester . . . The King of the Jews, who was reported to be destroyed, is still living: the Grand Seignior having to go to Adrianople, to prepare against the Tartars, has sent him to a castle at Gallipoli, and allows him 50 aspers a day, the same as he does to his chiefest commanders. The removal is to avoid any tumults, Constantinople being full of strangers from all parts, who flocked to see and speak with him. He has assured the Jews that the redemption of Israel is at hand, as will be proclaimed to the world by great miracles, when the prophet Nathan arrives. At Constantinople he was in a palace of the Grand Seignior, with Rabbis and teachers, the books of the law, and the free exercise of ceremonies, and Jews might freely visit him. He had leave to go abroad in public, but refused it till the time came for him to manifest himself. A pillar of fire, with several stars, was seen hovering over the place where he was. He appeared in the (Grand) Turk's bedchamber, and several men sent by the Vizier to strangle him fell down dead in his presence.

Under October 11, 1666: "From Smyrna comes an account of a fresh gadding humour of the Jews to visit their imprisoned Messiah, whose authority is now so great with them as to turn their fast for the destruction of the Temple into a day of rejoicing, because it is his birthday."

B. The Calculators

1. *Ḥayyim Vital* (1543–1620), disciple and successor to Isaac Luria, who represents the Lurianic Kabbala in its extreme and most fantastic form, and who announced himself as the Messiah ben Joseph,[77] sets no definite year

[77] שבחי ר' חיים וויטאל, ed. Lemberg, 1862, p. 4.

for the advent of the Messiah, but states that he would surely come during his (Vital's) lifetime, if Israel would hearken to his call to universal repentance.

"In the year 1553," he writes, "a man from Persia, whose name was R. Shaltiel Alshaikh, who sees visions in his waking state, a wise and pious man, who fasts daily, told me that he was continually being informed (by visions) that the Redemption of Israel depends upon me (Vital) through my causing Israel to repent, and they also informed him concerning my excellence; and unto this very year (1610) he is still writing me letters about his visions regarding myself and the redemption which is depended upon me."[78]

In the year 1609, Vital writes in his characteristic conceit, a certain R. Sagura visited a magician and fortune teller to inquire about the Redemption. The demonic tribe was assembled and the inquirer was told by the spokesman that Israel's lack of repentance delays the advent of Messiah, but if they would hearken unto the great and heaven-esteemed Ḥayyim Vital, much good would come to them; that much suffering would befall them for their failure to listen to him; and that after these visitations four kingdoms would fall, the first of which would be Malta,[79] and then the Redemption would come. Prior to this event, however, ten great and perfect men would first have to join him. Seven of these are already born; some are in Damascus and some in Safed. Redemption being contingent upon these ten men joining Vital, the demonic powers were unable to inform the questioner concerning the exact time of the Redemption.[80]

2. *Isaiah Horowitz* (1555–1630), author of the famous *Shene Luḥot ha-Berit* (the *Shelah*), whose thought is saturated with Kabbala, and who frowned upon Maimonides, Ibn Ezra and Gersonides, as he did upon philosophy in general, does not specifically apply himself to Messianic

[78] *Ibid.*, p. 6; see also p. 14.

[79] It was during Vital's lifetime that the great struggle between the Christian and Mohammedan forces for the possession of Malta took place.

[80] *Op. cit.*, p. 10.

calculations. However, in connection with his defense of the *Zohar* and Kabbala, in which he says that "those who study Kabbala are tenfold more exalted than those who study the Bible and Mishna,[81] he states that the latter book remained hidden for centuries purposely. It was not to be revealed until the latter end. Prior to that it was to be with the angels for their particular study and delectation. With the approach of the End of Days "in which we now live," it was revealed to men so that they might engage in its study, and the merit accruing therefrom would hasten the day. The author refers to the Messianic calculations in the *Midrash ha-Ne'elam*,[82] where the Biblical phrase, "In this (הזא״ת=408) year of jubilee ye shall return every man unto his possession"[83] is adduced to prove that the Messianic year will be in 1648. The implication is clear. Isaiah Horowitz believed that the Messiah would come in the year 1648.

3. *Yom-Toḅ Lipmann Heller* (1579–1654), in his commentary on *Abot* also seems to designate the year 1648 as the Messianic year. Obadiah Bertinoro (15 c.), commenting on "There were ten generations from Adam to Noah to show how long-suffering God is,"[84] says, "Thou, too, therefore, do not wonder that He has permitted the wicked Kingdom (Rome) to rule so long over His children; for a longer period elapsed between Adam and Noah before they (the wicked ones) were drowned in the flood." Yom-Toḅ Heller adds, "The flood occurred 1656 years after Creation. Figure this out. Wait for Him, for He will not be long in coming."[85] Yom-Toḅ Heller wrote his commentary in the year 5377 A. M. (1617 C. E.). The destruction of the Temple was in the year 3828. Deduct 3828 from 5377 and you have 1549 as the time which elapsed since the destruction. The year 5408 A. M. (1648) was at this writing thirty-one years away. The total number of

[81] כי יש עשר ידות למארי קבלה על מארי דמקרא ומארי המשנה, see שני לוחות הברית, ed. Lemberg, 1860, I, p. 66a.

[82] פ׳ יצחק, p. 139a, b.

[83] Lev. 25.13.

[84] *Abot*. V, 2.

[85] *Abot*, V, 2, in *Mishnah*, ed. Prague, 1614–17, IV, p. 126a.

years of the present exile would therefore be 1580 (1549 + 31) i. e. less than the time from Creation to Noah, which was 1656 years.[86]

4. That the year 1648 was generally regarded as the miracle year is apparent also from the narrative of *Shabbetai Cohen* (1622–1662). Shabbatai Cohen, who wrote Seliḥot and Ḳinot on the persecutions of 1648, intimates in his *Megillat 'Afah*, a narrative of those tragic events, that all Israel expected the Messiah to come in the year 1648. "The year 1648, concerning which I thought 'on this (year בזא"ת=1648) will Aaron enter the inner sanctuary,' my harp was turned to mourning and my joy to sorrow, and the Israelites, Levites and Priests were offered up as burnt offerings."[98] That the succeeding decades also were regarded as Messianic is indicated in the inscription on Shabbetai Cohen's tombstone in Holleschau, where the year of his death is given in the Gematria of שנת היום" ב"א משי"ח לגאול (=1662): "Today is the Messiah come to redeem."[88] His commentary *Sifte Kohen* on the Shulḥan Aruk, *Hoshen Mishpat*, which was printed in Amsterdam in 1663, also carries the date in the Gematria of ימ"י המשי"ח (=1663): "The Days of the Messiah."

5. *Joseph Sambari*, who finished his *Chronicle* in the year 1672, likewise makes mention of the nigh universal anticipations which were entertained for the year 1648. Speaking of the persecutions of 1648, he says, "and they made a sign for this year 5408 וקוץ וד'ר'ד'ר' לפ"ק "Thorns and Thistles,"[89] for they had thought that that year would be the year of Redemption, according to the *Zohar*,[90] in the year of "the Children of Heth," (בני ח"ת=1648) and now it has turned into a thorn."[91]

6. *Isaac Cohen*, who was the first to publish Isaac Halevi's *Pa'aneaḥ Raza*, in the year 1607, adds his own calculations to that of the author. Before he embarks

[86] See David Holub, אגרת תימן, p. 63.

[87] App. to שבט יהודה, ed. M. Wiener, p. 139.

[88] See Bernhard Friedberg, ספר כתר כהנה, ed. Drohobycz, 1898 p., 19.

[89] Gen. 3.18, in Gematria, =1648.

[90] פ' חיי שרה, p. 129a.

[91] Neubauer, *Med. Jew. Chron.*, I, p. 149.

upon his task, he warns the reader not to lose heart if these calculations are found to be as futile as those of the original author. For when all is said and done, we do not know the *terminus a quo* for all our calculations. The important thing is not to lose hope. He then proceeds to suggest that the two exiles, the Egyptian (400 years) and the Babylonian (70 years), should be taken as a unit (470 years). "Time, times and half a time" would then be three and a half times 470=1645. This is the length of the exile. If this number is counted from the destruction, then the Messiah will come in the year 1713–14.[92]

But this date is so far off, says the author. Perhaps the reckoning is to begin with the year when the Sanhedrin was expelled, and met in the market place (forty years before the destruction).[93] Then the end would be in the year 1673.[94]

There is a possibility of even an earlier date, if the period begins with the time when the rabbis declared the lands of the Gentiles unclean (80 years before the destruction). The end would then be in 1633.[95]

7. *Nathan Nata Spira* (c. 1584–1633), Rabbi of Cracow, placed the Redemption year in 1725. He bases himself on Deut. 3.25: "Let me go over, I pray Thee, and see the good land" (ה'א'ר'ץ). The Gematria of ארץ integrated, i. e. אלף, ריש, צדי, is equal to 1725, whereas the letters לף, יש, די possess the same numerical value as those of מ'ש'י'ח' ב'ן' ד'ו'ד'.[96]

8. *Manasseh ben Israel* (c. 1604–1657) of all the Messianic speculators was perhaps the only one whose Messianic

[92] He gives Gematria for this figure: Deut. 30.3, ו'ק'ב'צ'ך' מ'כ'ל' ה'ע'מ'י'ם' =473=1713 C. E. Also verse 5, והיטבך והרבך מ'א'ב'ו'ת'י'ך'=473=1713 C. E. This means that Messiah would come in the 474th year. Hence Dan. 12.4. ותרבה הד'ע'ת',=473=1714 C. E.

[93] *'Ab. Zar.*, 8b.

[94] As proof he offers the Gematria, ת'נ'ל' העקרה בקיבוץ בניה=433=1673 C. E. Also Deut. 30.5, והביאך.. אל הארץ אשר ירשו א'ב'ו'ת'י'ך' = 1673 C. E.

[95] The Gematria for this figure is Deut. 30.5, והביאך ה' א'ל'ה'ך' א'ל' ה'א'ר'ץ' =393=1633 C. E. See פענח רזא (64b).

[96] מגלה עמוקות, Cracow, 1637, p. 165d:

ואראה את הארץ הוא סוד משיח בן דוד, ר"ל כשתמלא אותיות ארץ כזה אלף ריש צדי הנעלם שהיא ל"ף, י"ש, ד"י עולה משיח בן דוד בסוד.... וכבוד ה' מלא אר"ץ ר"ל אימתי יהיה כבוד ה' מלאה כשתמלא אותיות אר"ץ דהיינו כשיבא משיח שנרמז במילוי ארץ.

interest led to tangible results of historical value and benefit to his people. It was his firm conviction that the hour of redemption was near at hand, waiting only upon a complete dispersion of Israel throughout the world. This strong belief prompted him to petition Cromwell for the readmission of the Jews into England (1655).

In his *Vindiciae Judaeorum*, Manesseh writes: "For I conceived that our universal dispersion was a necessary circumstance to be fulfilled before all that shall be accomplished which the Lord hath promised to the people of the Jews, concerning their restoration and their returning again into their own land."[97] Though his petition was not formally granted, the way was paved for the unopposed infiltration of the Jews into England, and for their organization into community life.

Manasseh ben Israel was opposed to Messianic calculations,[98] but he was firmly of the opinion that the time of the Messiah's appearance was very near at hand. In his address to the Lord Protector he writes of "the approaching deliverance of Israel,"[99] and in his *Declaration to the Commonwealth of England* he gives as the second motive for his mission to that country, "because the opinion of many Christians and mine do concur herein, that we both believe that the restoring time of our Nation into their Native Country is very near at hand."[100] In section 29 of his *Mikweh Israel*, he writes: "Yet this I can affirm that it shall be at the end of this age . . . though we cannot exactly show the time of our redemption, yet we judge it to be near."[101] He gives four reasons for this belief: (1) The present fortunes of Israel are so low that they cannot be aught else, but the tribulations announced by the prophets as precedent to the advent of the Messiah. "Oh, how have we seen these things in the banishment of England, France and Spain!" The Inquisition, the un-

[97] See Lucien Wolf, *Manasseh ben Israel's Mission to Cromwell*, London, 1901, p. 143.

[98] See *infra.*, pp. 237-8.

[99] *Op. cit.*, p. 78.

[100] *Ibid.*, p. 79.

[101] *Ibid.*, p. 36.

numbered martyrdoms and the nigh universal persecutions are fulfilment of ancient prophecies. But "if the Lord fulfil his word in calamities, he will fulfil it also in felicities."[102] (2) Israel's constancy under such suffering is proof that God has reserved us for better things. The beginning of these better things in the midst of great misfortune is even now visible. He points to the favor in which certain prominent Jews have been held in recent times by rulers and peoples; to the Abarbanel family; to the diplomat Rabbi Solomon ben Nathan Ashkenazi; to Abraham Alhulu, treasurer to the Pasha of Egypt; to Don Joseph Nasi, and to many others.[103] (3) Israel must be scattered through all the corners of the world before they can be redeemed. This is clearly the meaning of Dan. 12.7; "And when the scattering of the holy people shall have an end, all these things shall have been fulfilled." "And this appears now to be done when as our synagogues are found in America." According to Deut. 28.64, the dispersion must be "from one end of the earth to the other." The Jews were now in the one extreme end of the earth—America. If they could also be established in the other—England—the prophecy would be fulfilled.[104] (4) It is now clear that the prophecy of the two legs of the

[102] *Ibid.*, p. 48. This belief, which was universally held, is succinctly summarized by one of the Rabbis: אמרו ישראל רבש'ע אימת את גואלינו. א'ל לכשתרדו לירידה התחתונה אותה שעה אני גואל אתכם (*Mid. Sh. Ṭob. Tehil.* 45).

[103] *Op. cit.*, pp. 48–51.

[104] *Ibid.*, p.52. The thought that the presence of Jews in the extremes of the earth is tantamount to their dispersion in every land is already found in *Mid. Shir R.* 2.19: דומה כמו שגליתם כולכם.. ונשתעבדתם בע' אומות (Sarmatia) אחד מכם גולה לברברי ואחד מכם לסמטרי (see also *Pesiḳ. R.*, ed. Friedmann, chap. 15, p. 71b. Here a late version is quoted which substitutes לברטניא (Britain) for לסמטרי). A mystic explanation of this belief, rather widely held, is given by Vital in his לקוטי תורה וטעמי המצות. Israel must be scattered among all the nations, in order that it might bring up again the "sparks of holiness" which fell among these peoples and it is sufficient if only one Israelite is found among each people to accomplish this: וע'כ נגזר על ישראל שישתעבדו בע' אומות כולם להוציא הניצוצין שנפלו בכל אומה ואומה (*ibid.*, ed. Wilna, 1879, p. 131a). Jacob Anatoli (first half of 13c.) suggests as the reason for the universal dispersion at the time of Redemption the possibility of converting the whole world to God: "and the fact our being scattered among all the nations at the time of the Redemption will be instrumental in 'turning to the peoples a pure language that they may all call upon the name of the Lord'" (Zeph. 3.9; see מלמד התלמידים, ed. Lyck, 1866, p. 97a).

image of Nebuchadnezzar, which is to be overthrown by the Fifth Monarchy, refers to the Ottoman race. This clear understanding of prophecies hitherto obscure is a sign of Messianic times, for so says Dan. 12.4: "Then knowledge shall be increased."[105]

Manasseh devoted a whole book to the interpretation of the Image of Nebuchadnezzar—*Piedra Gloriosa o de la Estatua de Nebuchadnesar*[106] which he dedicated to Isaac Vossius and for which Rembrandt made four etchings.

Manasseh thus sums up his thesis in this book:

> Whereby one sees in this prophecy five propositions diffusely expressed, namely:
>
> I. That by those four figures of beasts the four Monarchies are signified, as it says in verse 17: these beasts are four, four monarchies, this being described with all the circumstances and typified by the Statue of Nebuchadnesar.
>
> II. That the fourth Monarchy will be divided into two nations, of different laws, this division being made by the little Mohammedan horn, and they are the two legs of the Statue.
>
> III. That this Roman empire will be divided into ten kingdoms, which are the ten horns derived from that beast and the ten toes of the Statue.
>
> IV. That after the termination and destruction of these kingdoms there will follow the Monarchy of Israel, as it is the holy people and the stone which turns into a mountain, filling up the whole world.
>
> V. That this Monarchy of Israel will be temporal and terrestrial, as it says "under the heaven"; all that which the Lord revealed to Nebuchadnesar, in a general way, as to a heathen, he explained again with more diffusion and latitude and other circumstances perfectly to Daniel, revealing to him at the same time the duration of the fourth Monarchy, although in such enigmatic terms that he alone understood them and kept them in his heart, as he affirms himself in the last words of this chapter.[107]

[105] *Op. cit.*, p. 52.
[106] Amsterdam, 1655.
[107] *Op. cit.*, pp. 254–5.

Manasseh was greatly impressed by the story told to him in 1644 by Antonio De Montezinos (Aaron Levi), who claimed to have discovered during his travels in Peru natives who recited the Shema‘, who said that they were descendant of Abraham, Isaac and Jacob, and who observed the Jewish faith. Whether Montezinos was himself deluded,[108] or the deliberate fabricator of a legend for personal gain, it is difficult to say. Manasseh clearly believed his account: "I, myself, was well acquainted with him for six months together that he lived here, and sometimes I made him take an oath in the presence of honest men that what he had told was true. Then he went to Farnambuc (Pernambuco, in Brazil) where two years after he died, taking the same oath at his death. Which, if it be so, why should not I believe a man that was virtuous, and having all that which men call gain."[109]

Manasseh offers other arguments to prove that the Indians belonged to the Lost Ten Tribes: "The West Indies were anciently inhabited by a part of the ten tribes which passed thither out of Tartary by the Strait of Anian."[110]

In the approaching restoration these "sons from afar"[111] are to be gathered "from the Islands of the sea" (i. e. West = ים Is. 11.11), and brought to Palestine.[112] They will be the first to return[113]. They shall assemble together with the others of the Ten Tribes in Assyria and Egypt[114] under the leadership of Messiah ben Joseph, who shall come out of the tribe of Ephraim and shall be the captain of the Ten Tribes. From there they will go to the Jerusalem, where they will be joined by the returning exiles of the other two tribes. Then the "twelve tribes shall be joined together under one Prince, that is under Messiah, the son of David."[115]

[108] *Cf.* Wahlman, עשרת השבטים, p. 79.
[109] *Mikweh*, Sect. 13, p. 28.
[110] Bering Strait (*ibid.*, p. 53).
[111] Is. 43.6.
[112] *Op. cit.*, p. 42.
[113] *Ibid.*, p. 44.
[114] Is. 27.13.
[115] *Op. cit.*, p. 53.

A fellow countryman of Manasseh's, Jacob Judah Aryeh de Leon, prompted by the thought of the imminence of the Restoration and by the solicitations of the Dutch mystic Adam Boreel who was deeply interested in the restoration,[116] made a model of the Temple of Solomon, and in 1642 published tracts in Spanish and Dutch, describing it.

9. *Samuel Ha-Kohen*, of Pisa, wrote a commentary on Ecclesiastes and Job in 1640[117] in which he states his belief that the Jews of his day were living in the "End of Days," and that the advent of the Messiah was near at hand.

The Jews are now scattered everywhere to the extreme ends of the earth. The prophecy[118] has therefore been fulfiled and the Redemption must now come. "I, myself," he writes, "call heaven and earth to witness that I once found myself in a place whose very name meant the end of the earth.[119]

"We find ourselves in the sixth millennium," he writes. "More than a third of it has already passed. It is quite possible that the men now living will live 600 years until the close of this millennium, when they will die and be resurrected. For if in Messianic times a man of 100 years will be accounted a lad,[120] then an old man in those times may very well be 600 years old."

[116] See Walther Schneider, *Adam Boreel*, Giessen, 1911, p. 43.

[117] צפנת פענח, Venice, 1656.

[118] Deut. 28.64.

[119] פיני"ש טירר"ה, probably Finisterre (=the end of the world) in Spain, the most westerly point of the continent of Europe (*op. cit.*, 10b).

Part II

OPPOSITION TO MESSIANIC CALCULATION

CHAPTER VIII

A. TALMUDIC

Messianic calculation did not go unchallenged in Israel. In fact, it was consistently and vehemently opposed right through the ages. This opposition varied in intensity as the need for it changed, but it was never missing.

The opposition was largely inspired by the fear that such calculations might awaken false hopes, which, if defeated, would tend to demoralize the people. This is forcibly expressed in the malediction which Rabbi Jonathan (2–3 c.) hurled against all those who calculated the end. "Perish all those who calculate the end, for men will say, since the predicted end is here and the Messiah has not come, he will never come."[1] In the *Mekilta de R. Simeon* this thought is further elaborated. Following up the declaration that the sons of Ephraim miscalculated the end and left Egypt thirty years before the appointed time and were therefore killed,[2] the writer says: "The matter may be deduced *a minore ad majorem*. In the case of the Egyptian exile, the duration of which was definitely revealed, they nevertheless erred in their calculation and left sooner than they should and perished. How much more so in the case of our exile, concerning which it is written, 'For the words are shut up and sealed until the time of the end;'[3] must the calculators err. Hence it was said, 'Perish all those who calculate the end; rather let a man wait and believe, and the good is bound to come.'"[4]

There was also constantly present the fear that some

[1] תיפח עצמן של מחשבי קיצין (*San.* 97b).

[2] *San.* 92b.

[3] Dan. 12.9.

[4] מכילתא דרבי שמעון בן יוחאי, ed. Hoffmann, Frankfurt, 1905, pp. 37–38. See also *Shir R.* 2.18.

unscrupulous pseudo-Messiah would exploit the desperate longing of the masses. At times the opposition was the result of Christian polemics; for the church fathers and later Christian writers, and more especially those among them who were apostate Jews, utilized the selfsame Biblical prophecies and cryptic dates to prove the Messiaship of Jesus. This seems to be the implied meaning of the saying attributed to R. Ḥiyya bar Abba (3–4c.): "When Jonathan ben Uzziel sought to make public a translation of the Hagiographa, a voice from heaven cried out, 'Desist'! What was the reason? Because it contains the date of the Messiah's advent."[5] The Palestinian Amora R. Levi (3 c.), is quoted as saying that three of the oaths implied in the Song of Songs (2.7), "I adjure you, O daughters of Jerusalem, etc.," were that they should not make public the end, nor force it, nor reveal the secret to the gentiles.[6]

The first Christian centuries were centuries of bitter theologic and Scriptural controversy between Christians and Jews. In the early Church, through the first five centuries, chiliasm was very widespread, and Messianic computation was freely indulged in to prove the Messianic character of Jesus, as well as his second advent. The church fathers used the same technique and aimed at the same objectives as the Rabbis. Both the latter and the former were dreaming of the Millennium; both were expecting the advent of the Messiah. In the case of the church fathers it was the *second* advent.

Taking into account these three reasons, one can understand the sharpness of tone and the asperity of judgment which one finds in a saying such as this. R. Jose (2 c.) declared: "He who calculates the end will have no portion in the world to come."[7] God refused even Jacob the right to reveal the end. "Jacob sought to reveal the end to his children,[8] but it was suddenly hidden from him."[9]

[5] משום דאית ביה קץ משיח (*Meg.* 3a).

[6] שלא יגלו את הקץ ושלא ידחקו את הקץ ושלא יגלו הסוד לע״כ (*Ket.* 111a).

[7] *Derek Ereẓ R.* chap. 11.

[8] Gen. 49.1.

[9] *Ber. R.* 98.3.

The opposition began with the first appearance of Messianic leaders in the first century. It expressed itself in various ways: (1) Some denied the coming of the Messiah altogether, and thereby aimed at demolishing completely the whole structure of Messianic speculation; (2) others tried to accomplish the same purpose by maintaining that the Bible contains no Messianic references touching this last exile, and that there is no oral tradition for it; (3) others, while acknowledging the presence of such Messianic prophecies in the Bible, insisted that they are undecipherble and purposely "hidden"; (4) and still others declared that Redemption is contingent entirely upon repentance, and that there can therefore be no set time for Redemption.

1. The most outspoken and fearless representative of the first group, whose clear and unequivocal denial of the entire Messianic belief as it concerned the future startled even those who were opposed to Messianic calculations, was the Amora Hillel.[10] He declared: "The Jews have no Messiah to expect, for they have already consumed him in the days of Hezekiah."[11] R. Joseph, who in this matter undoubtedly represented the prevalent Rabbinic view of his day, prayed that God might forgive Hillel for entertaining such erroneous views.[12] Hillel was probably driven to take this radical position by the intense Christian polemics of his day. The major effort of most of the New Testament writers, the apostolic fathers and the church fathers of the first centuries, was to "Christianize" the Bible, and the Rabbis were constantly engaged in opposing their views.

The brave exponent of this radical view remained, however, an almost solitary figure in his age and in many subsequent ages. The people did not accept his view, nor did their leaders. The belief in the Messiah was all too

[10] It is difficult to determine which Hillel this was. There is a Babylonian Amora Hillel and there are two Palestinian Amoraim by that name. Bacher (*Agada der pal. Amoräer*, III, p. 703) thinks that the author of this statement was possibly Hillel the son of Samuel b. Naḥman, hence of the fourth century.

[11] *San.* 99a.

[12] *San.* 99a.

desperately needed in their sad and troubled lives. It was their one hope and mainstay.

2. One of the earliest representatives of the second group was the Tanna R. Nathan (2 c.). R. Nathan declared: "The following verse goes to the heart of things: 'For the vision is yet for the appointed time, and it declareth of the end and doth not lie. Though it tarry, wait for it, because it will surely come. It will not delay.'[13] (This means that we are to do) not like the Rabbis who interpreted 'until a time, times and half a time' (as holding a Messianic date for the future), and not like R. Simlai[14] who interpreted "Thou hast fed them with the bread of tears and given them tears to drink in a large (three-fold, שליש) measure,[15] nor like Akiba, who interpreted, 'Yet once, it is a little while, and I will shake the heavens and the earth.'[16] But (we are to take these passages as referring to events now past), the first kingdom (Hasmonean) lasted seventy years; the second kingdom (Herod) fifty-two years, and the kingdom of Ben Kosiba, two and a half years."[17]

R. Nathan forcibly contends here that all attempts which have been made by his colleagues and predecessors to locate Messianic allusions in Sacred Writ are futile, as all such allusions refer to events which have already taken place.

R. Nathan, too, had few followers. In the Middle Ages we shall see his position strongly championed by Moses ibn Gikatilla, Ḥayyim Galipapa, certain Karaite leaders, and, at times, by ibn Ezra and Joseph Albo, but his position was never popular, and for the same reason which militated against the acceptance of Hillel's viewpoint. The people needed the Messianic faith, and it also needed and desired Biblical authority and divine sanction for it.

The dominant and popular view of his day and of the

[13] *Hab.* 2.3.

[14] Probably R. Ishmael (2c.). See Klausner, הרעיון המשיחי בישראל, Jerusalem, 1923, p. 25.

[15] Ps. 80.6.

[16] *Hag.* 2.6.

[17] *San.* 97b.

succeeding centuries is expressed in the *Pesiḳta.* "R. Ḥanina bar Papa said: 'The children of Israel said to Isaiah: "Isaiah, our master, perhaps thou didst come to comfort only the generation living at the time of the destruction." He replied: "I have come to comfort all generations. The verse does not read: אמר אלהיכם 'your God said' but יאמר אלהיכם 'your God will say.'"[18] 'Rabbi Ḥanina bar Papa said: 'In eight places is it written: "Your God will say", even as there were eight prophets who prophesied after the destruction: Joel, Amos, Zephaniah, Haggai, Zechariah, Malachi, Ezekiel and Jeremiah.'"[19] The meaning is clear. The prophecies of all these men refer to the *future* and to the *final* Redemption.

3. As belonging to the third group, which maintained that, regardless of whether there are future Messianic prophecies in the Bible or not, the time of the end is hidden intentionally and by the will of God, may be mentioned the following Baraita: "Seven things are hidden from men—(1) the day of death, (2) the day of consolation (resurrection), (3) retribution, (4) what is in the heart of one's neighbor, (5) whence one's livelihood will come, (6) *when the kingdom of David will be restored,* and, (7) *when the guilty kingdom (Rome) will be destroyed.*"[20] These things are known to God alone.

The same thought is expressed by the Palestinian Amora, R. Yoḥanan (3c.). Commenting on Is. 63.4: "For the day of vengeance that was in my heart and my year of Redemption are come," he says that the true meaning of this verse is: "To my heart alone have I revealed it (the hour of Redemption), not even to my limbs."[21] The secret lies hidden in the heart of God. Rabbi Yoḥanan is elsewhere quoted as declaring: "In the case of the men of the first Temple whose sin was open, the end of their exile was also revealed, but in the case of the men of the second Temple whose sin was secret, the end of the exile

[18] Is. 40.1.
[19] *Op. cit.*, ed. Buber, Lyck, 1868, p. 128b.
[20] *Ibid.*, p. 54b.
[21] *San.* 99a.

was likewise left secret."[22] A contemporary, R. Simon ben Lakish, following the same trend of thought, adds: "To My heart alone have I revealed it, not even to the ministering angels."[23] R. Zeïra (3 c.), on finding a group of Rabbis engaged in Messianic speculation, urged them not to force the end, and quoted an earlier saying to the effect that three things cannot be anticipated: (1) the Messiah, (2) a find, and (3) the sting of a scorpion.

A view similar to that of R. Yoḥanan is found in the *Tanna debe Eliyahu:* "Twice were the children of Israel exiled, once at the destruction of the first Temple, and once at the destruction of the second Temple. In the first instance a set time (for Redemption) was given them; in the second instance *it was not given.*" The reason for it is that "the men of the first Temple, although they were idolators, had 'derek ereẓ' (good manners, in the highest sense of the word), kindliness and charity."[24]

We have seen that in Christian circles this view was expressed as early as the first century by the author of the Acts of the Apostles: "When they therefore were come together, they asked of him, saying, Lord, wilt thou at this time restore again the kingdom of Israel? And he said unto them, It is not for you to know the 'times' or the 'seasons,'[25] which the Father hath put in his own power."[26] The most outspoken though not the most consistent opponent among Christian writers was St. Augustine, who declared: "In vain, then, do we attempt to compute definitely the years that may remain to this world, when we may hear from the mouth of the Truth (Jesus) that it is not for us to know this. Yet some have said that 400, some 500, others a 1000 years may be completed from the ascension of the Lord up to his final coming. But to point out how each of them supports his own opinion

[22] *Yoma* 9b.

[23] *Ibid.*

[24] תנא דבי אליהו, ed. Zolkiev, 1798, chap. 14, p. 40a.

[25] This clearly refers to the "times and seasons" of Daniel which already in the first century intrigued the speculative ingenuity of men. χρόνους η καιροὺς = עדן and מועד (see *supra*, pp. 8-11).

[26] Acts 1.6–7.

would take too long, and is not necessary; for, indeed, they use human conjecture and bring forward nothing certain from the authority of the canonical Scriptures. But on this subject He puts aside the figures of the calculators *and orders silence*, who says, 'It is not for you to know the times, which the Father put in His own power' "[27] Opposition to Messianic calculation in Christendom was largely responsible for the repudiation by many Christians of the Book of Revelations, as early as the second and third centuries

4. Of the fourth group, the most prominent spokesman is R. Eliezer (c. 80–120), pupil of Yoḥanan ben Zakkai. His famous disputation with R. Joshua is symptomatic of the bitter controversy which was to rage clear down the ages. "R. Eliezer said: 'If Israel will repent they will be redeemed; if not, they will not be redeemed.' Rabbi Joshua replied: 'If Israel will repent, they will be redeemed; if not, God will raise over them a king whose decrees will be as severe as those of Haman. Then Israel *will* repent.' Rabbi Eliezer said: 'Only if Israel will repent will they be redeemed, as it is written,' "Return, ye backsliding children, and I will heal your backsliding."'[28] R. Joshua replied: 'Has it not also been declared, "Ye were sold for naught, and ye shall be redeemed without money?"'[29] Ye were sold for naught, that is, for idolatry, and ye shall be redeemed without money, that is, without repentance and good deeds.' R. Eliezer replied to R. Joshua: 'Has it not also been declared, 'Return unto me, and I will return unto you?'[30] R. Joshua replied: 'Has it not also been declared, "For I am a Lord unto you and I will take you one of a city and two of a family and I will bring you to Zion."'[31] R. Eliezer made answer: 'Has it not also been declared, "Through repentance and quietude shall ye be redeemed."'[32] R. Joshua replied: 'Has it not

[27] *De Civ.* XVIII. 53.
[28] Jer. 3.22.
[29] Is. 52.3.
[30] Mal. 3.7.
[31] Jer. 3.14.
[32] Is. 30.15.

already been declared, "Thus saith the Lord, the Redeemer of Israel, and his Holy One, to him also who is despised of men, to him who is abhorred of nations, to a servant of rulers, kings shall see and arise, and princes, and they shall prostrate themselves because of the Lord who is faithful."'[33] R. Eliezer replied: 'Has it not already been declared, "If thou wilt return, O Israel, said the Lord, then wilt thou return unto me."'[34] Then R. Joshua made answer: 'Hath it not already been declared, "And I heard the man clothed in linen who was above the waters of the river, when he lifted up his right hand and his left hand unto heaven and swore by Him who liveth forever, that it shall be for a time, times, and a half, and when they have made an end of breaking in pieces the power of the holy people, all these things shall be finished."' Then R. Eliezer was silent."[35]

One wonders whether R. Eliezer's silence was due to weariness or acquiescence. Certainly R. Eliezer's voice was not silent in the succeeding ages. This prolonged debate is not without its significance. It is a struggle between the ethical conception of the Messiah idea and the purely empirical and physical one. The portentous array of Biblical data marshaled by the opposing sides is evidence of the earnestness with which they searched Sacred Writ for confirmation of their views.

The same controversy was waged a hundred years later between Rab and Samuel. "Rab said: 'All the forecasts are at an end (i. e. they apply to events since past). The matter now depends entirely upon repentance and good deeds.' But Samuel said: 'It is enough for a man to mourn as long as the period of his mourning lasts.'"[36] There is a definite period set for all mourning, and there must be a definite end to the mourning of the people of Israel.

That Redemption does not depend upon merit is also expressed in *Shir R.* 2.19, and in the *Pesiḳta R.*, where this view is attributed to R. Judah, R. Neḥemiah or R. Naḥman

[33] Is. 49.7.
[34] Jer. 4.1.
[35] *San.* 97b–98a; see also *Jer. Ta'an* 1.1.
[36] די לאבל שיעמוד באבלו (*San.* 97b).

and others.[37] The opposite view is beautifully voiced in *Mid. Tehil.* 45.3: "God said: everything depends upon you. Just as this rose grows with its heart toward heaven, so do you repent before me and turn your hearts heavenward, and I will thereupon cause your redeemer to appear."[38]

There were those who tried to harmonize these opposing views. They wished to retain the hope of an ultimate unconditional Redemption, while at the same time stressing the importance of repentance. Among these was R. Joshua ben Levi (3 c.), who explains Is. 60.22, "I, the Lord, will hasten it in its time," to mean that if the children of Israel are deserving, then Redemption will be hastened (אחישנה); if not, then it will come at the appointed time בעתה.[39] Similarly, he explains the apparently contradictory verses, "And there came with the clouds of heaven one like unto a son of man"[40] (the Messiah came swiftly like the clouds of heaven), and "behold thy king cometh unto thee . . . lowly and riding upon an ass"[41] (the Messiah came slowly like a man riding upon an ass). If the children of Israel are found deserving, then the Messiah will come swiftly (with the clouds of heaven); if not, then slowly like a lowly man riding upon an ass.[42]

An analogous textual contradiction in the case of the Egyptian exile is similarly adjusted. "Rabbi said: (It is written), and they shall serve them, and they (the Egyptians) shall afflict them 400 years,[43] and it is again written, 'and in the fourth generation they shall come back hither.'[44] How are these two verses to be reconciled? If they will repent (said the Lord) I will redeem them according to the number of generations; if not, according to the number of years."[45]

[37] הואיל וחפץ בגאולתכם אינו מביט במעשיכם הרעים (see פסיקתא רבתי, ed. Friedmann, Vienna, 1880, Chap. XV, p. 71a).

[38] See also *Deut. R.* 5.6.

[39] *San.* 98a.

[40] Dan. 7.13.

[41] Zech. 9.9.

[42] *San.* 98a.

[43] Gen. 15. 13.

[44] Gen. 15.16.

[45] מכילתא, ed. Weiss, Vienna, 1865, p. 19b.

That repentance will hasten the "day" is also suggested in the following legend built around R. Joshua b. Levi. R. Joshua discovered Elijah at the entrance to the cave of R. Simeon ben Yoḥai. . . . He thereupon asked him, "When will the Messiah come?" Elijah answered, "Go and ask him (the Messiah)." "And where was he sitting?" "At the gates of the city (Rome)". . . . He went to him . . . and asked, "When will my master appear?" He replied, "Today." He returned to Elijah, who asked him what the Messiah had said. He replied that he had lied to him, for he had said that he would come today, and he has not come. Elijah then said to him, "This is what he said to you: '*Today* if you will hearken unto His voice.'"[46]

Another Rabbi declared: "Were the children of Israel to observe fully two successive Sabbaths, they would immediately be redeemed."[47] And still another propounded this conviction in an homily on Gen. 1.2: "And the spirit of God moved upon the face of the waters: This is the spirit of King Messiah . . . through what merit may this spirit be accelerated, through repentance which is likened unto water, as it is written: 'Pour out your heart like water.'"[48]

This attempt at synthesizing the two views is evident also from the following passage in the *Pesiḳta Rabbati.* On the verse: "In thy distress, when all these things are come upon thee, in the end of days, thou wilt return to the Lord thy God, and hearken unto His voice. For the Lord thy God is a merciful God . . . nor forget the covenant of thy fathers,"[49] the following interpretation is placed. Five things bring about the Redemption: (1) suffering ("In thy distress"), (2) *the appointed end* ("In the end of days"), (3) *repentance* ("Thou wilt return unto the Lord, thy God"), (4) mercy, ("For the Lord, thy

[46] Ps. 95.7; *San.* 98a.
[47] *Sab.* 118b.
[48] Lam. 2.19; *Ber. R.* 2.5.
[49] Deut. 4.30, 31.

God, is a merciful God") (5) the merit of the fathers ("Nor forget the covenant of thy fathers").[50]

Opposition was also expressed to the impatient hopes entertained not only by the masses but by some outstanding Rabbis regarding the Messiah's advent. Some Rabbis felt called upon to caution the people against such ebullience. Thus one Midrash reads: "The Redemption of Israel is likened to a grain-harvest, a grape-harvest, a field of spice and a woman in confinement. A field which is harvested before the proper time, even the straw from off of it is poor. A vineyard which is gathered in too early, even the vinegar made out of its grapes is poor. Spices gathered before they are full grown and dry will lack their true odor, and an aborted child dies."[51]

But this view did not go unchallenged. An opposite view is expressed. On Ps. 73.27–8; "For, lo, they that go far from Thee shall perish. . . . But as for me the nearness of God is my good," an anonymous Rabbi comments: "Balaam was asked: 'Have they (the children of Israel) an end to their Redemption?' He answered, 'Yes,' They asked, 'When?' He replied, 'It is far off.' "I see it, but it is not now; I behold it, but not nigh."'[52] He postponed the end. They asked the prophets of Israel. They answered, 'It is near.' "The day of their calamity is at hand."'[53] Jeremiah[54] came and said, 'Howl ye, for the day of the Lord is at hand.'[55] Malachi came and said, 'It is near,' For behold, the day is come. It burneth as a furnace."[56] Joel came and said in the same way, 'Blow ye the horn in Zion . . . for the day of the Lord is come.'[57] Therefore David said, 'For, lo, they that postpone Thee[58]

[50] *Pesiḳ. R.*, ed. Friedmann, p. 184b; *cf.* also p. 144b, תורתי בידכם והקץ בידי ושנינו צריכים זה לזה, of which another version is found in the *Pesiḳta* קיצי בידך וקיצך בידי, ed. Buber, p. 131b.

[51] *Shir. R.* end.

[52] Num. 24.17.

[53] Deut. 32.35.

[54] Should be Isaiah (see note 29, *Pesiḳ. R.*, ed. Friedmann, pp. 173b–174a).

[55] Is. 13.6.

[56] Mal. 3.19.

[57] Joel 2.1.

[58] רחקיך (lit. "Go far from thee").

shall perish' . . . This refers to Balaam and his followers who postponed the end and were therefore destroyed. But Thou didst show goodness to the prophets of Israel because they announced that the end was near. Show mercy also unto me, for I, too, believe in the nearness of the end."[59]

[59] קרבת אלהים לי טוב (lit. "the nearness of God is my good"), *Pesiḳ. R.*, pp. 173–174.

CHAPTER IX

B. POST-TALMUDIC

Some of the expressions of opposition which we have quoted undoubtedly come from a period later than the Talmudic, as late as the tenth century. From the tenth century, we have records of Karaite opposition.[1]

1. *Japheth Halevi* devotes considerable space in his commentary on Daniel to refute the Messianic calculations based on the "times" and "seasons" passages of that book. He insists throughout that the "days" mentioned are to be taken literally as days and not as years and that they refer to contemporaneous events, and he briefly reviews the numerous false calculations which had been made.

> We have explained this chapter in accordance with what we have heard from the teachers of the Captivity, or read in their books, so far as those theories seemed probable. God will forgive and pardon any slips or errors in His goodness and gentleness. We shall now follow this with a statement of the views of others about these times and the end, that anyone who cares to know them may do so. The scholars who preceded Joseph ibn Bakhtawi explained the 2300, 1290 and 1335 as *years;* the Rabbanites, too, spoke of the *end*, and fancied that from the third year of Cyrus to the *end* would be 1335 years; the term is passed some years since, so that their opinion has been disproved, and that of their followers; similarly El-Fayyumi explained it years, and has been proved false; he had however some marvelous inven-

[1] It might here be noted in passing that similar opposition developed early among the Arabs, who likewise had their Messianic beliefs and calculators. "Just as in Judaism the 'calculators of the end of time,' as they are called, encountered severest reproaches, so the orthodox authorities of the moderate Shi'ites have branded the 'time determiners' (al-wakkatun) as liars, and have found in utterances of the Imams the condemnation of such speculation" (Goldziher, *Mohammed and Islam*, p. 243).

tions with reference to *the time and times.* He was answered by Salmon ben Jerucham; whom we need not in our turn answer, since his term is past and the end not arrived. Certain of the Karaites, too, made the 2300 years date from the exodus from Egypt; that term too is past years ago, and their prophecy not come true. Salmon ben Jerucham, in his Commentary on Ps. lxxiv. 9, denied that it was possible to ascertain the *end;* but on Ps. cii. 14 he offered a date which is passed and falsified. He agreed with many others in interpreting the 2300 and 1290 as days, but differed about the interpretation of the *time of the removal of the continual* which, he thought, meant the *destruction of the second Temple.* Benjamin Nahawendi agreed with him in the latter point, but differed from him about the days being days and not years. Benjamin took a separate view in believing that they were years. Salmon ben Jerucham referred the 1290 to the three and a half spoken of in Chap. x. 27 ("for half of the week he shall cause the sacrifice and the oblation to cease").

Each of the commentators has taken a different line, and all have gone wrong in making the days years. Benjamin Nahawendi, indeed, made the 2300 date from the destruction of Shiloh, and *from the time of the removal of the continual* from the destruction of the Second Temple; this leaves still some 400 years; but this is a delusion.

All these theories are confuted by two facts:

(1) Their inventors profess to know the *end,* whereas the Scripture says that the matter is *closed and sealed;* any one therefore who professes to know it before *the time of the end* is professing what cannot be true.

(2) They make the days years. Now we know that where he speaks of *weeks of years* he expressly distinguishes them from *weeks of days;* consequently none of the three sums mentioned (2300, 1290, 1335) can be years. All must be days.[2]

[2] See Jephet Ibn Ali, *Commentary on Daniel,* edited and translated by Margoliouth, Oxford, 1889, p. 86. See also Pinsker's *Likkute Kadmoniot,* p. 82.

2. *Moses ibn Gikatilla* (11 c.) was not an outspoken opponent of Messianic calculations, but his remarkable Scriptural exegesis was a clear denial of the right to employ Biblical texts for that purpose. Grammarian, commentator, poet, ibn Gikatilla was the most thoroughgoing and consistent representative in the Middle Ages of that critical-historical school of thought whose spokesman in Talmudic times was R. Nathan.[3] All the prophecies of the Bible, he maintained, refer to contemporaneous events. None refers to the Roman exile. Only those prophecies which are specifically introduced by a phrase such as "And it shall come to be in the end of days" (והיה באחרית הימים) have any eschatological significance. Such exegesis is fatal to Messianic computation based on sacred texts. He was bitterly denounced for it. His contemporary, Ibn Balaam, accused him of deliberately employing this historical method in order to dishearten the people, whose sole hope was the Messiah. Abarbanel charged him with lack of faith.[4]

The prophecies of Isaiah, especially the famous chapter eleven: "And there shall come forth a shoot out of the stock of Jesse . . ." refer to events in the times of the prophet Isaiah, to King Hezekiah, to Assyria, and to political conditions of that day.[5] The verse "Awake, awake, put on thy strength, O Zion"[6] applies to the Babylonian captivity.[7] Similarly the prophecies of Joel. On 3.1: "And it shall come to pass afterward that I will pour out my spirit upon all flesh," ibn Gikatilla remarks: "R. Joshua said that this entire prophecy refers to the future, but if that were so, why does he say, 'And it shall come to pass *afterward*,' and not 'and it shall be in *the end* of days'? This prophet lived in the days of Jehoshapat. He therefore mentions the valley of Jehoshapat." Also the whole

[3] See *supra*, 198.

[4] See Poznanski, *Ibn Chiquitilla, Nebst den Fragmenten Seiner Schriften*, p. 28; also *J. Q. R.*, New Series, XV, No. 1, pp. 51–52, "The Arabic Commentary of Ibn Balaam on the Twelve Minor Prophets."

[5] See Poznanski, *op. cit.*, p. 99.

[6] Is. 52.1.

[7] Poznanski, *op. cit.*, p. 101.

of chapter 4 refers to events in the reign of that king.[8] Obad. 1.17: "But in Mount Zion there shall be those that escape," refers to the days of King Hezekiah. "And the captivity of Jerusalem" (verse 20) refers to those who were exiled at the destruction of the first Temple."[9] Micah 4.11: "And now many nations are assembled against thee," refers to the second Temple and to Zerubbabel.[10] Zech. 9.9: "Rejoice greatly, O daughter of Zion . . . behold, thy king cometh unto thee," refers to Nehemiah, who in the Book of Ezra is called King of Judah.[11] This interpretation was so drastic and revolutionary that even Ibn Ezra opposed it. Ibn Balaam is vituperative in his denunciation.[12] Ibn Gikatilla wrote a commentary on Daniel, of which only a few insignificant fragments have come down. He undoubtedly pursued his critical and scientific method in the interpretation of this book, too. This brilliant exegete of Spain proved to be the model and inspiration of the opponents of Messianic computation in the following centuries.

3. The fine sanity of Gikatilla is sustained by *Moses ibn Ezra* (c. 1070—after 1138). Belonging to the critical school of grammarians and rhetoricians, he could not tolerate the pseudo-scientific methods of the Messianic calculators, who seemed to be numerous in that century, and who employed Gematria and Notarikon in their exposition of the Bible. In his study of Hebrew prosody, *Kitab al-Muhadarah wal-Mudhakarah*, he writes: "R. Samuel Gaon mentioned in his commentary on the Pentateuch portion, אלה הדברים, that Moses hinted in the phrase ונושנתם בארץ[13] that the duration of the Jewish state would approximately equal the number of years suggested in the word ו'נ'ו'ש'נ'ת'ם' (852 years). Other commentators maintain that the time of the duration of the first Temple

[8] *Ibid.*, p. 103.
[9] *Ibid.*
[10] *Ibid.*, p. 104.
[11] *Ibid.*, p. 105.
[12] See *op. cit.*, pp. 157–159.
[13] Deut. 4.25.

is implied in the word ב'ז'א'ת' in the verse בזאת יבא אהרן.[14] Others believe that the word רחם in the verse ברגז רחם תזכור[15] refers to Abraham, the Gematria of whose name is equal to that of רחם (248). Concerning these matters it can truthfully be said that they are a form of ignorance which does no harm, and a form of wisdom which does no good. The worst feature about it is that some of them attempt by means of these methods to deduce the time of the end from the dates found in Daniel and in other books. The fact is that not even one of these calculations has come out right. . . . The recent computators took no counsel from the mistakes of the earlier ones, but each one followed his own bent and exceeded the limit without explaining anything. God does not hide a matter from His prophet and does not inform him that it is a secret, only to reveal it, through such feeble means, to men who are many degrees lower than the prophet."[16]

4. *Judah Halevi* (1080–1141), in his *Kuzari*, speaks frequently of the exile, but only sparingly of the Messiah. Halevi urges upon men to suffer the exile in patience.[17] He who grows fretful and impatient is in danger of losing both worlds.[18] He speaks of the purpose of the exile[19] and of the cause of its long duration.[20] The Kuzari reveals Halevi's passionate longing and love for the Holy Land, "the land where heart and soul are pure and clean, sanctified as it is by the presence of God," and of his great eagerness to go there.[21]

Halevi does not in the *Kuzari* indulge in Messianic computation. Perhaps the reason for it is to be found in the last paragraph of the book: "It is written, 'Thou wilt arise and have compassion upon Zion, for it is time to be

[14] Lev. 16.3.
[15] *Hab.* 3.2.
[16] See Halper's ספר שירת ישראל, which is a Hebrew translation of Ibn Ezra's *Kitab*, pp. 165–166. Also. *R. E. J.*, xxii, p. 71.
[17] *Op. cit.*, 3.11.
[18] *Ibid.*, 3.12.
[19] *Ibid.*, 4.23.
[20] *Ibid.*, 1.115.
[21] *Ibid.*, 5.23 *et passim.*

gracious unto her, for the appointed time is come. For thy servants take pleasure in her stones and love her dust.'[22] This means that Jerusalem will really be rebuilt when the children of Israel will long for her with such perfect longing that they will take pleasure in her stones and her dust," i. e. go there themselves and rebuild it.[23]

But as in the case of Maimonides, Halevi, too, could not resist the great temptation of discovering the specific year for the final Redemption.[24] The times were full of trouble and unhappiness, and the people needed a definite promise to sustain and inspirit them.

5. *Abraham ibn Ezra* (1092–1167), while acknowledging that the Book of Daniel contains Messianic prophecies, nevertheless insists that neither Daniel nor anyone else knew or knows their true interpretation. That must remain hidden until the day of deliverance. In his commentary on Dan. 11.31, he broadly and categorically asserts that all the Messianic calculators, including Abraham ibn Alfakar, Solomon ibn Gabirol, Abraham bar Ḥiyya, Isaac ben Lev[25] and all others who tried to discover the end by means of astrology and the mysticism of letters and numbers are "pursuing vanity and chasing the wind." Of Ibn Alfaker[26] he says, "The son of the Potter composed a book on the appointed end, but I shattered his arguments like a Potter's vessel, proving that his expected end is already past."

Ibn Ezra, however, suggests certain interpretations of the visions in the Book of Daniel. He believes that the four kingdoms are Babylon, Persia, Greece and Ishmael. During the latter's reign, the deliverance of Israel will occur.[27] "The time, times and half a time," are the three and a half years which will precede the end, during which

[22] Ps. 102.14–15.

[23] *Op. cit.*, 5.27.

[24] See *supra*, p. 68.

[25] Probably Isaac ben Labi, Spanish liturgical poet of the eleventh century, whom Abraham Ibn Ezra quotes elsewhere in his Biblical commentary. His Messianic calculations are unknown to us.

[26] Arabic אלפכאר; Hebrew היוצר= The Potter, (a family name), died c. 1231.

[27] Com. on Dan. 7.13.

period great suffering will come upon the Children of Israel, but no one knows when this period will begin.

The "days" mentioned in Daniel are to be taken throughout literally as days and not years.[28] The "week," however, unless supplemented by the word "days" (as in 10.2) means seven years.[29]

The second vision of Daniel (chapter 8) leads up to Antiochus. The 2300 evenings and mornings (verse 14) are approximately the six years of Antiochus' cruel rule over Israel.[30]

The third vision (chap. 9) leads up to Titus and the destruction. The figure "70 weeks" he finds difficult to explain.[31] He suggests that they may represent the number of years (490) from the time of this vision of Daniel to the second destruction. The seven "weeks" (verse 25) are the 49 years between the time of Cyrus' proclamation and the coming of Nehemiah to Jerusalem. The 62 "weeks" are the 434 years of the duration of the second Temple. The "one week" are the seven years preceding the destruction, during which time Titus made a treaty of peace with Israel. The "half week" are the three and a half years prior to the destruction, when the continual burnt offering was discontinued.[32]

6. *Moses Maimonides* (1135–1204) is very firm and definite in his insistence on the dogmatic character of the Messiah belief: "He who does not believe in him and who does not wait for his coming, denies not alone the later prophets, but the Torah and Moses himself."[33] Faith in the Messiah is one of his thirteen articles of faith But he reduced the concept to its irreducible minimum. He strips of it all Midrashic adornments. Here, as elsewhere, he rationalizes with a vengeance: "Let not a man think that in the days of the Messiah the accustomed order of things will be changed. . . . The world will go

[28] ודע כי ימים לעולם ימים ולא שנים.

[29] Com. on Dan. 9.24.

[30] *Ibid.*, 8.24.

[31] רק פירוש אלה השבועים השבעים קשה עד מאד (*ibid.*, 9.24.)

[32] Com. on Dan., 9.24, 25.

[33] *Yad. Hil. Melakim* 9.1.

on as usual. . . . Only Israel will be at peace with the nations of the world, and these will accept the true faith. . . . All else written of the Messiah are only by way of parables. . . . Some of the sages say that before the coming of the Messiah, Elijah will appear; but concerning this and all else like unto it, no one knows exactly how they will come to be, since they are hidden with the prophets, and even the sages, have no certain tradition on the subject . . . hence the contradiction in views. . . . At best, the sages' attempted detailed presentation of the subject cannot be regarded as a fundamental principle of our religion. Furthermore, a man should not spend much time on the *Aggadot* and *Midrashim* which treat of this matter, nor regard them as important; for they lead neither to the fear nor to the love of God. *Nor should a man calculate the end.* He should wait and believe in the essential fact (of his coming, alone).[34]

Maimonides is particularly set against computing the end. In his commentary on *Sanhedrin*, he writes: "It is fundamental dogma to believe in the coming of the Messiah; even if he is delayed long, wait for him. But no one should attempt to fix the time, nor find Biblical texts from which to deduce the time of his coming."[35]

And yet Maimonides, too, under the strain and duress of his age, suggested a Messianic year.[36] Maimonides apparently relents the rigor of his views. As a philosopher and Halakist, his Messianic opinions are thoroughly disciplined. But when he writes not abstractly but purposefully, aiming at strengthening the faith of his brethren and at comforting them in their hour of tribulation, as in the case of the Yemenites, he is far less austere and exact. In his letter to the Yemenites, while warning them against the dangers of pseudo-Messiahs, he nevertheless urges upon them an elaborate Messianic belief as a great fundamental of Judaism. He states that the Messiah will appear in the

[34] *Ibid.*, 21.1–2.

[35] ולא ישים לו זמן ולא יעשה לו סברות במקראות להוציא זמן ביאתו (chap. 10, toward end, under היסוד שנים עשר).

[36] See *supra*, p. 75.

hour of greatest oppression, when the sway of Edom and Arab will extend all over the world. The Messiah will be wiser than all men, greater than all the prophets (except Moses). He will perform miracles. At his appearance all the nations of the earth will be terrified and subdued.

7. *Abraham ibn Daud* (1110–1180) makes no mention at all of the Messiah in his *Emunah Ramah*, and the Messianic interpretation of Zech. 11.7, found in his *Sefer ha-Kabbalah*, is not found in all the manuscripts and is not authentic.[37] In this latter work he interprets all the dates found in Daniel to refer to events preceding the destruction of the second Temple, thereby precluding all Messianic romancing on the basis of these figures.[38]

8. *Judah ben Samuel He-Ḥasid* (13 c.), author of the *Sefer Ḥasidim*, was a strong opponent of Messianic calculation. He refused even to mention the calculation of another man in his transcript of the account of the *Travels of Petaḥia.*[39] In his *Sefer Ḥasidim* he is quite outspoken about the entire subject: "If you see a man prophesying about the Messiah, know that he is either a sorcerer or engaged in witchcraft. . . . Demons come and teach him calculations and hidden things to his own confounding and that of the people who believe in him. . . . For no man knows anything about the coming of the Messiah."[40]

Again, commenting on the closed letter *Mem* in the words לם"רבה המשרה,[41] he remarks that the phrase refers to the Messiah, "whose end is hidden (closed) just as the *Mem.*"[42]

9. *Ḥayyim Galipapa* (c. 1310–c. 1380), Spanish Rabbi and commentator, followed Moses ibn Gikatilla and Ibn Daud in ascribing the so-called Messianic passages of the prophets and of Daniel to events which occurred during the existence of the second Temple. He wrote a tract on

[37] See Neubauer, *Med. Jew. Chron.*, I, Pref. xiii.

[38] *Ibid.*, ספר הקבלה לרב אברהם בן דוד, pp. 49–51. See also Mann, "Early Karaite Bible Commentaries", *J. Q. R.*, New Series, XII, pp. 450–51.

[39] See *infra*, p. 259.

[40] כי אין אדם יודע על ביאת משיח (see ספר חסידים ed. Wistinetzki, 1924, pp. 76–77, par. 212.)

[41] Is. 9.6.

[42] *Op. cit.*, p.364, par. 509.

Redemption called *Iggeret ha-Ge'ulah*, which is mentioned by Albo in his *Iḳḳarim*. From Albo's quotations we learn of the contents of this tract. All the Messianic prophecies of Isaiah, Galipapa maintained, allude to the period of the second Temple. Dan. 7 refers to Antiochus and the Hasmoneans. The four beasts are therefore not those usually given by commentators, but Babylon, Media, Persia and Greece, all of whom ruled during the second Temple.[43] It is clear that this interpretation undermines all the orthodox Messianic speculations which based themselves primarily upon the Bible.

10. *Ḥasdai Crescas* (1340–1410) does not include the belief in the Messiah among the six fundamental doctrines of Judaism. He regards it, however, as an essential truth of the faith. He who doubts it is a *Min*, a heretic. He states the irreducible minimum of the Messianic faith upon which all are agreed. He will be of the stem of Jesse. He will restore all Israel and Judah to the Holy Land and will set up a dynasty which will never be destroyed. All else predicated concerning the Messiah is debatable and a matter of private opinion.[44] All attempts to discover the end are vain, wearisome futilities Both Holy Writ and Rabbinic law frown upon such enterprize.[45]

Why is the exile so long? In comparison with the Babylonian its duration is appalling. Crescas suggests various explanations. The secret is with God. We can no more understand it than we can understand "the peace of the wicked and the suffering of the righteous." One must not attempt to compare the length of the exile with the degree of the sin which provoked it. For while the exile was the natural consequence of sin, the Redemption will be a miraculous act of God, dependent altogether upon His will and the merits of the people. And lastly, our present exile may only be a continuation of the Babylonian, which really never ended. For all the people were not

[43] ספר העקרים, Part IV, chap. 42.

[44] אור יהוה, ed. Wien, 1860, p. 81.

[45] אמנם הדבור בהגבלת זמן בואו הוא לאות ויגיעה לריק אם מצד הכתובים שלא פירש הזמן בהם .אבל העירו על העלמו באמרו ואני שמעתי ולא אבין כי סתומים וחתומים הם הדברים עד ועת קץ .ואם למה שאמרו רז׳ל תיפח רוחן של מחשבי קצין (*Ibid.*)

redeemed at that time, nor did Israel gain full independence then or thereafter.[46]

11. *Joseph Albo* (1380–1440), author of the *Sefer ha-Iḳḳarim*, goes a step further. He is more outspoken than Crescas. He not only ignores the whole Rabbinic superstructure built on the Messiah idea, but he also denies the dogmatic character of the belief. The Messianic hope is not a "root" principles. It is only a branch."[47]

A man should believe in the Messiah. "It is a faith held by the nation that every believer in the law of Moses ought to believe in it."[48] Also, "It is clear that he who does not believe in the coming of the Messiah denies the works of the prophets and contravenes a positive command; but, nevertheless, the belief in the Messiah is not a principle which, if a man denies, he denies the Torah. . . . A man who denies the coming of the Messiah cannot be called a כופר בעקר—one who denies the fundamental faith".[49]

Albo thus takes issue with the orthodox opinion of his day, an opinion which, by the way, had persisted for nigh unto a thousand years. The reason for it may be found in the supreme importance which the subject had assumed in the Judaeo-Christian disputations of his day. Albo participated in the famous disputation held by Pope Benedict XIII at Tortosa (1413–14). He is quoted by Astruc as having replied to the apostate Joshua Lorki by giving the true interpretation of two Messianic passages in the Talmud.[50] Lorki essayed to prove from Talmudic sources that Jesus was the Messiah. Albo sought to weaken all such Christian apologetics by denying the dogmatic importance of the whole subject, as far as Judaism is concerned.

Albo affirms that the date of the end cannot be known, not even from the definite Biblical prophecies which speak of the end. Biblical apoclayptic passages may very well

[46] *Op. cit.*, p. 82.
[47] *Op. cit.*, 1.22.
[48] *Ibid.*, 1.23.
[49] *Ibid.*, 4.42.
[50] ספר העקרים, ed. Wilna, end.

be taken to refer to events long since passed. He quotes Ḥayyim Galipapa, among others, as his authority.

12. There is a denial of Messianic calculation also in the *Zohar Ḥadash.* It is difficult to determine when this work was written. It is clearly much later than the *Zohar* proper.

"Rabbi Isaac said: 'It is written, "He was buried in the valley of the land of Moab over against Bethpeor, and no man knoweth of his sepulcher unto this day."[51] God said: "*Fools are they who calculate the time of the Messiah,* a thing which I never revealed, as it is written, 'For the day of vengeance is in my heart,' and have not revealed it even to the mouth, and these men would try to discover the end. In this instance (the place of the burial of Moses) I gave three distinct indications, (1) in the valley, (2) in the land of Moab, and (3) over against Bethpeor, and yet men could not discover his burial place, for I did not reveal it. How much less can men discover the end (which I completely hid)... " Hence it is written: 'The Burden of Dumah. One calleth unto me out of Seir':[52] This is Israel calling unto God from under the heavy yoke of Seir. 'Watchman, what of the night'? Lord of the universe, Thou art the watchman of Israel, we are in this exile which is like unto night, tell us what of the night? When wilt Thou lead us forth from this night? See what follows: 'The watchman said: The morning came and also the night.' I brought you out of exile before, but you were not deserving, and so I brought on the night again. . . . 'If ye will inquire, inquire ye,—if ye wish to know the time of your Redemption, when it will be, and when ye will return to your land, 'return, come.' Turn in repentance and it will come immediately. For this is what R. Jehudah said: The end of the exile depends upon repentance only, as it is written: 'Today, if you will hearken unto His voice.' Even at the time of the Creation of the world was this great secret hinted at among the hidden things. 'And God said, Let there be light, and there was

[51] Deut. 34.6.
[52] Is. 21.11.

light.' This means, Let it be a secret (רז). For רז and אור are one and the same thing (=207). 'And God saw the secret, and behold it was good.' It is well that it should be a secret unrevealed to any man, for if it were known many of the indiscreet among our people would go to perdition."[53]

That the last exile has no fixt duration is again stated in *Zohar Ḥadash*: "R. Eliezer said: 'For all the exiles of the congregation of Israel, God set a time and an end, and Israel always repented; but this last exile has no time or end, but everything depends upon repentance.'[54] God is merciful. If only the leaders of the congregations, or if only one congregation would fully repent, God would redeem the whole people. If Israel would but open the door of repentance the width of the eye of a needle, God would open for Israel mighty gates."[55]

13. *Isaac Arama* (c. 1420–1494), Spanish Rabbi and philosophic preacher, while not averse to the theosophy of Kabbala, notwithstanding frowns upon all attempts at Messianic computations. This in spite of the fact that his Messianic interest was intense, as witness his commentary on The Song of Songs, which makes of the latter an outright apocalyptic work. [56]In his "*'Aḳedat Yiẓḥaḳ*" Arama attacks all those who calculate the end, and specifically, by name, Abraham bar Ḥiyya. The latter was wise enough, Arama claims, to make his calculations fit in with events which had already happened, but as to future events, all his calculations went awry. Many worthy men were similarly misled, and unintentionally they spread falsehoods. The hour of Redemption is not contingent upon any heavenly constellation, but upon the free will of God.[57] The hour has not been revealed. "The nature and the bliss of the Messianic times we are aware of, for

[53] זהר חדש, ed. 1663, p. 12c.

[54] *Ibid.*, p. 37b.

[55] *Ibid.*, 37b; *cf. Shir R.* 5.30.

[56] At the conclusion of this commentary Arama writes: ובזה נשלם העולה בידינו מביאור זאת המגלה המעולה המגלה סוד הגאולה. See Com. on Song of Songs, ed. Warsaw, 1911, p. 32.

[57] *Op. cit.*, p. 296, par. פקודי.

they have already been explained by all the prophets, but the exact day and hour are hidden and unknown."[58] Arama justifies this mystery on ethical grounds. Were the time of Redemption fixed and known, men would cease to fight sin and evil and forego the struggle for moral perfection, which must precede the hour of Redemption. Knowledge of the exact day of deliverance would lead to moral anarchy.[59]

In the last chapter of his *Ḥazut Kashah* he is drastic in his denunciation of all those who declare that the fortunes of Israel are dependent upon the heavenly bodies. He denounces the writers who would substitute for the providential care of the Almighty the dominion of constellations. Especially is he severe with those who try to delude the people with the idea that their Redemption is contingent upon certain major or minor conjunctions. Such men actually delay Redemption, for they turn the minds of men away from the one thing which can hasten the glorious day—repentance.[60]

14. *Lipmann-Mühlhausen* (Austria, 14–15 c.) author of the *Nizzaḥon* (written in the first decade of the 15 c.), the outstanding polemic against Christianity, which evoked a whole literature of rebuttals from Christian apologists, quite naturally devotes considerable space to the Messianic theme. The author is especially interested in proving that the closing prophecies of Daniel refer to the future Redemption from this last exile and not, as the Christians claim, to Jesus.

He adopts Saadia's and Baḥya's interpretation of "time, times and half a time." The first עדן refers to the period from the Exodus to the building of the first Temple = 480 years. The second to the duration of the first Temple = 410 years. Half of עידן is therefore 445 years. The total 1335 years. This will be the duration of the present exile, *but no one knows when this period begins.*[61]

[58] *Ibid.*, p. 398, par. ויחי.

[59] ויהיה היתר רצועה בעיניהם הבלתי רואים שום תועלת בהיטיב את דרכם ולא שום רע בהשחיתה (*ibid*).

[60] חזות קשה, ed. Sabbioneta, 1552, p. 29b.

[61] ספר נצחון, ed. Amsterdam, 1711, p. 102a, par. 331.

He apologizes for the many calculators of the past whose prophecies have not come true. Even Daniel miscalculated. These calculators, like Baḥya, did not mean to imply that their calculations were absolutely certain. They merely tried *to guess at* the end. Some of them, like Rashi, merely tried to explain the meaning of those Biblical passages which contained prophetic dates. It is likely, too, that their prophecies would have come true had the people merited Redemption. As it is, they will have to wait upon another terminus, for there is more than one possible terminus to the exile.

He expresses the view that it is not at all desirable to calculate the end. The people will despair if the appointed time fails to materialize the Messiah. He notes the expectations popularly entertained in his day that the Messiah would come not later than the year 5170 = 1410 C. E. The basis of this belief was that the third Temple would last as long as the durations of the first and second Temples combined (410+420 = 830 years). The world must end in the year 6000; hence the Messiah must come not later than the year 5170 (6000–830) = 1410 C. E.[62]

But he insists that there is no binding authority to this belief. It is sufficient to believe that God will hasten the day according to His own pleasure. Redemption depends entirely upon the merit of the people. *It may come just one day prior to the close of the sixth millennium.*

15. *Abraham Saba* (15–16c.), preacher in Castile and Spanish exile, author of the commentary on the Pentateuch, *Ẓeror ha-Mor*, Kabbalist and mystic, expresses opposition to Messianic speculation. His commentary is replete with Messianic allusions. The theme of Redemption runs through it all like a golden thread. Hardly a passage but what contains some animadversion upon it. Whenever the number 4 is suggested in the Bible, Saba finds an allusion to the four kingdoms. And yet he deprecates calculation. He follows Naḥmanides and Baḥya in his interpretation of the sixth day of Creation, finding in it a

[62] *Ibid.*, p. 104a.

reference to the Redemption which will take place in the sixth millennium.[63] The Redemption will follow hard upon the fall of Rome.[64] Saba wrote after the fall of Constantinople in 1453, and Jewry read in this event the beginning of the end.

But the time of the end is hidden. Commenting on Deut. 32.24, "Is it not hidden with Me, sealed up in My treasures?" Saba writes, "And if a man will ask how long, O Lord?" or "When will be the end of the wonders?" He answered, 'Thou hast not asked wisely. For this is a thing which no eye has beheld and it is hidden with Me, sealed up in My treasuries. I have not revealed it *to any man*. I alone foresee it.'"[65]

16. *Azariah dei Rossi* (c. 1513–1578), author of *Me'or 'Enayim,* was clear and outspoken and systematic in his condemnation of all Messianic speculation. Dei Rossi devotes four chapters in his book to this subject, and his is the first thoroughgoing and elaborate criticism of it. He marshals his facts admirably, and his arguments are crushing. His approach is novel. He begins with a critical analysis of Jewish chronology. He demonstrates that our calendar—the *Aere Mundi*—is inaccurate and that more years have elapsed since Creation than the calendar would indicate. This leads him to the statement that all those who had based their Messianic computations on the Creation calendar have clearly gone astray, and that the Messianic year 5335 A. M. (1575 C. E.), eagerly awaited by his contemporaries, is now long since passed.

He maintains that his findings are not hostile to the highest interests of the people. On the contrary, they will save many from the dangers which always lurk in Messianic calculation. Hastily he reviews the history of Messianic computation from Talmudic times to his own. He shows where all prognostications have proved futile. He points to the Rabbinic prohibition of computation. The calculators of his own day are permitting themselves to violate

[63] צרור המור, ed. Warsaw, 1879, I, p. 67.
[64] כי עיקר גאולתנו תלויה בחורבן רומא.
[65] *Op. cit.*, V, p. 68.

the injunction of the Rabbis. Especially erring were those men who, like Abraham bar Ḥiyya and Isaac Abarbanel, had endeavored to derive their knowledge of the end from astral calculations. This, according to Dei Rossi, is clear heresy. Their writing should be "hidden."[66] Israel is not subject to astral influences, and God does not speak through the signs of the Zodiac. He quotes Halevi, Bar Sheshet, Arama, Ibn Ezra and Maimonides to prove his contention. "The fortunes of Israel and their hope of Redemption do not depend upon planetary computations. The Lord alone is our salvation, and He alone knows the time thereof." There is here a remarkable consonance of views between the Jewish critic and his Christian contemporary, Montaigne, who also attacks all forms of prognostication and astrology, in the ninth chapter of the first volume of his essays. The present day calculators, continues Azariah, should have learnt their lesson from those who preceded them. Naḥmanides, the wise and the learned, who wrote a book on Redemption which was so convincing that, were the author a contemporary of his, he would have believed in his calculations, maintained that the Messiah would come in the year 1358. Others, according to Isaac Abarbanel, believed similarly: Saadia, Abraham bar Ḥiyya, Rashi, Gersonides, Baḥya. Abraham Zacuto and Abraham Halevi calculated that he would come in the year 1530. They all had a sweet but unreal dream. Their hopes were vain. The present writers might have learned wisdom from them. They commit an additional wrong in prognosticating a day that is near at hand. What will happen if these prognostications are proved false? What disillusionment would overtake the people!

One need not accept his premise. The calendar may be right or wrong. His contention is nevertheless true. One should not fix his hope upon a definite year, but only upon a general faith in Redemption which the Lord will effect in His own time. The statement of Maimonides in *San.* 10

[66] הלא הספור כלו חתיכא דאסורא וראוי לגנוז שלא יראה החוצה, see מאור עינים, ed. Wilna, 1865, II, Chap. XLIII, p. 98.

sums up his views completely. Azariah apologizes for Maimonides' lapse from his own position in giving a Messianic date by adducing the troubled conditions in Yemen as extenuation.[67]

A contemporary of Dei Rossi, and a fellow countryman, who likewise evidences the broadening influences of the culture of the Italian Renaissance, was the eminent preacher of Mantua, Judah Aryeh Moscato (d. before 1594). Like Dei Rossi, he was a student of classic literature, and his sermons, for all their orthodoxy and mysticism, are distinguished by a refinement and elegance which are rare in the homiletical literature of the sixteenth century. In one or two instances Moscato indicates his opposition to Messianic calculation. On the text of Is. 21.11–12, he builds his homily, "The burden of Dumah" (in Hebrew דומה = silent). This refers to the last exile in which Israel must be silent, not knowing when the end of its exile would be—for it was revealed to no one. This last exile cries unto God, "Watchman, how much longer will this exile, likened unto night, still last?" And the Guardian of Israel replies, "The morning cometh, and also the night." At any given moment it is both morning and night. For everything depends upon repentance. You have the power to cause the sun of your Redemption to shine even in the middle of the night—"if ye will inquire"—if ye will seek God and return unto Him.[68]

17. *Elijah de Vidas* (16 c.), disciple of Isaac Luria, in his *Reshit Ḥokmah*, an ethical treatise of primary importance and strongly tinged with Kabbala, makes the Redemption entirely contingent upon the perfect observance of the moral law. This is significant, coming as it does from a Kabbalist and a follower of Luria. "If you will keep these two, charity and justice, at once will I (God) redeem you in perfect Redemption."[69]

18. *Isaac ben Abraham Troki* (1533–1594), anti-Christain polemist, in his *Ḥizzuḳ Emunah* is not primarily inter-

[67] *Ibid.*, Chap. XLIII, *passim.*
[68] ספר נפוצות יהודה, Venice, 1588, p. 230; also p. 207.
[69] ראשית חכמה, ed. Constantinople, 1736, p. 277a.

ested in the subject of Messianic speculation, but in the process of refuting the tenets and claims of Christianity. He is inevitably led to a discussion of the conflicting Jewish and Christian views concerning the Messiah. He desires also to persuade his people not to despair because the exile lasts so long.[70]

Chapter VI of his work is a reply to the Christian contention that the Biblical prophecies of restoration refer to the Babylonian exile and to the first restoration and not to the present exile. He reviews briefly the Biblical passages and shows wherein the prophecies were not fulfilled in the first exile and the first restoration. He follows closely the argument of Abarbanel's *Announcing Salvation*, though he does not mention him by name. He enumerates twenty distinctive features of the Redemption based on the prophecies of the Bible, none of which has as yet been fulfilled. Abarbanel enumerates fourteen.[71] Troki is elaborating also on the eight features enumerated by Joshua Lorki in his letter to Solomon Ha-Levi, the apostate (Pablo de Santa Maria), written at the close of the fourteenth century.[72]

These features, according to Troki, are: (1) the return of the Lost Ten Tribes,[73] (2) the destruction of Gog and Magog;[74] (3) the Mount of Olive shall be cleft asunder;[75] (4) the Red Sea and the Euphrates shall be dried up;[76] (5) living waters shall go out from Jerusalem and prodigious fertility shall be in the land;[77] (6) ten men out of all the nations shall take hold of the skirt of him that is a Jew, saying, "We will go with you";[78] (7) the yearly pilgrimage of the nations to Jerusalem;[79] (8) the nations shall worship

[70] ולאמץ ברכים כושלות מאורך קץ גליותינו (see חזוק אמונה ed. Sohran 1873, p. 8).

[71] See משמיע ישועה, pp. 39a–41a.

[72] See אגרת ר' יהושע הלורקי, ed. Landau, 1906, pp. 5—12; also ויכוח הרמב"ן, pp. 12–13,17.

[73] Ezek. 37.15–22.

[74] Ezek. 38.3.

[75] Zech. 14.4.

[76] Is. 11.15.

[77] Zech. 14.8; Ezek. 47.1.

[78] Zech. 8.23.

[79] Zech. 14.16.

God in Jerusalem on Sabbaths and New Moons;[80] (9) the destructions of all idols, false prophets and unclean spirit;[81] (10) one religion throughout the world, and that the religion of Israel;[82] (11) one sovereignty of the whole world, and that the sovereignty of Israel;[83] (12) universal peace;[84] (13) peace established between wild and domestic animals;[85] (14) a sinless world and more especially a sinless Israel;[86] (15) no suffering or sorrow or worry in the land of Israel;[87] (16) the Shekinah and prophecy will return to Israel and knowledge will be increased;[88] (17) the prophet Elijah will appear; [89] (18) the rebuilding of the Temple;[90] (19) the division of the land among the twelve tribes;[91] (20) resurrection.[92]

Chapter VII is a reply to the question, "Why is this exile so long?" The Egyptian exile lasted four hundred years. The Babylonian, seventy years. This exile has already lasted 1500 years. Again, in the case of both the earlier exiles, the length of each was revealed beforehand. Abraham knew that Israel would remain in Egypt 400 years, and Jeremiah knew that Judah would remain in Babylon 70 years; but the extent of this exile was revealed to no one. Troki replies that the extent of the first exile was made known to Abraham in order to confirm the promise which was made that his children will inherit the land of Canaan, though not immediately. The term of Babylonian exile was revealed in order to let the people know that it was an atonement for their sin of the neglect of the Sabbatical year.[93] But the present exile is punish-

[80] Is. 66.23.
[81] Zech. 13.2; Ezek. 2.18.
[82] Is. 45.23; Zech. 14.9.
[83] Is. 49.29; 60.10–12; Dan. 7.27.
[84] Is. 2.4; Mic. 4.3; Hos. 2.20; Zech. 9.16.
[85] Is. 11.69; Hos. 2.20.
[86] Deut. 30.6; Is. 60.20; Jer. 3.17; Ezek. 36.25; Zeph. 3.13.
[87] Is. 65.16–22.
[88] Ezek. 37.26, 39.29; Is. 11.9; Jer. 31.34.
[89] Mal. 3.24.
[90] Ezek. 40–45.
[91] Ezek. 47.11 ff.
[92] Deut. 42.39; Is. 26.10; Dan. 12.2 (*op. cit.*, pp. 56–62).
[93] Lev. 26.34; II Ch. 36.21.

ment for *all* the sins of the people, from the day they entered Canaan until they were driven from it. The exile is long because the sins were many. Israel is to remain scattered and dispersed until the people are purged of all their wickedness. Persecution and massacre are cleansing and purifying them. Redemption depends, then, on their repentance. It lies in their hands. God, therefore, did not reveal the end to anyone, not even to his prophets. "Our redemption from this exile depends upon complete repentance . . . and repentance depends entirely upon our own choice and will. It is, therefore, *impossible to place a definite time for the duration of the exile*, inasmuch as we have the power to shorten it . . . although the end is known to God, yet we are in possession of the freedom of choice."[94]

Furthermore, a revelation of the exact day of deliverance would only have proved a stumbling block in the way of the people, for many would have despaired because of the length of the exile and renounced their faith. Therefore the prophecies of Daniel are intentionally couched in obscure terms and their meaning is sealed. "The gates leading to a true understanding of the promised end (in Daniel) are barred not only to the men of average intelligence, but also to the men of profound intelligence."[95] Even Daniel did not know it.

Troki, being a Karaite, is under no obligation to explain away the many Messianic prognostications found in the Talmud. He finds it, therefore, a comparatively easy task to maintain his position on Biblical grounds. He quotes Deut. 32.34: "Is not this (i. e. the end) laid up in store with Me, sealed up in My treasures?" And Dan. 12.9: "For the words are shut up and sealed until the time of the end."

Troki devotes Chapter XXVI to refute those who, basing themselves on Jer. 17.4, claim that the present exile will last forever. This passage reads: "And I will cause thee to serve thine enemies in the land which thou knowest

[94] *Op. cit.*, p. 73.
[95] *Ibid.*

not; for ye kindled a fire in my nostrils which shall burn forever" (עד־עולם).

Troki contends that עולם is often used for an indefinite period, not necessarily for eternity, and quotes in proof the Christian scholar Martin Czechowic.

Chapter XXVII is an elaboration of Chapter VII. Troki meets the argument of those who declare that the Biblical promises of Redemption are contingent upon the merit of the people. Since Israel, however, has proved unworthy, those promises are now null and void. Troki agrees that the promises are conditional. "We do not believe that these good promises will come to us under any and all circumstances, even when we do that which is evil in the sight of God . . . but we trust that after we shall have turned to Him wholeheartedly, He, likewise, will turn to us . . . and fulfil the good promises which he made to his prophets. . . . All the prophets warned us that the good promises wait upon our repentance."[96] There are, however, certain prophecies which are clearly unconditional, in which God *swears* that the children of Israel will be redeemed.[97] This proves that the Redemption of Israel is absolutely certain. The exact hour, however, is known to God alone. Israel may hasten the day through repentance. When the appointed day arrives, God will redeem Israel, even if *all* the people are not altogether cleansed of all their sins, for God is merciful. "However, after those who remain shall have borne their punishment and atoned for their sins with the suffering of the exile, when the appointed end of the exile arrives, known to Him alone, even if they are not *altogether* meritorious, He will redeem them for the sake of His name."[98]

In his discussion of the prophecies of Daniel, and in his attempt to refute the claim of the Christians that Dan. 9.25–26 ("and after the three-score and two weeks shall an annointed one be cut off") refers to Jesus, Troki follows the arguments of Abarbanel very closely. In this instance

[96] *Ibid.*, pp. 175–176.

[97] E. g., Ezek. 36.7–12; Is. 54.9–10; Jer. 31.35–37.

[98] *Op. cit.*, pp. 184–185.

he mentions Abarbanel by name, as well as the latter's book, *The Wells of Salvation.*[99] Troki accepts all the figures which Abarbanel used in his calculations, but whereas the latter attempted to give a *terminus a quo,* Troki maintains that such a starting point was never revealed, not even to Daniel.[100]

19. *Isaac ben Samuel Adarbi* (16 c.), preacher in Salonica, devotes the last two of the twenty-nine sermons which comprise his *Dibre Shalom* to the subject of the Redemption. Adarbi was a pupil of Joseph Ṭaiṭazaḳ, the great Talmudic scholar, who fell under the spell of the Messianic preachments of Solomon Molko, when the latter visited him at Salonica. Adarbi's opposition to Messianic calculations may, therefore, be interpreted as a direct attack upon Molko and his followers. He maintains that the people may be redeemed at any time if they will repent: "Israel, even though they are in exile, and thick darkness is in their habitations, have it within their power to return to their former splendor at any time. . . . This (Redemption) does not require a specific time, only contrition of heart. For this there can be no set time. It can take place at any time."[101]

When Isaiah said, "Comfort ye, comfort ye my people," he used a transitive verb (נַחֲמוּ), and thereby implied that God was saying to Israel, "*Bring ye about your own comfort,* for everything is in your hands."[102] "The Redemption has no fixed hour. It can happen today if you will but hearken to His voice. Even today he can bring you the Redemption."[103]

20. *Moses Alshaikh* (second half of 16 c.) lived in Safed, the hotbed of Kabbala, and was the pupil of Joseph Caro and the teacher of Ḥayyim Vital, and yet his commentaries are singularly free from excessive mysticism. This is especially evidenced by his commentary on Daniel,

[99] *Ibid.,* p. 252.

[100] *Ibid.,* Chap. XLII.

[101] ולזה אין צריך זמן כי אם בהרהור הלב לבד בלי זמן ובכל מקום (see דברי שלום, ed. Warsaw, 1892, p. 263).

[102] *Ibid.,* p. 264.

[103] ואין לגאולה זו זמן מוגבל בהכרח (*ibid.,* p. 265).

Ḥabaẓelet ha-Sharon, printed in Safed in 1563. Here he does a remarkable thing. He deliberately refrains from commenting on the last two chapters of Daniel, for they are eschatological in character, avowedly cryptic, and thus beyond the grasp of human comprehension. "I tried, he declares in his Introduction, "to put forth my hand into the valley of the king (the latter part of the book), but I found that my hand could not grasp, and so I turned back (to the first part). I said to myself that the interpretation of the last words of Daniel belong to the Lord. And so I divided the book, part of it to the Lord, and part of it to me." The first part he calls the Rose of Sharon and the last part the lily of the valley (עמק = deep = hidden). No one can reach down to those depths.[104] The first part is quite clear and easily comprehended. The second part is sealed, seal within seal. As regards the visions of the end, no man knows his right hand from his left. That must wait until the coming of the Messiah.[105]

His son, R. Ḥayyim, bears testimony to his father's aversion for Messianic speculation and excessive Kabbalism in Biblical interpretations. He calls attention to the fact that his father refrained from commenting on the Chariot vision of Ezekiel for the same reason.[106]

Alshaikh seems to be aiming his shafts at the computers Abraham Halevi and Isaac Abarbanel. He was prompted to study the Book of Daniel more intensively, he writes, after the failure of the Messianic prophecies contained in the *Mashmia' Yeshu'ah and Ma'yene ha-Yeshu'ah* of Abarbanel, and in the *Mashre Ḳiṭrin* of Halevi.[107]

21. *Jacob ben Isaac Luzzato* (16 c.) another of the mystic group of Safed, author of *Kaftor we-Feraḥ*, devoted largely

[104] כי אין איש יגיע יראה מטה מטה ללקוט שושנים כי עמקו מאד עד אפס מקום.

[105] כי סתומים וחתומים הדברים חותמו חותם בתוך חותם כי לעת קץ החזון אשר לא ידע איש בין ימינו לשמאלו עד כי בא שי'לה ויקרא בגרון (see חבצלת השרון, ed. Venice, 1592, p. 2b.)

[106] See Moses Alshaikh's Commentary on Isaiah and Jeremiah, מראות הצובאות ed. Venice, 1605, end; also S. A. Rosanes, דברי ימי ישראל בתוגרמה, Husiatyn, 1913, Part III, pp. 210–212.

[107] והואיל משה באר ופשפש ולא מצא יאריך ירחיב למשרי קיטרין ויתורין וחסורי מחסרא. ומה גם עד אשר לא בא בן ישי משמיע ישועה במעיני הישועה ואתנה אל לבי לשום שכל והבין במקרא (*ibid.*).

to a defense of the many of the Agadot of the Talmud which were subjected to Christian condemnation, expressed himself strongly against Messianic computations. Commenting on the famous Agada of R. Jose, who met Elijah in one of the ruins around Jerusalem and from him learnt three things: the first of which was that we should not enter a ruin,[108] Luzzato writes: "There is an implication here that one should not enter upon a consideration of the reason for the long-deferred coming of the Messiah, and that one should not belong to them who calculated the end. Rather wait for him even if he is delayed."[109]

This outright proscription of calculation is surprising, coming from Jacob Luzzato, who edited and wrote an introduction to Molko's *Sefer ha-Mefo'ar* which contains a very definite Messianic calculation.[110]

22. *Judah Löw ben Bezalel* (d. 1609), Austrian Talmudist and preacher, around whom the "Golem" legends are built, devotes his entire book, "*Neẓaḥ Yisrael,*" to the Messiah saga. Because of its comprehensive scope and the thoroughness of its treatment of the Messianic idea, it must rank with Abarbanel's famous trilogy. It excels the latter in some regards. It is not at all concerned with Messianic divination or with the solution of the cryptic prophecies of the Bible. It deals broadly with the content of the Messiah idea and with its profound spiritual implications. It is less polemic and hortatory and more analytical and rational.

His main thesis is indicated in the title of the book, *The Eternity of Israel.* In the introduction he defines his purpose in writing this book "to establish that God bestowed eternal life upon Israel.[111] Israel is eternal because its existence is of God and in God. Israel by itself has no existence and no reality outside of God."[112] Israel is

[108] *Ber.* 3a.

[109] האחד שאין נכנסין לחורבא רמז שלא יכניס אדם מחשבתו לשאול טעם לאריכות ימי המשיח, גם שלא להיות ממחשבי קצין רק אם יתמהמה חכה לו (see כפתר ופרח, Basel, 1580, p. 6b).

[110] See ספר המפואר, ed. Cracow, 1570.

[111] נצח ישראל, p. 1b.

[112] *Ibid.*, 22a.

the essence and goal of all creations.[113] This should be taken literally not as a figure of speech.[114] "God cannot forsake Israel any more than Israel can permanently forsake God. They cannot be separated.[115] In exile God is still with Israel.[116] The exile was brought about by sin and is an atonement for sin. Israel suffered most because it should have sinned least of all peoples.[117] Suffering brings them nearer to God and assures them immortality."[118] Again, this mundane world[119] is not meant for Israel. His is the other, the spiritual world. Israel should not ask for material well-being here and now. One cannot feast at two tables.[120]

The exile itself is proof of ultimate Redemption.[121] Exile is an "unnatural" condition. The natural state is for each people to dwell on its own soil.[122] The condition being unnatural, it is only temporary. As day follows night Redemption must follow the exile.[123] Similarly, the natural condition is for the Temple to be built and not to lie in ruins.[124] The present condition of Israel and of the Temple is "a break in the order of the universe"[125] which must be mended. The logic of things demands it. Redemption is therefore inevitable.[126] Israel will be redeemed by the will of God only. The final Redemption will be unlike the Redemption from Egypt, which was due to the merit of the Fathers.[127] That is why the term of the end of this exile was not revealed. The end was not revealed, too, because of the nature of the particular sin

[113] ישראל הם עקר המציאות, p. 18a.
[114] *Ibid.*, p. 30d.
[115] אי אפשר שיהיה בטול החבור הזה, p. 22d.
[116] *Ibid.*, p. 18d.
[117] *Ibid.*, p. 23.
[118] אדרבה הפרעניות והצרות שבא עליהם הוא קיומם (*ibid.*, p. 25a).
[119] *Op. cit.*, p. 26a
[120] *Ibid.*, p. 25b.
[121] כי הגלות בעצמו הוא ראיה והוכחה ברורה על הגאולה.
[122] *Op. cit.*, pp. 21b, 17c.
[123] *Ibid.*, p. 40a.
[124] *Ibid.*, p. 34d.
[125] *Ibid.*, p. 35a.
[126] הגאולה היא הכרחית (*ibid.*, p. 42c).
[127] *Ibid.*, p. 23b.

which brought about this exile. It was jealousy—a "hidden" sin, unlike the sins which caused the former exiles, such as idolatry, incest and murder, which are "open" sins.[128]

One should not labor to discover the end. This is an attempt to forestall the will of God, for the very knowledge of the end already brings with it emancipation and freedom, which God does not wish the people to enjoy until the exile is completed.[129] Calculation of the end is an "edifice in which those who labor, labor in vain."[130] Even Jeremiah was not privileged to reveal the end. Whatever our sages may have said concerning the time of the end was said not as a certain and definite prognostication, but merely as an indication that the Messiah could not come before a certain time. Thus we were told that the Messiah will come within the last two millennia. He will not come before that time, but just when within that time we do not know. The end is one of the things which are hidden and cannot be revealed.[131] It is to be hoped that the end is near, for the age is beset with sin and suffering, which are the very foot-prints of the Messiah.[132] Judah Löw ingeniously remarks elsewhere in connection with his discussion of the relation of Redemption to the Messiah's coming, that the proclamation of the Jubilee year was fixed for Yom Kippur, for this form of Redemption (the freeing of the slaves), as well as every other form, is dependent upon repentance. Yom Kippur is meant to emancipate the soul, the Jubilee year the body.[133]

23. *Azariah Figo* (d. 1647), preacher at Venice, in his very popular collection of sermons, *Binah le'Ittim*, devotes four of his sermons to the subject of Redemption. They are his four discourses for the Sabbath of Consolation.

Figo speaks frequently of the peoples' unshaken faith in the coming of the Messiah in spite of the great length

[128] *Ibid.*, p. 6a; *cf. Yoma* 9b.
[129] *Ibid.*, p. 35c.
[130] *Ibid.*, p. 51a.
[131] *Ibid.*, p. 51c.
[132] *Ibid.*, p. 53a.
[133] See נתיבות עולם, ed. 1836, p. 73b.

of the exile: "In the former exiles it was not to be wondered at that the people remained steadfast in their hope and expectation, for they never lasted for many hundreds of years, and certainly never extended beyond a thousand years, but this exile in which the number has passed over a thousand years, it is an object of wonderment that they, the children of Israel, are still clinging to their hope and that they are not weakened, and that despair has not entered their hearts. Especially since there be those who use this (the great length of the exile) as the strongest argument against the hope of Redemption.[134] He applies himself zealously to the task of refuting the argument of those who deny the future Redemption of Israel, of those who claim that the Messianic promises of the Scriptures do not refer to Israel and of those who claim that these have but a spiritual significance, not to be taken literally.[135] Abarbanel, too, attacked those who, like Pablo de Santa Maria, attempted to *spiritualize* some Messianic passages.[136] Christian apologists felt constrained to interpret "spiritually" those Messianic promises of the Bible which were not fulfilled with the coming of Jesus. Paulus devotes the fourth and fifth parts of his *Dialogue* to this task.[137]

Figo comforts his people. After the long delay Redemption is sure to come. Their very suffering which has come to pass according to the prophecy should be indicative of the great joy which awaits them, also according to the prophecy.[138] Why does God delay it so long? One might as well ask why did God create the world on a certain day and not before or after? It is His will. We cannot understand it: "Why do you sin and inquire concerning the Messianic times, saying 'Why do their feet linger'? Why don't you ask concerning the first days of

[134] בינה לעתים, ed. Warsaw, 1866, p. 53a; see also pp. 56b and 58c.

[135] *Ibid.*, pp. 56b and 57a.

[136] לא כפי דרך חכמי א"ה בגאולתם הרוחנית (see משמיע ישועה, p. 41a).

[137] Thus the thesis of the third chapter of the fourth part is: "ut per terram Israhel et Jherusalem et templum dei ubi prophete dicunt congregandos fore omnes Israhelitas, intelligendum est de celesti beatitudine in qua sancti spiritualiter congregantur."

[138] *Op. cit.*, pp. 56b–57a.

Creation? Why were they not earlier? From this (argument) you can learn how deep are the thoughts of the Omniscient, for He alone apprehends the true end.[139]

The sins of Israel are responsible in a large measure for the long delay: "For the postponement of the end and the continuation of the exile, we ourselves are responsible."[140] Figo specifically mentions three of these major sins which delay the end: (1) Contention, strife and hatred, which are widespread in our midst. (2) Failure to realize the purpose of the exile, which is to teach us humility and discipline. We do not seem to feel the exile. We do not regard ourselves as slaves far removed from all the pleasures of life and from high position. . . . We seem to have fulfilled in exile the saying, "All Israel are sons of kings"; our houses are filled with all good things; we and our sons and daughters dress in silks and ornaments like the nobility, and we bring to our table royal delicacies like Solomon in all his pomp, just like in the time of our prosperity when we lacked nothing."[141] (3). Immorality.[142]

24. *Leon de Modena* (1571–1648), the most outspoken and relentless opponent of Kabbala in his day, in his classic polemic *Ari Nohem* does not directly attack the Messianic calculators, but in exposing the whole technique of Kabbalistic speculation, which, in his day, was largely based on arithmetical and alphabetic mysticism, deals a severe blow to the whole enterprise. Having demonstrated that Kabbala is neither a science nor an authoritative tradition,[143] he proceeds by logic and ridicule to expose its preposterous technique. Kabbala, itself based on untenable postulates, attempts to prove these postulates by methods equally unsound:

"Their method is as follows: they seek to find proof for their ideas in the Bible by means of substituted words Names, Gematria, Notarikon, Ẓiruf and Ḥilufim. All these methods are postulates, arbitrary assumptions and

[139] כי הוא לבדו מחשב הקץ האמתי (*ibid.*, p. 58c).

[140] *Op. cit.*, p. 42a.

[141] *Ibid.*, p. 43a.

[142] *Ibid.*, pp. 43b–44b.

[143] ארי נוהם, ed. Fürst, 1890, Chaps. IV–V.

pure inventions. It is by way of fitting the foot to the shoe or fashioning a shoe into which any foot can go.[144] Anyone may discover anything he wishes by such means and prove any falsehood and any outlandish notion. Such methods may be employed to prove and disprove one and the same thing.

How heavily this attack bears upon Messianic calculations becomes clear when one realizes how largely dependent that pseudo-science was upon the technique of Gematria in all its ramifications.

25. *Simeon Luzzato* (d. 1663), the friend of Leon Modena, unequivocally asserts his opposition to construing the prophecies of Daniel so as to make them apply to the present exile. He belongs to the historico-scientific group of Biblical interpreters. "It is apparent that Luzzato was a thinker and a believer as well; he did not share Manasseh ben Israel's dream that the Ten Tribes still exist together in some part of the world. He maintained that Daniel's revelation refers not to a future Messiah but to past historical events."[145]

26. *Solomon Ephraim of Łęczyca* (d. 1619), preacher at Prague, whose book of sermons, *Sifte Da'at*, printed in Prague, carries the date in its colophon י'ב'א' מ'ש'י'ח' (= 1610–11), "May the Messiah Come," devotes much space to the subject of Redemption. He believes firmly that there is a fixed time for the coming of the Messiah. The merit of the generation may hasten his advent, but the sins, even if universal, will not postpone it beyond the appointed hour.[146]

Elaborating upon the Rabbinic saying that Jacob wished to reveal the future to his children, but it was suddenly withdrawn from him, he says that great harm might be caused by revealing the time of the end, for the men who would know that the Messiah would not appear in their lifetime would not pray to God for His coming, and the men who would know that the Messiah would come in

[144] *Ibid.*, p. 24.
[145] *J. E.*, VIII, p. 227.
[146] שפתי דעת, ed. Prague, p. 94a.

their lifetime would not find it necessary to pray for him. This is exactly what happened in Egypt when the exact duration of the exile was made known. Those living in the years prior to the fixed time of the Exodus made themselves thoroughly at home in Egypt and built for themselves beautiful and permanent homes, as if the Messiah would never come, even as some Jews are doing today.[147] God desires His children to turn to him in prayer and repentance. The revelation of the end would render this impossible.

The author follows closely the reasoning of Isaac Arama[148] whom he quotes on this subject.[149] In his *'Ir Gibborim* the author sums up his position in the form of a clear prohibition: "It is forbidden to search and inquire after the coming of the redeemer . . . for if he does not appear at the expected time the people will despair of him. The matter does not depend upon calculation but upon repentance and good deeds."[150]

27. *Manasseh ben Israel* was opposed to Messianic calculations. In his Mikweh Yisrael[151] he writes: "It is given to none to know the time thereof (the Return), neither is it revealed to Rabbi Simeon ben Johay, the author of the *Zohar:* because that God hath reserved that mystery to himself, as Moses saith, 'It is hid with me.' And Isaiah in chapter 63.4. 'For the day of vengeance is in my heart, and the year in which the redemption shall come.' Which the Rabbins thus interpret, 'I have revealed it to my heart and not to angels'; and elsewhere, 'If any man tell you when Messiah shall come, believe him not.' So also the angel saith to Daniel, chap. 12.9, 'All things are closed up and sealed to the time of the end.' Therefore all those, who search after that time, as Rabbi Seadiah, Moses Egyptius (Maimonides), Moses Gerundensis (Naḥ-

147 *Ibid.*, p. 27c, d.

148 See *supra*, p. 220.

149 See his כלי יקר on Par. ויחי in the מקראות גדולות, ed. Warsaw, p. 258.

150 עיר גבורים, ed. 1580, p. 28a.

151 Spanish, Amsterdam, 1650; English, London, 1650, trans. Moses Wall, third ed. 1652. This last edition, printed in Lucien Wolf's *Manasseh ben Israel's Mission to Oliver Cromwell*, London, 1901, is quoted here.

manides), Selomoh Jarchi; Abraham bar Ribi Hijah, Abraham Zecculo (Ab. Zaccuto) Mordehai Reato (Mor. Dato), and Isaac Abarhanel, have been mistaken; for that they would go beyond human capacity, and reveal that which God concealed. And even to Daniel himself (to whom was made known the secret of the change of the four Monarchies) it was so revealed to him, that he confessed he did not understand it. Our Ancients did point at this from the letter (m) in Is. 9.7 where he saith 'Of the increase of his government:' which (m) in the Hebrew, being such an (m) which they write only in the end of words, and a closed letter, yet is put in the middle of the word, against common practice; because that the time of the fifth Monarchy shall be hid, till the time when it shall begin."[152]

This probably accounts for the fact that Manasseh does not even attempt to harmonize the conflicting apocalyptic passages of Daniel in his *Conciliator*.

28. *Moses ben Menaḥem* (Präger, end 17 c.), author of two Kabbalistic works, *Wa-Yaḳhel Moshe* (a treatise on the *Zohar* in the style of the Lurianic Kabbala), and *Zera' Ḳodesh*, states in his Introduction to the former work that his purpose in writing the book is to hasten the day of the coming of the Messiah by means of popularizing among Israel those Messianic teachings of the Kabbala which are potent enough to effect the advent. He believed with the earlier Kabbalists that the study of *Zohar* was of sufficient merit to bring about the Redemption:[153] "The sin of not knowing the true (Kabbalistic) method of praying is sufficient to delay the days of the Messiah, the rebuilding of the Temple and the ingathering of the people."[154] He was convinced that Israel would never leave the exile unless it studied Kabbala.[155]

He, nevertheless, bitterly denounced those charlatans who, using the art of Gematria and Notarikon, delude

[152] *Ibid.*, Sect. XXVIII, p. 45.

[153] ויקהל משה, ed. Dessau, 1699, p. 7c.

[154] *Ibid.*, p. 4b.

[155] ואין אנו יכולים למיפק מגלות אלא בלימוד הזה (*ibid.*, p. 11b).

the masses with fictitious promises which they received neither from the earlier nor from the later Kabbalists. These men dare to reveal the future and calculate the end and confuse and mislead the people. Concerning them and their kind the prophet said, "They have seen vanity and lying divination."[156] They make a living out of it. Their lying prophecies have more than once thrown the people into terrible confusion and despondency."[157]

Moses ben Menaḥem undoubtedly refers to the Shabbetai Zebi fiasco, and his sentiments may be taken to represent the reaction which set in after the tragic collapse of the Shabbetian movement, which was so largely built upon the extensive Messianic calculations of the seventeenth century. The opinion of this Rabbi is highly important. He was an extreme Kabbalist of the Lurianic school. Through Kabbalistic incantation he is credited with having exorcised an evil spirit from a lad in Nikolsburg.[158] He regarded Luria as being higher than an angel, and as having revealed more truth than any prophet in Israel.[159] and yet he so vehemently attacked the whole adventist enterprise. Evidently the Shabbetian affair had sobered the minds even of some of the most extreme Kabbalists.

[156] Ezek. 13.6.
[157] *Op. cit.*, p. 16.
[158] See מעשה ה' כי נורא הוא, App. to זרע קדש, ed. Fürth, 1696.
[159] ויקהל משה, p. 7a.

Part III

METHODOLOGY

CHAPTER X

THE FIVE METHODS

Messianic calculators may be said to have employed five methods in their technique.

A. The Book of Daniel

The most common and the earliest was to decipher the specific dates given in the Book of Daniel. As early as the first century, men were already engaged in this work. The Book of Daniel gives at least six Messianic dates:[1] (1) time, times and half a time, (2) 2300, (3) 70 weeks (also 7 weeks, 62 weeks and 1 week), (4) season, seasons and half a season, (5) 1290 days, (6) 1335 days. These were challenging and tantalizing figures. What were the terminals of these cryptic dates? Surely they cannot be mutually exclusive. They must all be graded historical moments in the great drama of Israel's Redemption leading up to the ultimate Messianic day. Do the days mean years? Do the weeks mean seven years? How long is "time"? Is "times" the same as "seasons"? Is "time, times and half a time" equal to two and a half, or three and a half times? Were there perhaps more than one Redemption year given, dependent upon the merit of the people? What are the four kingdoms and the four beasts? And who is "the little horn"? And who is the king of the South and the king of the North, and all the other persons and powers alluded to in the revelations? Above all, what is the starting point from which all these periods of time are to be reckoned? These and numerous other questions presented themselves to those who embarked upon the fascinating enterprise of unraveling the great mystery.

[1] See *supra*, p. 124.

B. Other Biblical Texts

A second method was to determine from Scriptural passages (other than those of Daniel), phrases or words, especially those alluding to the future and redolent of promise, the length of the Messianic age, and to fix upon a certain important moment in the history of the people as the starting point from which to reckon this age. Many such *termini a quo* were fixed upon by the calculators through the ages.

C. Other Exiles

The third method was to turn to the earlier exiles, the Egyptian and the Babylonian, and from their duration and attendant circumstances learn the secret of the third exile. Clearly there was some divine logic in fixing the term of the Egyptian exile to 400 (also 210 and 430) years, and that of the Babylonian to 70 (also 52) years. A similar logic undoubtedly controls the duration of this last exile. What is it?

D. Gematria

One of the most fruitful methods employed by Jewish adventists in their calculations was Gematria (the interpretation of a word according to the numerical value of its letters), and its related pseudo-sciences, Notarikon (taking each letter of a word as the initial of some other word=acrostics), Ẓiruf or Ḥiluf (the interpretation of a word by transposing its letters=anagram), and Temurah (substituting one letter for another). Gematria was a never-failing medium and its scope was limited only by the ingenuity of the speculator.

It was a time-honored device, and the medieval student had ample authority for employing it. R. Eliezer ben Jose, the Galilean (second half of 2 c.), had included Gematria among the thirty-two hermeneutic rules by which the Torah may be interpreted. R. Yoḥanan ben Zakkai studied Gematria.[2] This device was actually used

[2] *B. B.*, p. 134a.

in connection with redemption from exile—in this case the Egyptian exile. R. Abba bar Kahana interpreted the word[3] רדו as indicating the number of years (210, in Gematria) which the children of Israel would remain in Egypt.[4] R. Levi pointed out that the word בזאת[5] indicated the length of the duration of the first Temple, 410 years.[6] It is of interest that both of these Gematriot were frequently used by later calculators.

R. Yoḥanan, quoting R. Jose ben Zimra, proved that Notarikon is found in the Torah.[7] There are close to a hundred and fifty cases of Gematria in Talmudic literature.

The science of Ẓiruf was employed in discovering the will of God through the Urim and Tumim. R. Yoḥanan declared that the answer to the High Priests' query was given by the letters thrusting themselves upward. Resh Lakish said by the automatic combinations of the letters.[8]

That number mysticism was also employed by the early Christians in connection with the Messiah is evident by the sharp and lengthy criticism which Irenaeus (2 c.) directs against it.[9]

Under the influence of Kabbala this science was highly developed and elaborated in post-Talmudic times. The *Sefer Yeẓirah*, the *Otiot de R. Akiba* and many other treatises on alphabetic theosophy gave great impetus to Gematria. The *Sefer Yeẓirah* declared, "By means of 32 mysterious paths of wisdom did the Lord of hosts . . . ordain and create his universe" (i. e. the 22 letters, plus 10 sefirot, or vowels).[10] "The 22 fundamental letters God appointed, established, combined, weighed and changed them, and through them He formed all things existent and

[3] Gen. 42.2.

[4] *Ber. R.* 91.2.

[5] Lev. 16.3: בזאת יבא אהרן.

[6] *Lev. R.* 21.8.

[7] *Sab.* 105a: מנין ללשון נוטריקון מן התורה; see also the six Notarikons given in that passage.

[8] כיצד נעשית: רבי יוחנן אומר בולטות. ריש לקיש אומר מצטרפות (*Yoma* 73b).

[9] "Against Heresies," Bk. II, Chaps. XXIV–XXV in *The Ante-Nicene Fathers*, I.

[10] *Op. cit.*, 1.1.

destined to exist.[11] The planetary system, the Zodiac, the days of the week, the organs of the human body and all the moral qualities were fashioned by the aid of the basic alphabet. Similarly, the *Otiot de R. Akiba* declared, "R. Akiba said: 'the 22 letters by which the Torah was given to Israel are engraved with a flaming pen upon the fearful and awful crown of God; and when God wished to create the universe, all the letters descended and stood before God, and each one said, 'Through me create thou the universe.'"[12]

Letter mysticism made tremendous strides during the Middle Ages. Hardly a Biblical commentary outside the classic Spanish school but what employed alphabetic metaphysics on a smaller or larger scale. In the thirteenth century Abulafia maintained that letters, vowels and numerals are the highest subjects of speculation, and their mystic interpretation the profoundest tradition of the prophets.[13] In the sixteenth century Cordovero declared that the letters have their source in God and from Him they emanate as very light spirits and descend in successive stages until their pilgrimage is ended.[14] The vowels have even a higher mystic value.[15] Likewise are the accents of supreme mystic import. They belong to the very source of the first sefirah. Cordovero characterizes the letters as persons (נפשות), the vowels as powers (כחות), and the accents as souls (נשמות).[16] In the *Tikkune ha-Zohar*, one of the Zoharitic compositions, it is stated that the accents are the souls (נשמתין), the vowels are the spirits (רוחין) and the letters are the persons (נפשות).[17] This is an interesting application of the doctrine of the three souls, sensuous, emotional and intellectual, of the Platonic system. The *Sefer ha-Bahir*, a pre-Zoharitic Kabbalistic

[11] *Ibid.*, 2.2; 6.9.

[12] מדרש אותיות דרבי עקיבא, Cracow and Amsterdam version, ed. Wertheimer, Jerusalem, 1914, p. 59.

[13] See ספר האות, App., p. 86.

[14] שיעור קומה, ed. Warsaw, 1885, p. 169a.

[15] *Ibid.*, p. 174b.

[16] *Ibid.*, p. 175a.

[17] תקוני הזהר, ed. Amsterdam, 1719, Intro., p. 7b.

text book, declared that the vowels are like the soul which lives in the body of a man.[18]

The true interpretation of the Torah, declared Cordovero, can be had only through the medium of letter mysticism in all its endless ramfications: "We can arrive at a knowledge of the secrets of our Holy Torah, by means of anagrams, Gematriot, substitutions, initial, middle and final letters, the beginning or ends of verses, skipping of letters and the contraction of letters. These matters are very exalted and occult, and their secret is beyond our full comprehension, for by means of these methods they may change endlessly and to infinity."[19]

David ben Solomon ibn Abi Zimra (1479–1589), teacher of Isaac Luria and author of a work on the mystic significance of the alphabet, accurately sums up the nigh universally accepted belief of the Middle Ages regarding the sanctity of the letters of the Hebrew alphabet. He quotes approvingly and substantiates Maimonides' opinion that "The script which we now employ is the Assyrian script,[20] and that it is the script in which God wrote the Torah."[21] "This is the script," writes the Radbaz, "in which the Torah and the Tables were given; and all the secrets of their forms, their flourishes and their crownlets, majuscular letters and minuscular, crooked and looped, bent and straight, and all their intimations and mysteries were revealed to Moses, just like all the rest of the oral law, and this script has a sanctity all of its own." והוא הכתב שיש בו קדושה מצד עצמו[22] So also Abraham Portaleone, the physician (d. 1612), writes in his שלטי הגבורים[23]: והנה זה משלמות התורה ומהרמזים הצפונים באותיותיה כי על כן באו בתורה אותיות הפוכות ותלויות וכן עקומות ומלופפות וכן גדולות וקטנות וכן מנומרות ומנוקרות כי יתגלו מתוכן חמשים שערי בינה שנגלו לו למשה. As late as the year 1863 Aaron Kornfeld wrote a book, ציונים לדברי הקבלה in which he catalogues over

[18] ודמיין באתוותא לנשמתא דחיי בגופא דאינשא (see ספר הבהיר, ed. Wilna, 1883, p. 23).

[19] ספר פרדס רמונים, ed. Koretz, 1780–1, Gate 30, p. 176b.

[20] כתב אשורי as against כתב עברי.

[21] *Yadayim* 4.5.

[22] מגן דוד, ed. Amsterdam, 1713, end of Intro.

[23] Ed. Mantua, 1613, p. 174a.

300 Rabbinic laws and interpretations derived *per Gematriam* from Biblical verses. He maintains that God in writing the Torah had intended that these verses should lend themselves to such use if for no other reason than as an aid to man's memory.[24]

ולסבה הזאת אין רחוק לומר כי ה׳ יתבר׳ בכתבו התורה כוון גם לזה למען יועיל לחרותם בזכרון לבלתי ישכח כל כך מהרה.

The Radbaz calls his book מגן דוד, because מ׳ג׳ן׳ suggests the three ways by which he intends to interpret every letter: מסורת (traditional sound and form of the letter), גימטריא (numerical value), and נוטריקון (initials).[25] "God is the whiteness of the parchment which underlies, penetrates and supports the letters of the alphabet."[26]

The Neo-Platonic influence which is strong in Kabbala, and which had incorporated the Pythagorean science of numbers and letters, gave to Jewish mysticism a strong impetus in this direction, although the origin of it need not be sought, as we have seen, outside of Jewish thought. It was well developed among the Rabbis of the early centuries of the common era, but whereas among the Rabbis this study was regarded as פרפראות לחכמה, mere after-courses to wisdom,[27] among the Kabbalists in the decadent period it had suplanted חכמה herself.

As regards this method of computing the end the Jewish adventists had a great advantage over the Christian. The latter, in their speculations, were limited to those passages in the Old and the New Testaments which contained clear Messianic references, where specific dates and figures are given, such as those of Daniel and Revelations. Few of them had access to the original Hebrew of the Old Testament. The Old Testament was known to them largely in the Latin translation, and the New in its Greek original, or in its Latin translation. They could not, by means of the highly elastic art of Gematria, force a secret from any passage they chose. The science of Anagram

[24] Ed. Prague, 1865, Intro.
[25] *Op. cit.*, p. 1a.
[26] *Ibid.*, p. 1b
[27] *Abot* 3.23.

and Gematria was, of course, known to them, but they were limited to the use of a language which was not "the language of God." The Jewish adventist was in possession of the divine speech itself. To him Hebrew was the language of God actually, not figuratively. To him the phrase, "by the word of God were the heavens created," was more than a figure of speech. The "word" was made up of letters and vowels. These letters and vowels were Hebrew letters and vowels—the twenty-two letters of the alphabet and the ten vowels. Not alone were words channels of revelation, but every letter of the Bible and every vowel held a profound mystery. Not alone did each word possess a literal meaning (פשט), an allegoric meaning (רמז), an homiletic meaning (דרוש) and an anagogic meaning (סוד), but the very letters of the word and their permutations, combinations and numerical value contained recondite truth—had, as it were, marvelous halftones and overtones. Not alone were the Biblical laws and teachings divine, but the very words which expressed them had a divinity of their own and a meaning of their own. Cordovero gives the most complete exposition of the spiritual autonomy of the Hebrew alphabet. It is altogether unlike the alphabet of any other language. All other alphabets are the formal and inert channels of thought. The Hebrew alphabet is thought itself. When a doctor writes a medical treatise his object is to suggest some cure. He does not intend to make *the book itself* a cure. When his thought is once grasped there is no more need for the book. Not so the Torah. It has an inviolable sanctity beyond the ideas which it conveys. So that even an ignorant man reading it without understanding is greatly benefited. The surface narratives and chronicles of the Torah, says Cordovero, elaborating upon a theme of the *Zohar*,[28] are only the outer garment (לבוש עליון), the legal and Aggadic interpretations of it are the body (גופא), the Kabbalistic interpretation of it is the soul (נשמה), but the mystic interpretation of its letters, their permuta-

[28] Par. בהעלותך, p. 152a.

tions and combinations, is the real spiritual essence of it (רוחניות), the knowledge of which would enable a man to create worlds.[29]

Every letter was a visible revelation of invisible truth. The Rabbis had already employed words and part of words in their hermeneutics and dialectics to expound the law and to develop it, as well as in their Aggadic peregrinations. The mystic employed the same strategy in his excursions. The letter never restrained him. On the contrary, he moved bravely on to his destination on a vehicle which always responded to his will.

This may perhaps account for the fact that the Jewish mystic seldom, if ever, found himself in direct opposition to the "written word." We find no Jewish mystic who attacked the Bible, but many of the Christian mystics fretted under the constraint of the "letter which killeth." The Jewish mystic could find his complete freedom in the Bible, for by means of his highly refined methodology the very letters dissolved into a world of spirituality. Spiritual autonomy, which is the very life-blood of mysticism, drove the Christian mystic away from the Book. It drove the Jewish mystic *into* the Book. Rufus Jones, in outlining Sebastian Franck's (16 c.) attitude to the Scriptures, accurately sums up the essential viewpoint of many of the Christian mystics: "Franck insists that from its inherent nature, a written Scripture cannot be the final authority in religion: (a) it is outward, external, while the seat of religion is in the soul of man; (b) it is transitory and shifting, for language is always in the process of change, and written words have different meanings to different ages and in different countries . . .; (c) the Scripture is full of mystery, contradiction and paradox, which only 'the key of David'—the inner experience of the heart, can unlock . . .; and (d) Scripture at best brings only knowledge."[30]

The Jewish mystic, however, said הפך בה והפך בה דכלא בה "Turn it about and about, for *everything* is in it". To

[29] פרדס רמונים, p. 167a, b, c.

[30] *Spiritual Reformers in the 16th and 17th Centuries*, p. 60.

the Christian mystic the Book was at best a temporary guide, a pedagogic help, a shadow of reality. To the Jewish mystic it was the *whole of reality.* It was the Living Word.

Jewish mysticism in general based its authority not upon vision or revelation, but upon an inspired and occult interpretation of the words of the Bible. When the Jewish adventist, therefore, sought the key to the solution of his problems, he felt free to go to any passage in the Bible, to the words or letters of any sacred text, which to him seemed freighted with mystery and prophetic of marvelous matter.

The rôle which Gematria played in Messianic calculations cannot be overestimated. Especially was it of importance in the seventeenth century and in the Shabbetian movement. It is astounding to see how often the weapons which were employed by the opposing sides in the Shabbetian controversy were those of Gematria.

Rabbi Joshua Neneto, of Alexandria, writing to the community of Leghorn, points to the numerous passages in the Bible which, *per Gematriam,* clearly establish the Messiahship of Shabbetai Ẓebi. He states that these passages are almost endless, and that they are sufficient and valid proof.[31] This view was shared by all the adherents of Shabbetai Ẓebi. They pointed with conviction to the fact that the name of Shabbetai Ẓebi, שבתי צבי was equal to the name of God, שדי taken in its integrated form: ש'י'ן ד'ל'ת' י'ו'ד'=814.[32] It is also equal to ו'ש'נ'ת' ג'א'ו'ל'י' ב'א'ה' =814 ("And my year of redemption is come").[33] Ẓebi (צבי) is also the Notarikon of צ'דיק ב'אמונתו י'חיה ("the righteous shall live by his faith").[34]

[31] ומצאנו בתורה נביאים וכתובים פסוקים נרמזים על שמו לאין חקר ולאין מספר (see קיצור צנ"צ, p. 25).

[32] *Ibid.*

[33] Is. 63.4. Emden's תורת הקנאות, ed. Lemberg, 1870, Chap. XVI, and Cahana's תולדות השבתאים והחסידים, p. 96.

[34] Hab. 2.4. There is another Notarikon for שבתי צבי in Ezek. 20.15: הביא אותם אל הארץ אשר נתתי' זבת' חלב' ודבש' צ'ב'י' (see A. Freimann, עניני שבתי צבי, p. 98; also the elaborate Notarikon built upon the two verses in Gen. 41.1, 2. ויהי מקץ שנתים, reprinted in Cahana's תולדות הש' והח', App. IV, pp. 142–3.)

The opponents countered by pointing out that שבתי צבי is equal to י'ו'ד'ע' צ'י'ד' א'י'ש ש'ד'ה' ("And he (Esau) was a cunning hunter, a man of the field").[35] Also that שבתי is equal to ב'ל'ע'ם' ר'ש'ע' = Balaam, the wicked. Also that שבתי צבי is equal to עמלק הרשע = Amalek the wicked, and ר'ו'ח' ש'ק'ר' = the lying spirit.[36]

The year of Shabbetai Ẓebi's revelation was also established by Gematria. It was based on the Zoharitic Messianic year 1648, which in turn was based on the verse בשנת היובל הזאת תשובו = 5408 = 1648 ("In this year of the Jubilee shall ye return").[37] This was the year when Shabbetai Ẓebi first began to reveal his true character to his disciples in Smyrna. It was in the eighth year of the Jubilee cycle. Within the remaining 42 years of that cycle, i. e. up to 1690, the restoration must take place. The year 1666, when Shabbetai again made public avowal of his Messiahship, was indicated in ישראל נ'ו'ש'ע' בה' = 1666 ("O, Israel, thou art saved by the Lord").[38] Nathan of Gaza proclaimed that the restoration will take place before the year 5430 = 1670.[39] When this year did not bring about the promised Redemption, the disciples found Gematria for other years: 1675, 1680, 1686, 1692, 1706, 1710.[40]

The extensive use of secret Gematria codes in the charms and amulets of the eighteenth century, coupling the name of Shabbetai Ẓebi with that of God, was responsible for the prolonged and bitter Emden-Eybeschütz controversy.

This method, of course, was not unopposed. There were many who sensed the menace of such a free and

[35] Gen. 25.27.

[36] קיצור, צנ"צ, pp. 63, 65–66.

[37] Lev. 25.13.

[38] Is. 45.17, קיצור צנ"צ, p. 13a.

[39] A Gematria was discovered for that year, too. כמגדל דוד צוארך בנוי לתלפיות אלף המגן תלוי עליו כל שלטי הגבורים ("Thy neck is like the Tower of David, builded with turrets, whereon there hang a thousand shields, all the armor of the mighty men," Songs of Songs, 4.4). The Tower of David is Shabbetai Ẓebi—The Messiah ben David—who will rebuild the Temple in the year (פיות) ה'ת'ל' = 5430 = 1670, according to the testimony (לתל) פ'י'ו'ת' of Nathan the Prophet, in the fifth millennium אלף ה'מגן (קיצור צנ"צ p. 8).

[40] See קיצור צ"צ, pp. 73, 77, 83; also ספר מריבת קדש in עניני שבתי צבי, pp. 12, 37.

undisciplined reading of sacred text. Maimonides, for example, was strongly opposed to the whole system of alphabetic theosophy. In his *Guide* he writes: "You must beware of sharing the error of those who write amulets. Whatever you hear from them or read in their works, especially in reference to the names which they form by combinations, is utterly senseless; they call these combinations "shemot" (names—combinations of the letters of the Tetragrammaton), and believe that their pronunciation demands sanctification and purification, and that by using them they are enabled to work miracles. Rational persons ought not to listen to such men, nor in any way believe their assertions."[41] There were many others who shared Maimonides' view. We have also seen the vigorous onslaught upon this pseudo-science by Modena. In spite of them this pseudo-science progressed unchecked in Jewry.

E. Astrology

Astrology was another means of Messianic calculation. It, too, was well grounded in Jewish tradition. We might with safety assume that already in their nomadic period the tribes of Israel, like almost all Semitic peoples, had developed some crude astrological system. The nomadic Hebrew undoubtedly shared in the pan-vitalistic supposition of primitive man. And this would inevitably result in ascribing life and conscious existence to the heavenly bodies. Under Canaanitish and Assyrian influence astral worship as well as astrology developed in Israel, for wherever there is worship of heavenly bodies there is also astral divination, i. e. astrology. The historical books of the Bible abound in references to this form of idolatry. In the period of the prophets the worship of the "host of heaven" was prevalent in Israel, and the prophets from Amos down exerted themselves to the utmost to suppress it. Amos and Isaiah denounced it.[42] Zephaniah and

[41] *Guide For the Perplexed*, Friedlander, London, 1910, Bk. I, Chap. LXI, p. 91.

[42] Amos 5.26; Is. 17.8.

Jeremiah inveighed against it.[43] Deuteronomy is strenuous in its opposition.[44] It is doubtful whether the Deuteronomic reformation succeeded in putting even a temporary check upon this idolatry. Deutero-Isaiah indirectly wages war upon it by insisting that Yahweh is the sole creator and Lord of all the hosts of heaven.[45] Job speaks of the sinfulness of it.[46] The worship in some form or another survived throughout post-exilic times and traces of it are found in very late Talmudic sources.

The official religion, under prophetic impetus, began quite early to oppose astrological divination. Occasionally, however, even in the Bible the predictive powers of the heavenly bodies are acknowledged. Thus in Gen. 1.14 it is declared: "And they (the sun, moon and stars) shall be for *signs* and for seasons." But as a rule the official religion frowned upon it, and at times vigorously opposed it. It compromised with the principle of monotheism, and it endangered the doctrine of free will and moral responsibility. Herein Judaism moved in advance of all the other religions of antiquity, which never outgrew it. Judaism, in keeping with its practice of ascribing to all forms of Israelitish idolatry a foreign nativity, branded astrology "a custom of the heathen." Thus Jeremiah urges upon the people, "be not afraid of the signs of the heavens," and calls it "the way of the heathen."[47] Judaism did not deny astral influences as such. It simply denied their efficacy in the case of Israel. Israel, being God's own people, was beyond the control of stars or planets. This was also the position taken in subsequent times. Abraham, the Rabbis held, employed astrology until he was favored with a revelation from Yahweh. With it came the command, "Forsake astrology."[48]

When the Christian Church in the early centuries was

[43] Zeph. 1.5; Jer. 7.18; 8.2; 19.15; 32.29.

[44] Deut. 1.19; 17.13.

[45] Is. 40.26; 45.12.

[46] Job. 31.26–7.

[47] Jer. 10.2.

[48] צא מאצטגנינות שלך (*Ber. R.* 44.14; *Sab.* 156a). See Philo *Migration of Abraham* XXXII; *Dreams* X; also Halevi, *Kuzari* 4.27.

confronted with the need of opposing astrology, it adopted a similar strategy. In the face of what seemed to be overwhelming evidence for astrology, it contented itself with declaring that astrology was the particular domain of the devil and other evil spirits, and that with the coming of Christ all astrological divination was prohibited. Thus Tertullian wrote: "One proposition I lay down: that those angels, the deserters from God, the lovers of women, were likewise the discoverers of this curious art (astrology), on that account also condemned by God. . . . But, however, that science has been allowed until the Gospel, in order that after Christ's birth no one should thenceforward interpret anyone's nativity by the heaven."[49]

The Sibylline Book III counts it among the virtues of "the race of most righteous men," the Jews, that they do not study the predictions of Chaldaean astrology, nor do they astronomize, for all these things are in their nature prone to deceive."[50] According to Enoch the evil spirit Baraquijal taught men astrology, and Kokabel the constellation.[51] But while the official religion proscribed it, the popular religion retained it.

The practice of forecasting the future by means of heavenly bodies was therefore not new in Israel. It gained widespread recognition among the people in the early centuries of the common era through Graeco-Roman influence. The thought of the Mediterranean world was thoroughly saturated with this pseudo-science, and its finest minds, such as Pliny, Seneca, Ptolemy, Galen, Plutarch, Lucian and many others believed in it and expounded it. Above all, it was universally accepted and practiced by the masses of the people of the Mediterranean world, and it was approved by the official religions of the day.

In spite of occasional expressions of opposition to astrology found in the Talmud and the Midrash, such as

[49] *On Idolatry*, chap. 9.
[50] The Sibylline Books III, l. 227–8.
[51] Book of Enoch 8.3.

"There are no planets for Israel,"[52] and "One must not consult Chaldeans," (astrologers)[53], the preponderately favorable allusions prove conclusively that it was widely held and practiced in Israel. Some Rabbis, like Samuel (3 c.), may have practiced it in their leisure time, when they were not engaged in the study of the Torah, and may have scrupulously refrained from combining the two studies.[54] But it is clear from statements such as the following that this science had a strong hold over the minds even of some of the leaders of the people. R. Simon said, "There isn't a blade of grass which has not a planet in the heavens which strikes it and commands it to grow."[55] Raba (4 c.) declared, "Life, offspring and sustenance do not depend upon merit but upon the planets."[56] Elsewhere in the Talmud we find quite an elaborate account of natal astrology.[57] as well as the categoric assertion of R. Ḥanina that "the planet makes a man wise and the planet makes a man rich, and there is a planet governing the fortunes of Israel." That certain constellations are good and certain others are evil[58] and that each nation is under the sovereignty of a particular star was widely held.[59] Both Philo and Josephus believed in some form of astrology. It is noteworthy, however, that we find in Talmudic literature no *Messianic calculation* based on astrology.

But it was in the Middle Ages under Arabic influence that the belief in astrology among the Jews became well-nigh universal. The Arabs appropriated the whole astrological gallery of the Graeco-Roman world and added thereto. Jews and Christians alike were their eager disciples. A perusal of the list of translations of astrological works made by the Jews of the Middle Ages, will

[52] אין מזל לישראל (*Sab.* 156a).
[53] אין שואלים בכלדיים (*Pes.* 113b).
[54] *Deut. R.* 8.6.
[55] *Gen. R.* 10.7.
[56] *Mo'ed Ḳat.* 28a.
[57] *Sab.* 156a.
[58] *Ta'an* 29b.
[59] See E. Bischoff, *Babylonisch-Astrales im Weltbilde des Thalmud und Midrasch*, Leipsig, 1907, pp. 115 ff.

indicate the high regard in which this science was held by them.[60] The Jews proved to be important channels through which this science invaded Christian Europe in the twelfth and thirteenth centuries. They came into vital contact with Arabic culture at a somewhat earlier time than the European Christians. Accordingly astrology was wide-spread among them at an earlier time.

Ibn Ezra, who at times practiced astrology as a profession, called the heavens the "Book of Life in which men's destinies are inscribed the day they are born."[61] He declared that "all the affairs below depend upon the powers above, and from the heavens are all deeds determined."[62] Also "good or evil, honor or disgrace, which befall a man are all the work of the conjunction of the stars."[63] The *Zohar* declared "everything depends upon the planets, even the Scrolls in the Temple."[64]

Abraham Bar Ḥiyya vigorously defended astrology in the twelfth century. In answer to an attack which was made upon him because he advised a bridegroom to postpone the hour of his wedding to a time when the constellation would be more propitious, he wrote a lengthy defense of astrology in a letter to R. Judah ben Barzillai.[65] He declared that he had studied this science all his life.[66] He finds it not at all incompatible with Judaism. The Rabbis engaged in it;[67] even Abraham studied it.[68] The powers of the heavenly bodies are of course granted to them by God.[69] Through righteousness and prayer their evil decrees may be averted. This is an especial favor

[60] See Steinschneider, *Die Heb. Übersetzungen des Mittelalters*, p. 525 ff.

[61] Com. on Ps. 69.29. See Krochmal, מורה נבוכי הזמן, Warsaw, 1894, pp. 306, 311 ff.

[62] Com. on Gen. 11.5.

[63] Comm. on Ps. 67. See also Ibn Ezra's ספר למשאלה בקדרות, ed. Manasseh Grossberg, London, 1902, p. 3, note 6.

[64] Par. נשא, p. 134a.

[65] Published by A. Z. Schwarz, in *Festschrift Adolf Schwarz*, Vienna, 1917, pp. 23–26.

[66] *Op. cit.*, p. 36.

[67] *Ibid.*, p. 26.

[68] *Ibid.*, p. 27.

[69] *Ibid.*, pp. 25, 30.

granted by God to Israel in which the Gentiles do not share.[70] He is convinced that Jews ought to study astrology and believe in it.[71]

In the thirteenth century Judah ben Solomon Ha-Kohen ibn Matkah of Toledo rose to a similar defense of astrology.[72]

Even those who opposed it did not entirely deny that the heavenly bodies were active intelligences. Thus Halevi gives astrology an ancillary position to prophecy, but he does not deny its validity. One cannot arrive at a knowledge of God or at religious truth by means of astrology any more than one can by means of philosophy. Even Maimonides, who alone among his contemporaries vigorously attacked genethlialogy and judicial astrology,[73] calling it "stupidity" and "falsehood," shared the universal belief that the heavenly bodies were living, active intelligences who controlled, through their influences, the mundane world.[74] Under the influence of Arabic thought the orthodox opposition to astrology in Israel well-nigh broke down, as was also the case in the Christian world.[75]

It is not surprising, therefore, that Jewish adventists resorted to this method in their calculations. It was employed by them before the days of Ibn Ezra.[76] It was extensively used in the fourteenth and fifteenth centuries.[77] It was generally held that the seven planets in their progress through the signs of the zodiac and in the variety

[70] *Ibid.*, p. 27.

[71] ומכל אשר קדמנו תבאר שחכמת הכוכבים ראויה ללמוד אותה ולהחזיק בה (*ibid.*, p. 18).

[72] See Alexander Marx, "The Correspondence Between the Rabbis of Southern France and Maimonides about Astrology," *Hebrew Union College Annual*, III, Cincinnati, 1926, p. 314.

[73] See his *Responsum* to the letter of inquiry sent to him by the Rabbis of Southern France concerning Astrology, published anew and corrected from new MSS. by Professor Alexander Marx (*op. cit.*, pp. 349 ff.). In connection with Maimonides' thoroughgoing opposition to astrology, Professor Marx states that to his knowledge only one other Hebrew writer—Isaac Pulgar (14 c.), author of *'Ezer ha-Dat*—fully endorsed Maimonides' position (*ibid.*, p. 324).

[74] See his *Guide Bk.* II, 2.5, and 10.

[75] See T. O. Wedel, *The Medieval Attitude Toward Astrology*, Yale Univ. Press, 1920, pp. 69 ff.

[76] See his Com. Dan. 11.29; see also *Me'or 'Enayim*, chap. 43.

[77] "Zunz, Eine merkwürdige Medaille," in his *Ges. Schr.*, III, pp. 94 ff.

of their conjunctions influenced the affairs of men and nations. Each stage in the progress and each conjunction had a particular significance. They predicted mighty events and great changes in the world. Of particular significance for Israel was the conjunction of the two highest planets, Jupiter and Saturn. This conjunction was regarded as significant also by Christians. Six years before the birth of Jesus, it was pointed out, such a conjunction took place in the tenth revolution of Saturn, which always predicts the advent of a great historic personage.[78]

The prevalence of this belief in the twelfth century is attested by Petaḥia of Ratisbon. In Nineveh the traveler Pataḥia consulted an astrologer *to learn the Messianic year:* "At Nineveh there was an astrologer whose name was Rabbi Solomon. There is among all the sages in Nineveh and in the land of Ashur none as expert in the planets as he. Rabbi Petaḥia asked him when the Messiah will come. And he told him, 'I have seen this often distinctly in the planets.' But Rabbi Judah the Pious (who probably transcribed Petaḥia's account of his travels) would not write it down, lest he should be suspected of believing the words of Rabbi Solomon."[79]

[78] See Thorndike, *Magic and Experimental Science,* II, p. 672; also p. 896.
[79] *Travels of R. Petachia,* trans. Benisch, London, 1861, p. 13.

INDEX

Coll.